Industrial Map of
China's
Financial Sectors

Industrial Map of
China's
Financial Sectors

China Industrial Map Editorial Committee
China Economic Monitoring & Analysis Center
Xinhua Holdings, China

World Scientific

NEW JERSEY · LONDON · SINGAPORE · BEIJING · SHANGHAI · HONG KONG · TAIPEI · CHENNAI

Published by

World Scientific Publishing Co. Pte. Ltd.
5 Toh Tuck Link, Singapore 596224
USA office: 27 Warren Street, Suite 401-402, Hackensack, NJ 07601
UK office: 57 Shelton Street, Covent Garden, London WC2H 9HE

British Library Cataloguing-in-Publication Data
A catalogue record for this book is available from the British Library.

中国金融产业地图 2010–2011
Originally published in Chinese by Social Sciences Academic Press
Copyright © Social Sciences Academic Press, 2011

INDUSTRIAL MAP OF CHINA'S FINANCIAL SECTORS

ISBN 978-981-4412-60-5

In-house Editor: Dong Lixi

Typeset by Stallion Press
Email: enquiries@stallionpress.com

Printed in Singapore by B & Jo Enterprise Pte Ltd

CONTENTS

Chapter 1

INTRODUCTION

On 26th December, 2010, when market expectation of an interest rate increase during the year weakened, Bank of China declared that it would be rounded up, each by 0.25%. Just on 10th December of the very month, the central bank released currency and credit data for November, which showed that the two indicators, M1 and M2, still remained at a relative upper bit, and that the newly added RMB loan was significantly beyond the limit. No sooner than the credit information was released, the central bank declared that the cash reserve ratio of financial institutions to increase by 0.5%.

The above two measures markedly manifests the dilemma faced by monetary policy, as well as for the finance policy as a whole in 2010. On one hand, the shadow left by the global financial crisis since the second half of 2008 was still looming, and the road of recovery by the developed economy with America as its representative was full of twists and turns. Thus export — one important engine on which the Chinese economy depended on during the past 30 years (especially the past 10 years) still faces indeterminacy to a large degree. On the other hand, there appeared the negative impact of significant fluxility exerted by the large-scale economic stimulus plan to counteract the impact brought by the global financial crisis, and price level and inflation were expected to witness a daily increase. Thus another important engine for Chinese economy, i.e. investment increasingly exerted negative impact on economic development. Faced with this dilemma, the urgent and important mission for the government, in particular the currency and finance supervisory authorities, for the year 2010 was how to weaken the negative influence of the economic stimulus plan as much as possible to downplay the harm resulted from salient fluxility while at the same time to enlarge the positive effects by the economic activation plan to the full so as to protect the outcomes from economic recovery and growth that came in no easy way.

Just as what the data in this book demonstrates, during the years from 2009 to 2010, since Chinese government decisively carried out the economic stimulus plan and a series of industry invigoration plans, together with the co-efforts made by Chinese laborers, enterprises and financial institutions, the Chinese economy has realised a V-shape inversion, and its economic growth has basically recovered to the level before the financial crisis. Nevertheless, certain problems concerning the Chinese economy that have accumulated for a long time still fail to be fundamentally solved, and are aggravated by the corresponding measures against the financial crisis, which brings to the future development of the Chinese economy and financial sector many problems that are in urgent need of solutions.

In the times of post-financial crisis, the Chinese economy will resultantly face a series of turns and transitions. The traditional increase pattern was characterized by expanding production capacity through adding investments and digesting production capacity through exports. Now this pattern is confronted with a bottleneck due to the following two factors: for one thing, the slow recovery of the developed market may exert negative influence upon its consumption demand, and the increasingly obvious trade protectionism will not consistently expand exports to provide space for economic policy; for another, the crowding-out effect exerted by high investment rate over consumption, especially domestic household consumption, leads to domestic under-consumption, which will possibly shake the base of long-term and sustained economic growth in China.

Under the circumstance of high-speed growth, the non-equilibration of Chinese economy is apparent, which from the perspective of macro-economy is the non-equilibration between consumption, investment and export. Since the outset of this century, the proportion of investment and export in GDP has continuously increased, while that of consumption faces a cut day by day, both of which lead to the non-equilibration of macro-economic drive. In terms of enterprise financing channels, the indirect financing channel — obtaining capital through bank credit is always the main means of capital gain for enterprises. On the contrary, the direct financing channel through the financial market is relatively narrow in scope and range. From the perspective of financial market, due to historical factors, the stock market was made to outshine the others while the bond market failed to develop with rapidity. In terms of the financial sector *per se*, there still exists a large-scale non-equilibration such as commercial banking and profits depending too much on loans and deposits business, non-interest business accounting for a small percentage in commercial banking income and profit, all of which, together with the current non-market rate system in China, make the relational degree between the profit of commercial bank and monetary policy oversized, and the base for the further advance of future profitability relatively weak, etc.

Moreover, similar problems of simplification in commercial banking also have their existence in the financial sector and other sub-sectors. For example, the securities industry depends too much upon securities brokerage, leading to a close relationship between the profit of securities business and the advance-decline of the stock market. In addition, the proportions of life insurance and industry business in the insurance sector are unbalanced, and there also exists severe business convergence in the fund industry. In a sense, the non-equili-bration of the financial sector is one embodiment of the non-equilibration of a three-dimensional economy. However, the non-equilibration of the finan-cial sector also has its unique factors and characteristics. In the age of post-financial crisis, to face and spare no efforts in elevating this non-equili-bration are the immediate challenges that the Chinese economy and the financial industry have to take up for the very present.

In the current economic environment, the "transition" of China's econ-omy has a double meaning. In the short run, China's economy is in need of getting out of the negative impact from the global financial crisis, restoring its trend of growth, to lay a solid material foundation for creating employ-ment opportunities and improving social welfare. According to recently-released macro-economic data, this short-term goal has been basi-cally achieved. In the long run, however, China's economy demands a "transition" of a deeper meaning: transiting from the model on which the Chinese economy in the past 30 years developed with success to gradually explore a new model that is adapted to the changed global economic pattern. Seen from the present situation, it still has a long way to go to realize this transition. What accounts for it lie in the following two aspects: firstly, the previous model of economic development largely stunted people's proactiv-ity to explore a new model; secondly, a series of fiscal policy and monetary policy taken to eliminate the impact of the global financial crisis in the short-est time possible reinforces the original model, adding more difficulty to the work of improving the original model. In other words, success in the short-term "transition" brings about, in a sense, negative effects to the long-term "transition".

As with real economy, the financial sector in China also needs to focus on the long-term transition. In a way, the financial sector collectively demon-strates the extensive model of development with investment as its core during the past several years. Both the industrial distribution of stock markets and the credit structures of banking reflect the influence of the orginal develop-ment model over the financial sector. When the transition of real economy is undertaken step by step, its postive and negative influences upon the finan-cial sector will come into being. For example, the change in speed in industrial development will be reflected by the degrees of valuation level of different industries on the stock market; the industrial policy taken by the government towards different industries would also be reflected in one way or another by the credit structures of banking, and even influence the profit model and profit level. The change in the financial market will ultimately lead to the salient changes in the various sub-sectors within the financial sector, such as banking, insurance, securities, fund, trust, etc.

The Chinese real economy should develop towards the more equilibrated direction. This equilibration includes the equilibration between investment and consumption, domestic demand drive and overseas demand drive, government expenditure and residents' expenditure, government industrial investment and public expenditure, manufacturing and service industries, capital-intensive and labor-intensive industries, and traditional and emerging industries, etc. Meanwhile, in order to meet the real economy's demand for diversified financial services, the financial sector itself should also develop in the direction of equilibration, which includes the equilibration between direct and indirect investment, equity financing and debt financing, large and small and medium-sized enterprises in issuing credit, capital-intensive industry and emerging industry in capital market financing, and the equilibration between high-risk and low-risk financial products, etc. Presently, the situation, in which banking functions as the main channel of fund providing, and stock issue as the main channel of direct financing, will unavoidably gradually transit to the pattern where multiple financing means coexist and multiple financial products coexist, and thence a diversified financial environment will be formed step by step.

No change comes all of a sudden. The data concerning macro-economy, financial market and financial sector entails the necessity of change from different perspectives, and the incoming change. The present book attempts to provide an overview of China's financial sector according to certain significant data about the Chinese financial sector and macro-economy during the years from 2009 to 2010, and to demonstrate, on the basis of comparision of historical data, the developmental trend of China's financial sector in recent years.

The financial sector is not only an industry closely related to the macro-economy, but it is also an industry of detailed internal division and micro-diversification. Traditionally, the whole financial system is divided into three general parts, namely, monetary policy, financial market and financial intermediaries. Actually, many kinds of businesses and contents within these three divisions interlock with each other. For example, stock investment belongs to the financial market, but also involves many financial intermediaries such as securities, fund industry and so on. Taking into consideration such financial institutions like banks and insurance as listed companies, stock investment also covers banking and insurance sector, etc. However, for the sake of organized and systemized narration, it's necessary to distinguish between the specific contents as the following example shows: the financial products on the market such as stocks, securities, commodity futures, are emphatically analyzed in the part of financial market, while the institutions (such as securities companies, fund companies, etc.) that provide financial products and services are the concern of the financial intermediaries. For certain sub-sectors, the emphasis is put according to their respective market features. Take commodity futures for instance. It is focused on the commodity futures market rather than on non-intermediary companies (futures companies), and thus in this book the search on market is stressed. In addition, in the fund industry, although fund products are closely related with the financial market, given that fund products have closer relation with their issuing agencies and fund companies in charge of products management, fund products are classified into the fund industry within the part of financial intermediaries for analysis.

The classification of the financial market is another significant issue in the division of contents in this book. Theoretically speaking, the money market that meets the demand of short-term financing and the capital market that meets the demand of mid-and-long term investment and financing are of two different natures. However, the characteristic of the Chinese financial market is that because of historical development and system design, the stock market is relatively developed while the securities market is relatively slow, and at the same time the market segmentation is relatively severe, for example, the securities market is segmented into inter-bank bond market and exchange bond market. Therefore, in China's financial market system, investors or financial regulators pay more attention to the features of financial products to investigate and analyze the market. Given this fact, this book takes the perspective of financial products as the main classification, together with the full consideration of the developmental degrees of different products on the financial markets, focusing on the analysis of stock markets and securities markets, while classifying other relevant markets in another category.

Based on the above principle, the contents of this book are divided into three general sections: firstly, the section of "monetary policy" focuses on the description of macro-economy, macro-financial and monetary policy, which lies in the second chapter of the present book; secondly, the section of "financial market" demonstrates the status quo and development of the financial market from the perspective of stock market, securities market, interbank lending market, repo market, interest-rate swap market and commodity futures market, etc., which is covered from the third chapter to the fifth chapter of this book; thirdly, the section of "financial intermediaries" discloses and analyzes the data relevant to various financial institutions within the financial sector from the perspectives of banking, insurance, securities, fund and trust industries respectively, which includes the sixth chapter to the eighth chapter.

The present book puts emphasis on the analysis of China's financial sector in 2010. For the sake of comparison, however, most chapters provide relevant data of the year 2009. Moreover, in some chapters, in order to further analyze the variation of the relevant data, it provides data of much earlier periods. Partial data, say international comparative data, because of data statistic cycle, covers only the data by the end of 2009. As for data acquired from certain relevant agency annual reports (such as financial data of listed banks, listed insuence companies and listed securities companines), due to the problem of annual disclosure time in 2010, such financial data were the relevant data published by the interim report of the year 2010.

At present, China's economy and financial sector are just like a travellor undergoing a very long journey and in bad need of a map to tell where he/she comes from, where he/she is and where the present road will lead to. Of course, economic phenomenon is different from natural phenomenon, the feature of the former lies in its large uncertainty and many possibilities. This book attempts to provide the above-said travellors with some useful information on the basis of objective data and thus help them to explore the road to the near future. This is probably one interpretation of what this book indicates — "A Map for China's Financial Sector".

Chapter 2

MACRO FINANCIAL ENVIRONMENT AND MONETARY POLICY

2.1 Macro-Economy in 2010: Coexistence of Recovery and Inflation

2.1.1 *Macro-economy gradually transits to normal*

After the global financial crisis in 2008, as a response to this crisis, the Chinese government issued a series of economic stimulus policies, including monetary policy and fiscal policy so as to avoid a substantial downturn and lay a foundation for economic recovery from 2009 to 2010. Based on the data of growth rate of GDP (YoY), the real economy basically reversed the slipping situation from the end of 2008 to the first half of 2009 and thus realized a V-shape reversal. The growth rate of GDP (YoY) in 2010 was 10.3%, this growth rate increasing 1.1% in comparison to that of 2009. The growth rate of GDP (YoY) in 2010 was above the mean value (10.29%) and median (9.8%) of the years 2009 and 2010, indicating that China's economy basically recovered to the economic status before the global financial crisis.

The recovery of the three categories of industry shows that in 2010: the primary industry syncronously grew by 4.3%, higher than the mean value (4.04%) and the median (3.94%) of the years 2009 and 2010; the secondary industry syncronously grew by 12.2%, higher than the mean value (11.19%) and the median (10.52%) of the years 2009 and 2010; the tertiary industry syncronously grew by 9.5%, lower than the mean value (11.24%) and the median (10.33%) of the years 2009 and 2010, which entails the further reinforcement of the development of the tertiary industry.

The macro-economic data of each month in 2010 directly reflects that the year-on-year growth data of value-added of industry in real economic growth consistently remained above 13% during the year, while the very data appeared in a high-to-low profile: from January to May, influenced by the radix of the previous year (i.e. 2009), the year-on-year growth rate of value-added of industry was relatively larger, all above 15%; from June onwards,

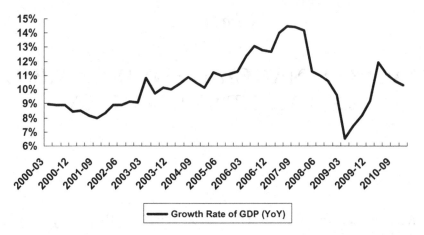

Figure 2.1.1.1   China's economy has recovered to the level before the global financial crisis
(*Data source*: National Bureau of Statistics)

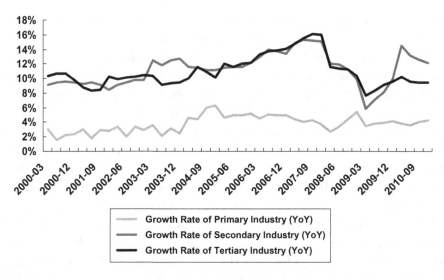

Figure 2.1.1.2   Three categories of industry all witnessed recovery to different extents
(*Data source*: National Bureau of Statistics)

under the double influence of regulation policy and the radix in 2009, the monthly year-on-year growth rate of value-added of industry fluctuated within the interval between 13% and 14%.

The Purchase Management Index (PMI) in manufacturing reflects the trend of economic recovery from another angle. In 2010, PMI in manufacturing was always within the boom range, namely, over 50. However, different from the value-added of industry, 2010's PMI in manufacturing appeared in a pattern that is high in the middle and low at both ends. Seen

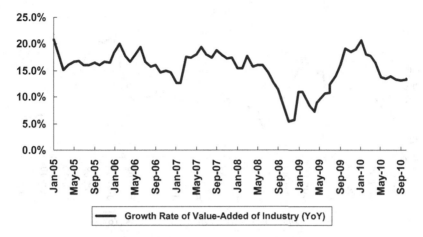

Figure 2.1.1.3 Growth rate of value-added of industry (YoY) remained stable
(*Data source*: National Bureau of Statistics)

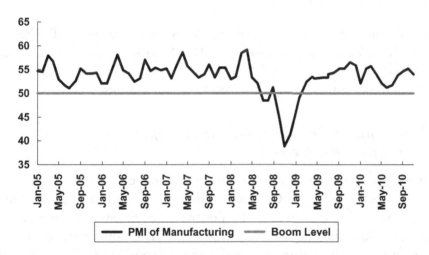

Figure 2.1.1.4 PMI in manufacturing remained above the boom level
(*Data source*: China Federation of Logistics & Purchasing)

from the year-end resumption of the uptrend, a stable economic growth can still be expected next year.

One important mark that indicates the gradual transition of macro-economy to normalization lies in the following fact: in 2010, the year-on-year growth of urban fixed asset investment fell month by month, with fluctuation within the interval between 24.5% and 26.5% in each month during the year; compared with the year-on-year growth rate of over 30% in most months during 2009, the data in 2010 demonstrates that the "hangover" left by the

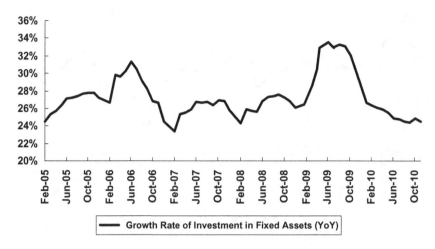

Figure 2.1.1.5   Growth rate of urban fixed asset investment (YoY) recovered to the normal status

(*Data source*: National Bureau of Statistics)

economic stimulus plan in respect to investment has gradually become smooth. According to the statistics, in 2010 the year-on-year growth rate of urban fixed asset investment in each month was below the mean value (27.4%) and median (26.8%) of the years ever since 2005.

2.1.2 *Increase in the price level, and the appearance of inflation expectation*

Along with economic recovery was an obvious increase in price levels. The year-on-year growth of the Consumer Price Index (CPI) and the Producer Price Indexes (PPI) transitted to be positive respectively in November and December, 2009, basically in an upward trend. The upward trend of CPI's year-on-year growth is more consistent and obvious, from 1% ~ 2% at the beginning of the year to over 5% at the end of it, while the year-on-year growth of PPI remained above 4% in 2010.

Seen from the specific indexes, since food price accounts for a major part in CPI composition, and the growth rate of food price in 2010 was relatively significant, it provided a driving force for CPI.

2.1.3 *Liquidity increased and monetary policy transitted to stability*

Due to the loose monetary policy to resist the global financial crisis at the end of 2008, the liquidity of the real economy was largely enhanced. Therefore,

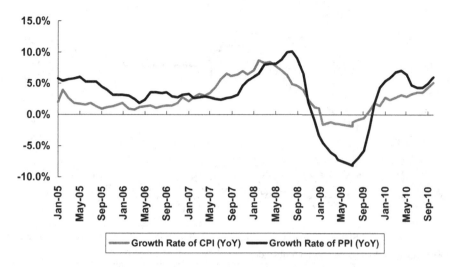

Figure 2.1.2.1   The price level obviously rose in 2010

(*Data source*: National Bureau of Statistics)

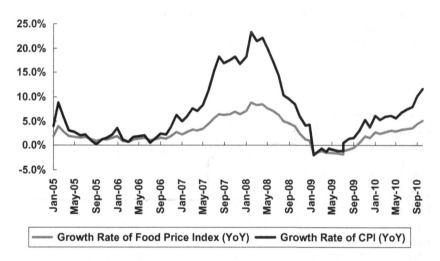

Figure 2.1.2.2   The stimulating function of food price rise towards CPI

(*Data source*: National Bureau of Statistics)

in 2010 the central bank constantly controlled this liquidity through the quantitative policy instrument (i.e. reserve requirements ratio policy) and price-based instrument (i.e. deposit and loan interest rate). In 2010, the central bank raised for 6 times the reserve requirements ratio of deposit of financial institutions, from 15.5% in 2009 up to 18.5%, the growth rate being 3%; meanwhile, the central bank raised the deposit and loan interest rate twice, raising one-year base interest rate of saving and one-year base interest

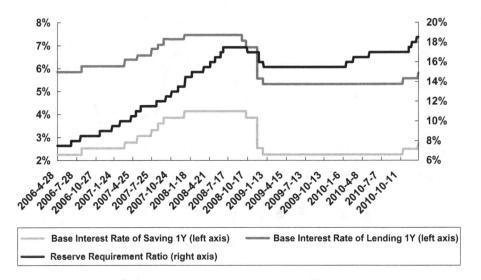

Figure 2.1.3.1   Change in reserve requirements ratio and one-year base interest rate of lending since 2006

(*Note*: the reserve requirements ratio after October, 2008 refers to the reserve requirements ratio of large deposit financial institutions)
(*Data source*: People's Bank of China)

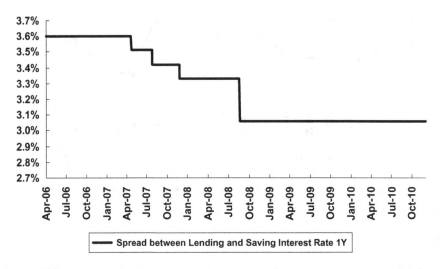

Figure 2.1.3.2   Spread between one-year lending and saving interest rate tended to be narrowed since 2006

(*Data source*: People's Bank of China)

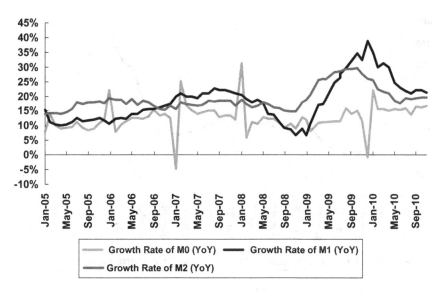

Figure 2.1.3.3 Money supply growth rate in 2010 represented a high fall-back situation as a whole

(*Data source*: People's Bank of China)

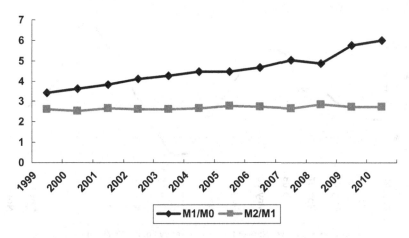

Figure 2.1.3.4 Large-scale elevation of the ability of the banking system to create current deposit in the past 10 years

(*Data source*: People's Bank of China)

rate of lending from 2.25% and 5.31% in 2009 to 2.75% and 5.81% respectively, the growth rate both being 0.5%.

Though the benchmark deposit and lending rate were raised two times in 2010, the one-year benchmark deposit and lending rates were raised at the same time, yet since 2006 the spread between one-year lending and saving interest rate (=one-year base interest rate of lending — one-year base interest

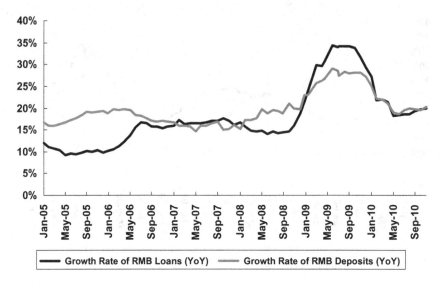

Figure 2.1.3.5   The growth rate of RMB credit scale underwent certain reduction yet still remained at a high level

(*Data source*: People's Bank of China)

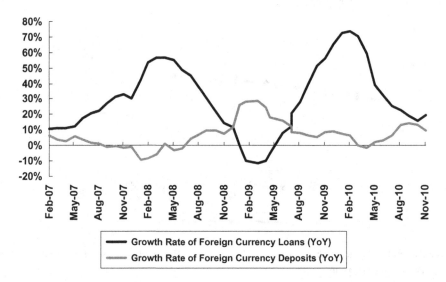

Figure 2.1.3.6   The loan scale of foreign exchange has fallen back to normal

(*Data source*: People's Bank of China)

rate of saving) gradually narrowed, from 3.6% at the beginning of 2006 down to 3.06% at the end of 2010, that is, narrowed by 54%.

The measures continuously taken by the central bank to tighten liquidity in 2010 were based on the rapid growth of money supply in 2009. The economic stimulus plan initiated from the end of 2008 led to the unprecedented

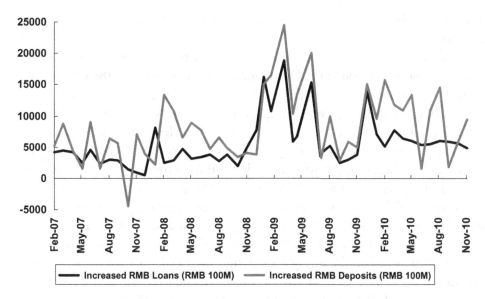

Figure 2.1.3.7   Increased loans in 2010 still kept at a relatively high level

(*Data source*: People's Bank of China)

growth rate of money issue during the whole year of 2009. Except in January, the year-on-year growth of M2 (i.e. cash in circulation + current deposit + fixed deposit) of the remaining months in 2009 were all above 20%, and even close to 30% at the year end, which brought great difficulties to the monetary policy in 2010. From the perspective of the situation in 2010, though M1 and M2 underwent a gradual fall back (from approximately 40% and 60% at the beginning of the year to 20% odd at the end of the year respectively), yet historically speaking, their acceleration still remained at a relatively higher level.

One phenomenon interrelated to the absolute increase of money supply is that the ability of China's banking to create money (more accurately speaking, the ability to create current deposit) is on a steady rise. The comparison of the data in 1999 and 2010 demonstrates that the ratio between M1 (cash in circulation + current deposit) and M0 (cash in circulation) was about 3.4, while in 2010, the above ratio approximated to 6. In other words, during these 10 years, the ability of the banking system to create current deposit has doubled. However, during the above-mentioned 10 years, the ratio between M2 and M1 basically fluctuated within the range from 2.6 to 2.8, which indicates that the rise of the ability to create money is almost attributed to the improvement of the ability to create current deposit. Undoubtedly, the enhanced ability of the banking system to create money adds difficulties, in a sense, to the implementation of monetary policy by the central bank.

The other side of the increase of liquidity in the economy lies in the constant expansion of credit scale. Under the circumstances where the year-on-year growth rate of loan balance during the second half of 2009 continuously surpassed 30%, although a seires of regulation measures were taken in 2010, the rise of credit scale still remained at a relatively high level. For example, during the first five months the year-on-year growth rate of RMB loan balance kept above 20%. Though this growth rate reduced during the second half of the year, it was still higher than the mean value (18.08%) and median (16.49%) of the years since 2005. The changing tendency of the year-on-year growth rate of deposit was similar to that of loan, and appeared in a high-to-low pattern.

Dissimilar to the high growth rate of RMB credit scale, the growth rate of the scale of credit in foreign exchange in 2010 underwent a relatively salient fall back. The growth rate in the fourth quarter was obviously below the mean value (29.82%) and median (27.80%) since 2007.

In 2010, the newly added RMB loan of the financial institutions was a total of 7.9 trillion and the newly added deposit was 12 trillion in total, with a reduction by 17.3% and 8% in comparison with a total of RMB 9.6 trillion and RMB 13 trillion for 2009 respectively. Nevertheless, the newly added deposit and loan for 2010 still remained at a high level, its average monthly newly added loan being RMB 0.6603 billion and newly added deposit being around 1 trillion, both higher than the monthly mean values of the time from February, 2007 to the end of 2009, RMB 0.5016 billion and RMB 0.7328 billion respectively. But compared with the monthly mean levels (RMB 0.7980 billion and RMB 1.1 trillion respectively) in 2009, these two mean values has certain reduction.

2.1.4 *Economic structure in need of equilibration and optimization*

Although China's economy is always in a tendency of high growth in recent years, correspondingly, structural problem is increasingly prominent. From 1990 to 2000, the average annual compound growth rates of the four elements comprising GDP, namely, household consumption, government expenditure, investment and net export, were respectively 17.1%, 19.5%, 17.8% and 16.7% (the average annual compound growth rate of GDP being 17.7%). The four elements basically kept a balanced increase. But during the period from 2000 to 2009, the average annual compound growth rates of household consumption, government expenditure, investment and net

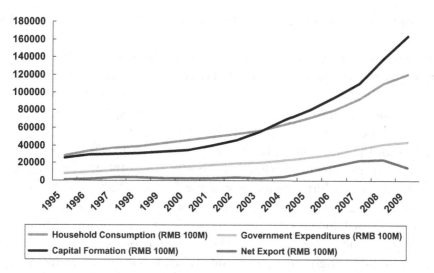

Figure 2.1.4.1 Rise in household consumption, government expenditure, investment and net export

(*Data source*: National Bureau of Statistics)

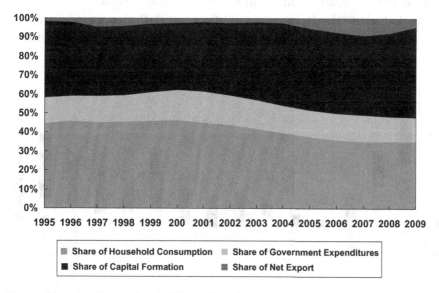

Figure 2.1.4.2 Share of capital formation obviously surpassed that of consumption

(*Data source*: National Bureau of Statistics)

export were respectively 11.4%, 12.3%, 18.8% and 22.7% (the average annual compound growth rate of GDP being 14.9%). Obviously, investment and net export became main factors to spur GDP growth, while the rise in household consumption largely fell behind GDP growth. Moreover, the growth rate of household consumption ranked at the bottom of those of the other three elements.

Seen from the proportions of the four elements in GDP, in 1990, the proportions of household consumption, government expenditure, investment and net export in GDP were respectively 48.8%, 13.6%, 34.9% and 2.6%. In 2000, the above proportions basically kept steady, being 46.4%, 15.9%, 35.3% and 2.4% respectively. But in 2004, investment surpassed household consumption for the first time. After it became the first in GDP proportion, the proportion of investment remained above 42%. In 2009, the proportions of the above-mentioned four elements became 35.1%, 12.9%, 47.7% and 4.4%. Investment and export (investment in particular) obviously became the main driving forces of China's GDP growth, while the proportion of household expenditure reduced year by year. The structural problem of the Chinese economy is increasingly prominent and its economic structure needs to be equilibrated and optimized.

In terms of the contribution made to GDP growth, during the period from 1990 to 2000, except for certain years, the growth in household consumption made greater contribution than capital formation, and was the element that made the largest contribution to GDP growth. However, after 2001, contribution made by household consumption was obviously lower

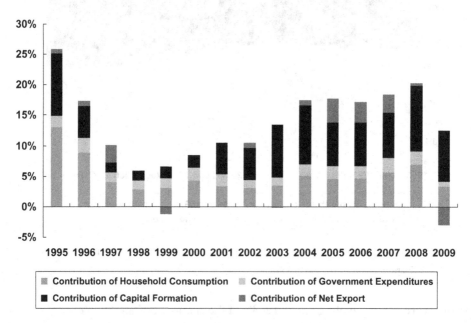

Figure 2.1.4.3 Contribution of capital formation to GDP growth was significantly greater than that of consumption

(*Data source*: National Bureau of Statistics)

than that of capital formation. The contribution made by household consumption growth to GDP growth in 2009 was 3.3%, while that made by capital formation reached up to 8.3%, which demonstrates an evident tendency of capital formation simulation. According to rough estimate, to the GDP growth rate of 10.3% for 2010, capital formation growth made a contribution of 5.6%, consumption growth (including growth in household consumption and government consumption expenditure) a contribution of 3.9%, net export of goods and services a contribution of 0.8%. Hence the contribution rate of capital formation growth to GDP growth were still high.

2.2 Exchange Rate Reform Restarted, and Pressure of RMB Appreciation Still Existed

2.2.1 Review of RMB exchange rate trend since the exchange rate reform in 2005

In July, 2005, RMB exchange rate initiated a mechanism reform, switching from USD peg to a directed floating exchange rate based on a basket of currencies. From then on till the end of 2010, the exchange rate of RMB against USD underwent three phases: in the first phase — from July, 2005 when the exchange rate mechanism reform was declared to 2008, the tendency of RMB against USD basically appeared in the form of unilateral appreciation; in the second phase — from the second half of 2008 when the global financial crisis

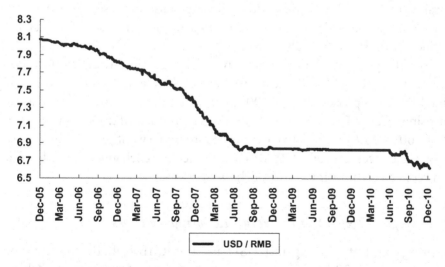

Figure 2.2.1.1 The three phases the exchange rate of RMB against USD underwent after the exchange rate mechanism reform

(*Data source*: State Administration of Exchange Control)

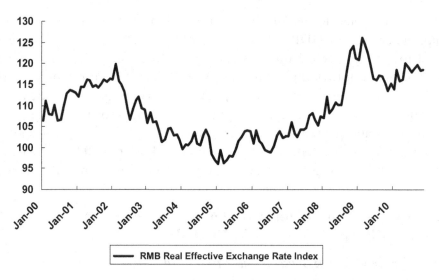

Figure 2.2.1.2   RMB tendency during the recent 10 years can be generally divided into two phases from the perspective of real effective exchange rate

(*Data source*: State Administration of Exchange Control)

broke out to 19th June, 2008 when central bank declared restarting RMB exchange rate, the exchange rate of RMB against USD fundamentally recovered the "dollar-peg" tendency, narrowly fluctuating within the small interval between 6.82 and 6.8; in the third phase — from 19th June, 2008 when the central bank declared restarting RMB exchange rate till present, the exchange rate of RMB against USD still appeared in a rising trend, and the exchange rate fluctuation still obviously increased.

From the perspective of real effective exchange rate, from 2000 till present, the tendency of RMB real effective exchange rate can be generally divided into two phases: before 2005, it appeared in a fall trend but basically kept rising after 2005. Although from the second half of 2008 to the second half of 2009 RMB real effective exchange rate underwent greater fluctuation, yet since the inception of 2010, RMB real effective exchange rate index once again recovered the rising trend of the past 5 years.

2.2.2 *Import/Export and foreign exchange reserves*

The rising trend of RMB against USD and the RMB real effective exchange rate index since 2005 reflects that, in a sense, the status of China's import/export and foreign exchange reserve in recent years. During the period from 2005 to the breaking out of the financial crisis (September,

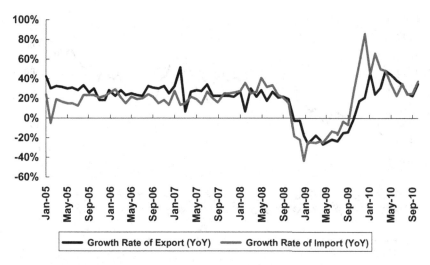

Figure 2.2.2.1　Year-on-year growth of imports and exports gradually recovered in 2010 (*Data source*: National Bureau of Statistics)

2008), the mean value of year-on-year growth in China's monthly total exports was above 26.6% (its median and standard deviation being 26.8% and 7.6% respectively), while that of the total imports was 21.5% (its median and standard deviation being 21.7% and 7.4% respectively). The average year-on-year growth rate of monthly total exports topped that of monthly total imports by about 5%. During the financial crisis, the year-on-year comparison of import and export both underwent a large-scale reduction, but with the implementation of the economic stimulus plan, the data of the above two items markedly recovered to rise. Entering 2010, with the elevation of the radix in the previous year and the gradual economic normalization, the growth rate of export approached step by step to the historical average level, the monthly average being 33.6% (about historical average +1 time of the standard deviation), while the growth rate of import remained relatively higher, the monthly average being 43.0%, mainly due to the higher growth rate of import in the first quarter. By the fourth quarter, the monthly average basically achieved uniformity of import/export year-on-year growth, with the growth rate of imports slightly higher than that of exports.

Seen from the absolute quantities of imports and exports, in 2010, China's total imports and exports basically recovered the rising trend, while seen from net exports, it underwent a temporary reduction since the growth rate of imports for the first quarter of the year was slightly higher than that of exports. However, since the beginning of the second quarter, it recovered the trend of exports being higher than imports. Continuously remaining at a

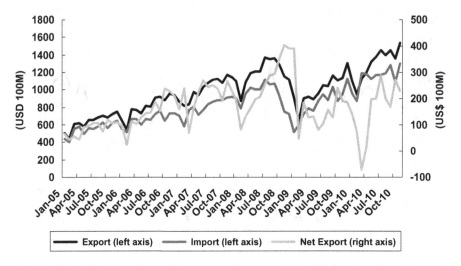

Figure 2.2.2.2 Total number of imports and exports in 2010 continued to rise and the growth rate of net exports tended to slow down

(*Data source*: National Bureau of Statistics)

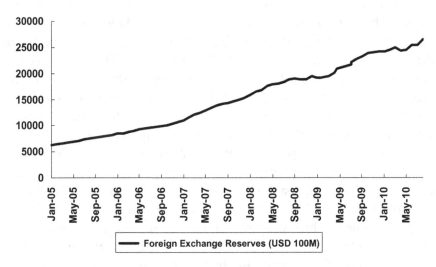

Figure 2.2.2.3 China's foreign exchange reserves continued rising

(*Data source*: State Administration of Exchange Control)

relatively high level of net exports (monthly average over USD 15 million) made RMB exchange rate still under the pressure of a rising trend.

One main reason accounting for the continuous rise of foreign exchange reserves lies in the contant high level of net exports. Since 2005, China's foreign exchange reserves increased from about USD 600 billion to USD 2.5 trillion, having quadrupled in 6 years. Besides, RMB issue caused by continuous increase of foreign exchange reserves was another factor leading to excess liquidity.

2.2.3 *RMB exchange rate after exchange rate reform restarted*

On one hand, since the restarting of exchange rate reform till the end of December 2010, the exchange rate tendency of RMB against the major currencies shows that the exchange rate of RMB against USD was in an obvious rising trend, its appreciation rate being 3%, but in a depreciation trend against

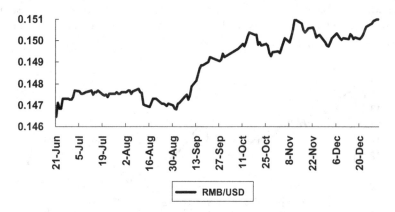

Figure 2.2.3.1-a Change in the exchange rate of RMB against USD after the restarting of exchange rate reform (calculated by RMB 1 converted to the corresponding foreign currency)

(*Data source*: State Administration of Exchange Control)

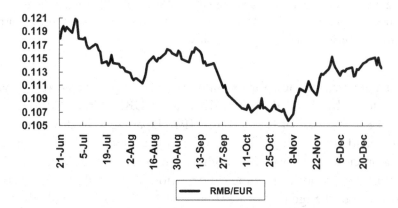

Figure 2.2.3.1-b Change in the exchange rate of RMB against euro after the restarting of exchange rate reform (calculated by RMB 1 converted to the corresponding foreign currency)

(*Data source*: State Administration of Exchange Control)

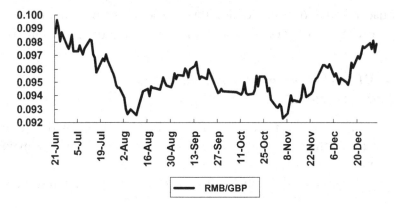

Figure 2.2.3.1-c   Change in the exchange rate of RMB against GBP after the restarting of exchange rate reform (calculated by RMB 1 converted to the corresponding foreign currency)

(*Data source*: State Administration of Exchange Control)

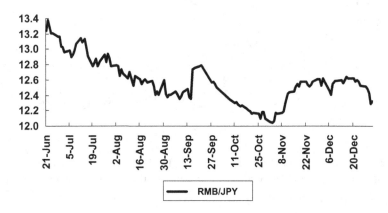

Figure 2.2.3.1-d   Change in the exchange rate of RMB against JPY after the restarting of exchange rate reform (calculated by RMB 1 converted to the corresponding foreign currency)

(*Data source*: State Administration of Exchange Control)

the other major currencies, for example, the exchange rate of RMB against euro was down by 3.7%, that of RMB against GBP (Great British Pound) down by 0.8%, and that of RMB against JPY (Japanese Yen) down by 7%. On the other hand, the change rate of the exchange rate of RMB against the other major currencies was also higher than that of RMB against USD. During this same period, the standard deviation of the daily change rate after the annualized exchange rate of RMB against USD was 2%, while that of the annualized change rate of RMB against euro and GBP was 11.6% and 9.1% respectively, that of the annualized change rate of RMB against JPY reached up to 9.7%, whose fluctuation was more significant than the case of RMB

Table 2.2.3.1 Statistics of change in exchange rates of RMB against major currencies after the restarting of exchange rate reform

21ˢᵗ June, 2010 31ˢᵗ December, 2010	RMB/USD (%)	RMB/euro (%)	RMB/GBP (%)	RMB/JPY (%)
Compound change rate	3.1	−3.7	−0.8	−7.0
Annualized average change rate	5.8	−6.5	−1.1	−13.4
Standard deviation of the annual change rate	2.0	11.6	9.1	9.7

Note: In the case of "annualization", the calculation takes 250 trading days as the base.
(*Data source*: State Administration of Exchange Control, Xinhua Finance)

against USD. Based on the above date of fluctuation rates, and given the basic depreciation tendency of USD against the major currencies during the afore-said period, it can be found that USD still accounted for a large proportion in the "reference basket" of RMB exchange rate.

2.3 Analysis of Macro Financial Environment in 2010

2.3.1 *Features and changes of the macro economic status in 2010*

The most fundamental elements comprising the macro economic environment include economic growth (or the growth of production and service activities), money supply and price level, etc. Therefore, to select the variables of the macro economy, these three aspects shall be taken as the main points of departure.

(1) Economic growth indicator: ususally including GDP, value-added of industry and so on. Since GDP is quarterly issued while value-added of industry can reflect the dynamic change in the present economy based on the monthly data, the latter is a sound alternative to GDP. Therefore, the "monthly year-on-year growth of value-added of industry" is selected as the economic growth indicator;

(2) Money supply indicator: ususally including M1, M2, loan balance, etc. Here "M1 monthly year-on-year growth" is taken as the money supply indicator, the main reason being that M1 is in certain sense the leading indicator of economic cyclic fluctuation; moreover, since M1 reflects the states of cash and current deposit, hence its higher liquidity, so it can directly reflect the influence exerted by money supply over capital market.

(3) Price level indicator: ususally including CPI, PPI, etc. Here "CPI
    monthly year-on-year growth" is chosed as the price level indicator, the
    main reason being that CPI fluctuation is relatively smoother than PPI
    fluctuation, beneficial to divide the economic stages and that CPI
    includes the prices of consumer goods and servies, etc. and its tendency
    is uniform with that of PPI.

To sum up, in "Xinhua Finance model of China's macro economic status", the "monthly year-on-year growth of value-added of industry" is
selected as the real economic growth indicator, "M1 monthly year-on-year
growth" as the money supply indicator, and "CPI monthly year-on-year
growth" as the price level indicator. In order to clearly observe the characteristics of the overall change in the macro economic indicators, Kalman filter
is adopted to smooth the monthly tendency of these three indicators, namely,
M1, CPI and value-added of industry.

According to the analysis of the time series data of the macro economic
variables after filtering, the following macro economic cyclic stages can be
found, as Table 2.3.1.1 shows.

It should be noted that because of the complexity of the economic operation and also the government regulation of macro economy, the cycle of
macro economy does not necessarily follows the cycle of "depression —
recovery — expansion — prosperity — inflation — stagflation". For example,

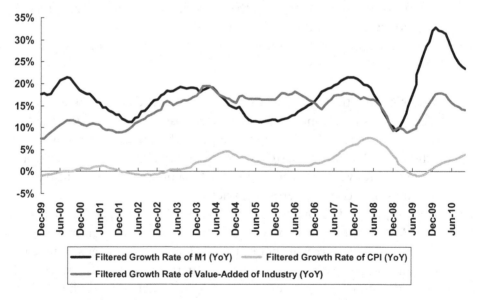

Figure 2.3.1.1 Cyclic changes of the main macro indicators of China's economy since 2000
(*Data source*: State Administration of Exchange Control, Xinhua Finance)

Table 2.3.1.1   Different stages and the features of the macro economic cycle

Stage	Characteristics of the change in the macro economic indicators
Expansion	Money supply significantly increases and price level keeps steady, with significant economic growth.
Prosperity	Money supply, price level and value-added of industry all undergo a rise.
Deceleration	Money supply and price level significantly increases while the growth of value-added of industry slows down.
Inflation	Due to the implementation of tight monetary policy by central bank, money supply significantly slows down, while price level continue to elevate because of policy lag. The most prominent feature of this stage is that CPI growth rate is significantly higher than M1 growth rate while value-added of industry keeps rising or remains stable.
Stagflation	Money supply undergoes a further shrink, but price level still lags and meanwhile economic growth begins to stagnate or reduce. The most salient difference of this stage from the stage of "inflation" is that here the growth rate of value-added of industry begins to depress.
Depression	Money supply undergoes a further shrink, price level begins to depress and economic growth undergoes a further drop.
Recovery	The shrinking tendency of money supply is curbed and even begins to rise, price level stops declining significantly, and value-added of industry significantly slows down its fall or slightly increases.

in the macro economic cycle showed above, the period from the second half of 2006 to the first half of 2007 witnessed a "deceleration" stage, the main feature of which is that although both money supply and price level increase, the growth of value-added of industry begins to decelerate. The feature of this stage can also be seen as a mixture of "prosperity" and "stagflation".

Table 2.3.1.2 demonstrates the different stages in the macro economic cycle during the period from December 1999 to December 2010. Since 2000, China's economy generally underwent less than 4 cycles. But during 2008 to 2009, the global financial crisis and the large-scale economic stimulus plan it led to brought about a change: thanks to the large-scale economic stimulus plan, there appeared large-scale money issue, infrastructure and the corresponding spur of the linkage in the industrial chain. Therefore, from March 2009 to February 2010, in about 1 year, China's economy underwent a "small cycle" from recovery to prosperity and caused inflation in the first quarter of 2010. Due to government property regulation measures, the real economy with value-added of industry as the symbol began to slowdown. Meanwhile, the effects of the economic stimulus plan over industry pull gradually declined while large-scale liquidity still pushed CPI to a new high so that the economy rapidly entered the stagflation stage.

Table 2.3.1.2 Macro economic cycle and the changes in macro economic indicators and securities markets at different stages since 2000

Period	Macro economic stages	Duration (month)	Change in monthly year-on-year growth of the macro economic indicators		value-added of industry (%)
			M1 (%)	CPI (%)	
December 1999–September 2000	Prosperity	9	3.1	1.0	4.6
October 2000–March 2001	Inflation	6	-3.4	0.8	0.1
April 2001–August 2001	Stagflation	5	-3.2	0.2	-4.0
September 2001–January 2002	Depression	5	-4.7	-2.0	1.2
February 2002–April 2002	Recovery	3	2.0	-0.3	2.8
May 2002–August 2002	Expansion	4	3.1	0.6	0.6
September 2002–August 2003	Prosperity	12	4.2	1.6	4.4
September 2003–March 2004	Inflation	7	1.3	2.1	2.3
April 2004–October 2004	Stagflation	7	-7.5	1.2	-3.7
November 2004–August 2005	Depression	10	-1.1	-3.0	0.3
September 2005–December 2005	Recovery	4	0.3	0.3	0.5
January 2006–July 2006	Expansion	7	3.5	-0.5	0.2
August 2006–March 2007	Deceleration	8	4.5	2.3	0.9
April 2007–2007November	Prosperity	8	1.9	3.7	-0.3
December 2007–June 2008	Stagflation	7	-7.7	0.1	-1.3
July 2008–February 2009	Depression	8	-3.3	-8.7	-5.0
March 2009–June 2009	Recovery	4	14.2	-0.1	-0.3
July 2009–August 2009	Expansion	2	2.9	0.5	1.6
September 2009–February 2010	Prosperity	6	7.3	3.9	8.4
March 2010–April 2010	Inflation	2	-3.7	0.1	-2.9
May 2010–December 2010	Stagflation	8	-10.1	1.8	-4.3

(*Data source*: National Bureau of Statistics, People's Bank of China, Xinhua Finance)

2.3.2 *Characteristic analysis of the financial environment in 2010*

According to the analysis of the indicators of macro economic stages, the macro economy during the 2009–2010 period can be said, in a sense, to be more of a manually-created fluctuation. The depression stage (which may be prolonged) brought by the global financial crisis was made by the economic stimulus plan into a small cycle, the formation of which was basically caused by money supply. At first, a substantial increase in money supply leads to economic "recovery"; then, when the substantial liquidity brought by money supply transmits to the main part of economy, value-added of industry increases, displaying the prospect of "prosperity"; lastly, the substantial liquidity transmits to the lower reaches, causing a rise in prices. Meanwhile, the effects of the economic stimulus plan weakens, which together with the conscious control by the government leads to a depression both in value-added of industry and money supply, while the price level becomes strong because of the lagged effects, thus the economy demonstrates the features characteristic of the "stagflation" stage.

The difficulty in taking the monetary policy at the "stagflation" stage lies in the fact that the policy needs to curb the liquidity through quantitative or price-based instrument so as to control the continued rise in price level while at the same time to be meticulously careful in order to avoid accidentally injuring the real economy. According to the macro economic information released in December 2010, the Consumer Price Index (CPI) for December underwent a year-on-year growth of 4.6%; after the high reached in November 2010 since the breaking out of the global financial crisis, namely, since August 2008, it still retained the tendency of high position. But the year-on-year growth of value-added of industry was 13.5%, lingering between the interval from 13%–14% for 7 consecutive months. According to the calculation of "Xinhua Finance model of China's macro economic status", for the change rate of the smoothed value-added of industry transits to be positive, the estimated time is about the first quarter of 2011, while the price index is synchronously raised, and the "stagflation" still fails to witness obvious improvement.

By comparing similar stages in history, we can spot the particularity of the present situation. For example, around September 2004 the year-on-year growth rate of CPI was about 5.1%, when M1 year-on-year growth was lower than the present level of 13.7%, while the growth of value-added of industry then was higher than the present level of 16.1%; between June and July in 2007, there also appeared a period when the year-on-year growth rate of CPI was around 5% (4.4% and 5.6% respectively), but M1 growth then was about 21%, slightly lower than the present level, while the growth of value-added of

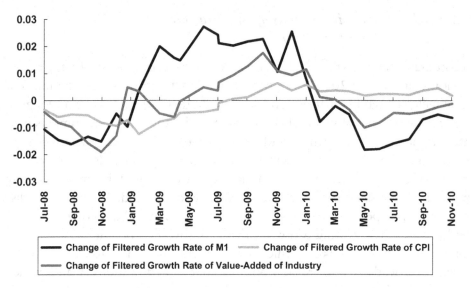

Figure 2.3.2.1   China's macro economy still at the "stagflation" stage

(*Data source*: National Bureau of Statistics, People's Bank of China, Xinhua Finance)

industry then was 18%–19%, higher than the present level. In August 2008, there also appeared a similar situation where the year-on-year growth rate of CPI was around 5% (i.e. 4.9%), but money supply and real economic growth both were lower than the present level (1.3% and 12.8% respectively). The present situation seems to be quite special: the real economy is always in a "base building" status while money supply is always wandering around the high position. For another, the reality the monetary regulatory authority is currently confronted with is never seen in history. During the first 10 years of this century, due to the constant rise in property price, a substantial liquidity is absorbed by the real estate; when the liquidity begins to overflow this time, the government is faced with an arduous task of regulating the real estate.

Obviously, the adequate liquidity in 2010 is the outcome of the economic stimulus plan initated at the end of 2008. The uncertainty of the global economic recovery determined that it is impossible for China to take radical retrenchment policy, or it will probably cause the rapid influx of hot money, making the economic stimulus plan go down the drain. This also accounts for the fact that in the second half of 2010, although price level was on a continuous rise, yet the central bank cautiously implemented the monetary policy and adopted more of quantitative regulation (namely cash reserve ratio) than price-based regulation (namely benchmark deposit and lending rate). In other words, this is one reason for adopting the quantitative regulation of "oriented absorption of liquidity".

Chapter 3

STOCK MARKET

3.1 Development of A-Share Market

3.1.1 Expansion of A-share market

In recent years, the scale of A-share has been constantly expanded. By December 2010, its total market capital value expanded to RMB 19.3 trillion. Compared with the previous 10 years (namely by December 2000), the total market capitalization increased by 4.5 times, and free float market capitalization increased by 11 times. Since the reform of stock right dividing has been basically completed, the free float market capitalization of A-share market has witnessed a steady rise in recent years and the present free float market capitalization reaches a new high of the latest 10 years.

The development of A-share market is shown not only in the expansion of total market capitalization and circulation value, but the gradual improvement of liquidity, especially after 2006. During this period, as the reform of stock right dividing pushes ahead, the proportion of negotiable share increases step by step, compelling the rise in its turnover to some extent. For example, during this period from 2001 to 2005, the monthly average turnover was about RMB 288.7 billion, which rose up to RMB 3.166 trillion during the period from 2006 to 2010. Seen from monthly turnover velocity (calculated by "monthly value of share trading/month-end free float market capitalization), it underwent significant twists and turns during the recent 5 years with the fluctuation of market tendency, while seen as a whole, the monthly turnover velocity still remained in a rising trend. For example, the average monthly turnover velocity of the period from 2001 to 2005 was 21.2%, while during the years from 2006 to 2010, this figure rose to 44.2%.

Market expansion is shown not only in the increase of the scale of market capitalization and the improvement of market liquidity, but in the rise in the quantity of financiers and investors. In the past 5 years (i.e. from 2005 to 2010), the quantity of listed companies on the stock market increased from 1,381 to 2,063, a rise of around 49.4%. Especially since the second half of

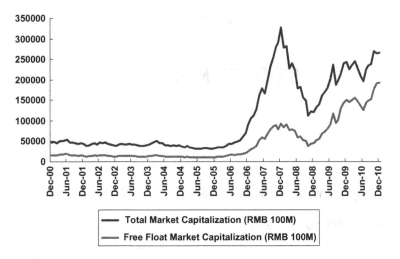

Figure 3.1.1.1 The scale of A-share market has been rapidly expanded during the past 10 years

(*Data source*: China's Securities Regulatory Commission)

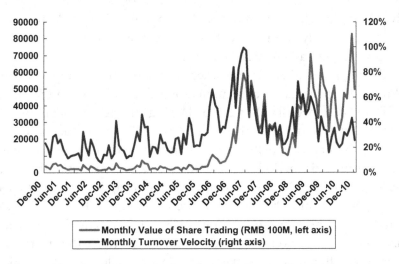

Figure 3.1.1.2 An obvious rise in the liquidity of A-share market during the recent 5 years

(*Data source*: China's Securities Regulatory Commission)

2009, the quantity of listed companies rapidly enlarged. For example, during the period from January to December in 2010, there were 345 newly added listed companies, an average of 29 in every month.

In correspondence to the steady increase in the quantity of listed companies was the rise in the quantity of investors. During the period from 2006 to 2010, the deposit amounts increased from 79 million to 158 million,

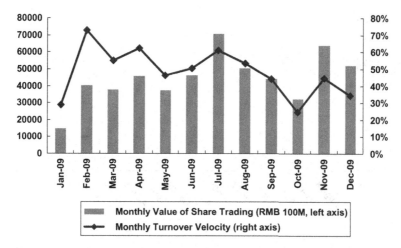

Figure 3.1.1.3-a   Liquidity of A-share market in each month of 2009

(*Data source*: China's Securities Regulatory Commission)

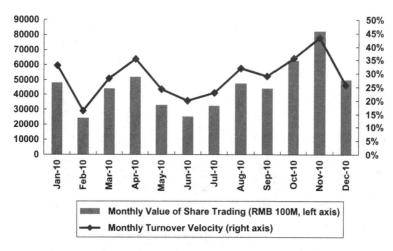

Figure 3.1.1.3-b   Liquidity of A-share market in each month of 2010

(*Data source*: China's Securities Regulatory Commission)

rising by 1.16 times. Presently, the deposit amounts of Shanghai Stock Exchange and Shenzhen Stock Exchange are 79 million and 78 million respectively, increasing by 1.15 times and 1.18 times respectively in comparison with those by the end of 2005. To be specific, from January to November in 2010, the newly–added deposit amounts of Shanghai Stock Exchange and Shenzhen Stock Exchange were 6.8 million and 6.79 million respectively, the average newly-added deposit amounts being 618 thousand and 617 thousand respectively.

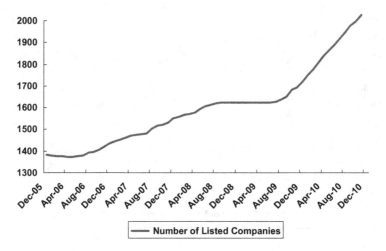

Figure 3.1.1.4   Significant increase in the number of listed companies during the past 5 years
(*Data source*: China's Securities Regulatory Commission)

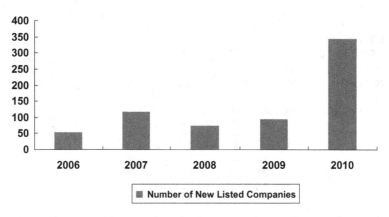

Figure 3.1.1.5   More significant increase in the number of listed companies in 2010
(*Data source*: China's Securities Regulatory Commission)

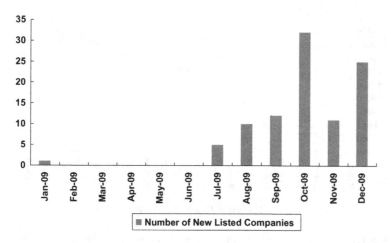

Figure 3.1.1.6-a   The number of newly listed companies in each month of 2009
(*Data source*: China's Securities Regulatory Commission)

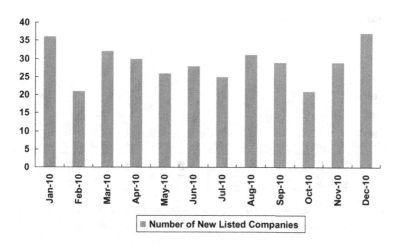

Figure 3.1.1.6-b   The quantity of newly listed companies in each month of 2010
(*Data source*: China's Securities Regulatory Commission)

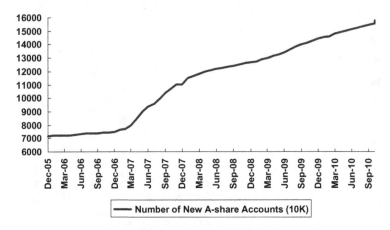

Figure 3.1.1.7 A steady increase in the number of investors during the past 5 years

(*Data source*: Shanghai Stock Exchange, Shenzhen Stock Exchange)

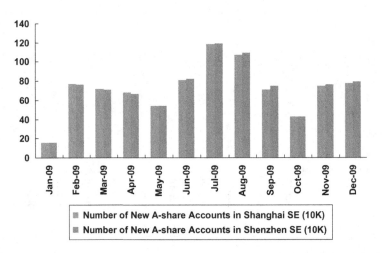

Figure 3.1.1.8-a Number of new A-share amounts in each month of 2009

(*Data source*: Shanghai Stock Exchange, Shenzhen Stock Exchange)

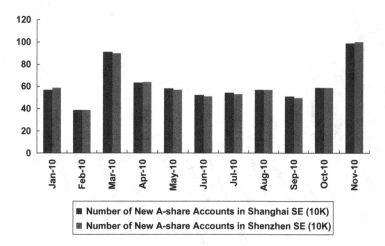

Figure 3.1.1.8-b   Number of new amounts in each month of the period from January to November in 2010

(*Data source*: Shanghai Stock Exchange, Shenzhen Stock Exchange)

3.1.2 *Construction of multi-level capital market — growth enterprise market*

In October 2009, Shenzhen Stock Exchange launched a board — "Growth Enterprise Market" (GEM) to accommodate those enterprises in the growth stage, of strong innovative capability and high growthiness. After this launch, A-share market initially formed the market levels of main enterpirses board, small and medium-sized enterprises (SMEs) board, and GEM board, etc. and thus further advancing the course of improving the multi-level capital market.

The industrial distribution of the listed companies on GEM to some extent embodies the characteristics of the listed companies at the start-up stage. Whether seen from the distribution of market capitalization or the quantitative distribution, the industries among the first six ranks are respectively machinery, information service, healthcare, electric equipment, chemical engineering, and technological equipment. The listed companies of these six large industries account for 86.7% and 84.3% in market capitalization and company quantity respectively. In a sense, the industrial distribution of GEM reflects the governmental policy of encouraging emerging industries. Hence companies belonging to industries such as equipment manufacturing (corresponding to machinery), information and electronics (corresponding to information service, electric equipment and information device industries), new materials (corresponding to chemicals) and biomedicine (corresponding to healthcare), etc. are evidently encouraged by such policy when entering GEM.

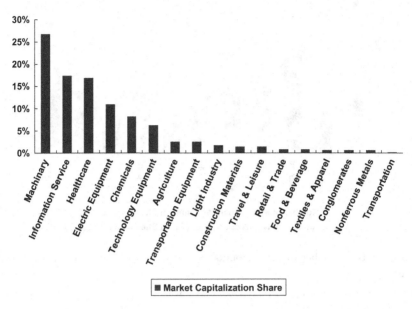

Figure 3.1.2.1   Industrial distribution of the market capitalization of the listed companies on GEM (adopting the Grade-A industrial distribution by Shenyin & Wanguo)

(*Data source*: Shenzhen Stock Exchange, Shenyin & Wanguo Securities)

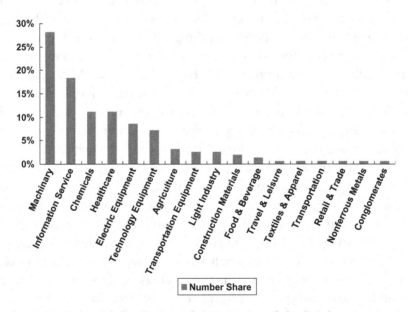

Figure 3.1.2.2   Industrial distribution of the quantity of the listed companies on GEM (adopting the Grade-A industrial distribution by Shenyin & Wanguo)

(*Data source*: Shenzhen Stock Exchange, Shenyin & Wanguo Securities)

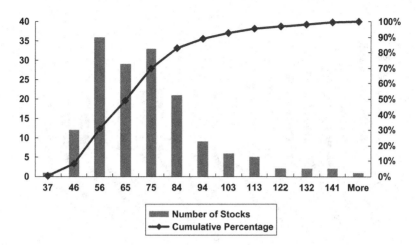

Figure 3.1.2.3 Distribution of the first p/e ratio (diluted) of the listed companies on GEM (*Data source*: Shenzhen Stock Exchange)

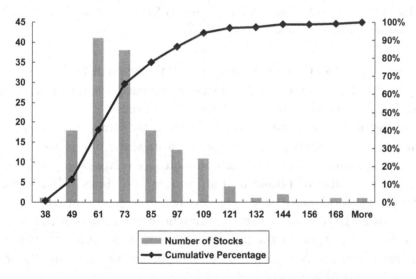

Figure 3.1.2.4 Distribution of p/e of the listed companies on GEM by the end of 2010 (*Data source*: Shenzhen Stock Exchange)

One major characteristic of the companies listed on GEM is their relatively high p/e (price/earning) ratio. According to statistics by the end of December 2010, the mean value of the first p/e ratio (diluted) of the listed enterprises on GEM was 69.3 times (the median being 65.6 times). About 90% of the companies listed on GEM achieved a first p/e ratio of over 50 times, and about 10% achieved a first p/e ratio of over 100 times.

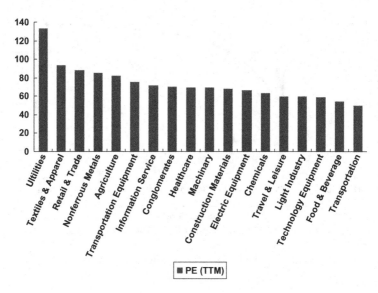

Figure 3.1.2.5   Industrial distribution of p/e of the listed companies on GEM by the end of 2010 (adopting the Grade-A industrial distribution by Shenyin & Wanguo)

(*Data source*: Shenzhen Stock Exchange, Shenyin & Wanguo Securities)

By the end of 2010 since the launch of GEM, the medial of the scroll p/e ratio (i.e. TTM p/e ratio) of the listed enterprised on GEM was about 65 times, and its mean value reached up to 71.5 times.

In terms of different industries, if adopting the Grade-A industrial distribution system by Shenyin & Wanguo Securities, the p/e ratios of public utilities, textile and apparel, retail & trade, etc. are relatively higher, among which, the p/e ratio of public utilities is over 100 times, while those of transportation, foods and beverage, and technology equipment, etc. are relatively lower. Except for transportation whose p/e ratio is at the bottom, the p/e ratio of the rest of the industries all surpasses 50 times. That is to say, at least from the perspective of p/e ratio, the valuation levels of the companies on GEM are quite high.

Given the characteristics of the high growthiness of the GEM companies, the indicators of growing forecast p/e ratio and PEG (=p/e ratio/growth rate) in future can, relatively speaking, reflect the value of a given company all the more. According to the data acquired by the end of 2010, for the listed enterprises on GEM, for the year 2012, the mean value of the forecast p/e ratio is 30.2 times (its median being 28.4 times), among which, for only about 20% companies, their forecast p/e ratio is below 25 times. On the contrary, for over 20% of companies, their forecast p/e ratio is over 35 times.

Seen from PEG data and according to the data by the end of 2010, for the listed enterprises on GEM, for the year 2012, the average PEG is about

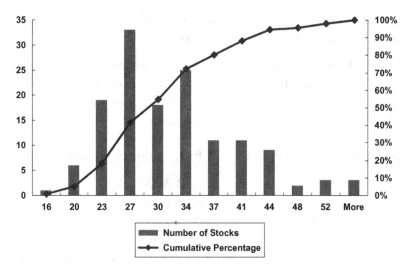

Figure 3.1.2.6 Distribution of the forecast p/e ratio of the listed companies on GEM for the year 2012, based on data by the end of 2010

(*Data source*: Shenzhen Stock Exchange, Xinhua Finance)

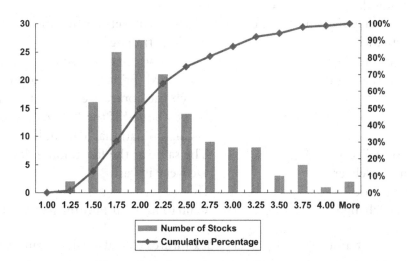

Figure 3.1.2.7 Distribution of the forecast PEG of the listed companies on GEM for the year 2012, based on data by the end of 2010

(*Data source*: Shenzhen Stock Exchange, Xinhua Finance)

2.2 (its median being 2.0). Almost all the enterprises' PEG is above 1, and there are only 10% of enterprises whose PEG is below 1.5. On the contrary, there are more than 10% of enterprises whose PEG is over 3. Adopting the evaluation standard that enterprises whose PEG is below 1 are of investment value will indicate that at least by the end of 2010, a majority of enterprises on GEM will be at an overvalued state.

3.1.3 *Aboundance in financial tools of capital market (1) — stock index futures*

In April 2010 stock index futures were officially issued, symbolizing that the investors on A-share market began to possess a short tool. The first stock index futures contract issued was "Shanghai-Shenzhen 300 Index Contract", whose relevant parameters are showed as follows:

Subject matter of the contract	Shanghai-Shenzhen 300 Index
Contract multiplier	RMB 300/point
Quote unit	Index point
Minimal change in price	0.2 point
Contract month	Current month, next month and the two months respectively at the end of the following two quarters
Trading hour	9:15–11:30 am.; 13:00–15:15 pm.
Trading hour on the last trading day	9:15–11:30 am.; 13:00–15:00 pm.
Limit to daily maximum price fluctuation	±10% of the settlement price of the previous trading day
Minimum trading margin	12% of the contract value
The last trading day	The third Friday of the month in which the contract expires; it would be postponed if the last trading day occurs on national legal holiday
Date of delivery	The same as the last trading day
Means of delivery	Delivery in cash
Trading code	IF
Listed exchange	China Financial Futures Exchange

From the tendency of the stock index futures after its issue, it can be seen that by the end of 2010, month contracts demonstated a positive basis on most trading days. The statistics show that: from 16th April 2010 (the day of issuing the stock index futures) to 30th December 2010, the mean value of basis of the month contract were 16.9 points (the median being 13.5 points); the trading days of positive basis accounted for more than 80% of all the trading days; the biggest positive basis is over 120 points, and the biggest negative basis approximated to 60 points. The proportion of the trading days with a positive basis of over 50 points was about 10%.

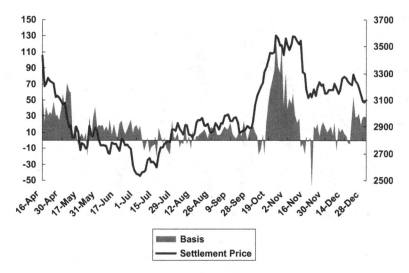

Figure 3.1.3.1 Settlement price tendency and change in basis of the month contracts from the issue of stock index futures in 2010 till year end

(*Data source*: China Financial Futures Exchange)

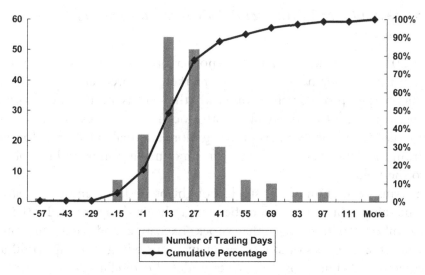

Figure 3.1.3.2 Basis distribution of the month contracts from the issue of stock index futures in 2010 till year end

(*Data source*: China Financial Futures Exchange)

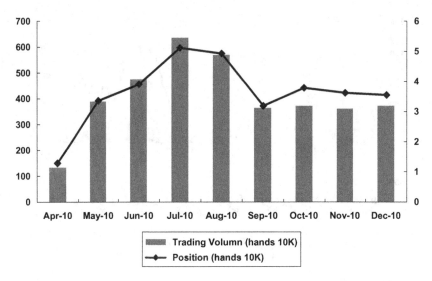

Figure 3.1.3.3   Trading volume and position of the month contracts from the issue of stock index futures in 2010 till year end

(*Data source*: China Financial Futures Exchange)

3.1.4 *Aboundance in financial tools of capital market (2) — margin*

March 2010 witnessed the lauch of another financial tool of great significance to the development of A-share market. Theoretically speaking, the issue of margin provides investors with the means of making short on the aspect of stock. Complemented with stock index futures, it can to some degree balance the mechanisms of doing more and making short. However, seen from the data of 2010, the mechanism of making short did not play its role to the full.

In terms of the number of stocks bought or sold, the amount of stocks under margin trading appeared to be in a gradually rising trend. By the end of December 2010, in Shanghai Stock Exchange and Shenzhen Stock Exchange, the amounts of stocks under margin trading were up to 50 and 39 respectively, while those of stocks under short selling were 9 and 15 respectively.

In terms of the trading volume, that of stocks under margin trading far outnumbered that of stocks under short selling. During the period from the issue of margin in March 2010 to year end, for Shanghai Stock Exchange and Shenzhen Stock Exchange, the mean values of the daily turnover of stocks under margin trading were RMB 230 million and RMB 150 million respectively (their medians being RMB 130 million and RMB

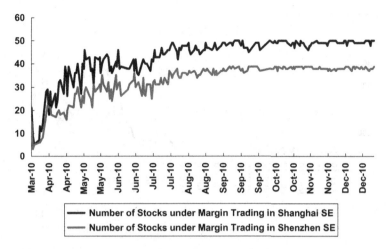

Figure 3.1.4.1   Number of stocks under margin trading after the issue of margin in 2010
(*Data source*: Shanghai Stock Exchange, Shenzhen Stock Exchange)

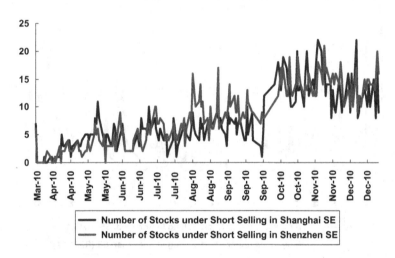

Figure 3.1.4.2   Number of stocks under short selling after the issue of margin in 2010
(*Data source*: Shanghai Stock Exchange, Shenzhen Stock Exchange)

90 million), while the mean values of the daily turnover of stocks under short selling both were around RMB 3 million (the medians both being about RMB 2 million), indicating a distinct gap between the two kinds of turnover.

The asymmetry of the businesses of financing and load securities is also embodied in the balance of financing and the balance of securities load of two cities, namely, Shanghai and Shenzhen. During the period from the

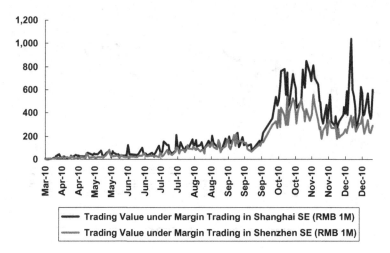

Figure 3.1.4.3   Daily trading volume of stocks under margin trading after the issue of margin in 2010

(*Data source*: Shanghai Stock Exchange, Shenzhen Stock Exchange)

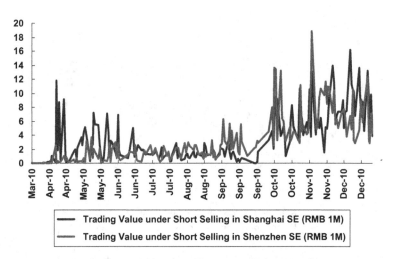

Figure 3.1.4.4   Daily trading volume of stocks under short selling after the issue of margin in 2010

(*Data source*: Shanghai Stock Exchange, Shenzhen Stock Exchange)

issue of margin in March 2010 to the year end, for Shanghai Stock Exchange and Shenzhen Stock Exchange, the mean values of financing were RMB 2.65 billion and RMB 1.54 billion respectively (the medians being RMB 1.95 billion and RMB 1.1 billion respectively). By the end of 2010, the financing balances of the above two exchanges amounted to RMB 8.43 billion and RMB 4.33 billion respectively. However, in the case

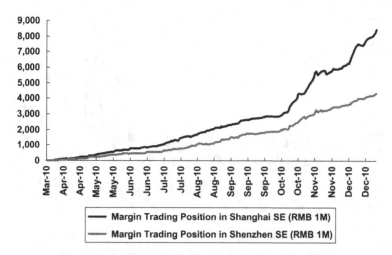

Figure 3.1.4.5 Margin trading position after the issue of margin in 2010

(*Data source*: Shanghai Stock Exchange, Shenzhen Stock Exchange)

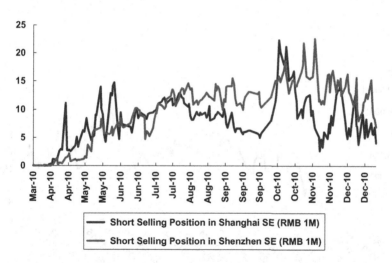

Figure 3.1.4.6 Short selling position after the issue of margin in 2010

(*Data source*: Shanghai Stock Exchange, Shenzhen Stock Exchange)

of securities load, during the year 2010, the average balances of securities load were RMB 8 million and RMB 10 million respectively (the medians being RMB 8 billion and RMB 1.11 million respectively). By the end of 2010, the short selling positions of the two exchanges were RMB 4 million and RMB 7 million respectively.

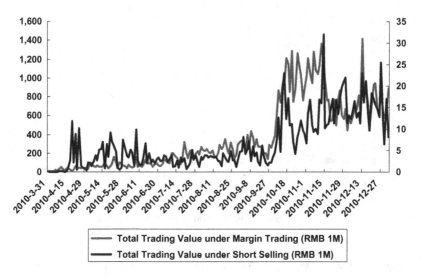

Figure 3.1.4.7   Comparison of the daily trading volume of stocks under margin trading and stocks under short selling in the two cities after the issue of margin in 2010

(*Data source*: Shanghai Stock Exchange, Shenzhen Stock Exchange)

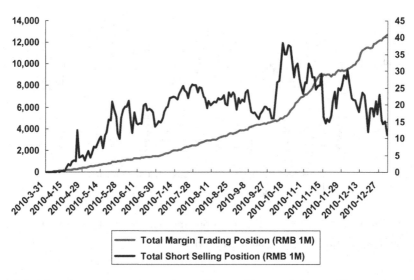

Figure 3.1.4.8   Comparison of margin trading position and short selling position in the two cities after the issue of margin in 2010

(*Data source*: Shanghai Stock Exchange, Shenzhen Stock Exchange)

3.2 Structural Characteristics of A-Share Market in 2010

3.2.1 *Overall valuation and fundamentals of A-share market in 2010*

One significant characteristic of A-share market in 2010 was the evident industrial differentiation (in a sense, the differentiation between market stocks and small-cap stocks is the demonstration of industrial differentiation). To understand the characteristics of industrial differentiation, this book adopts "Xinhua Industrial Differentiation System of China's A-Share Market" to differentiate the listed companies on A-share markets according to their industries.

In this system, the whole economic system is divided into four major systems, ten general industrial categories and 31 kinds of industries (some cross-industry listed companies are classified into "conglomerates" industry). Within this system, the four systems include the systems of energy, industry, consumption and economic support, among which the "industry" system is further divided into two industrial categories — "primary industrial product"

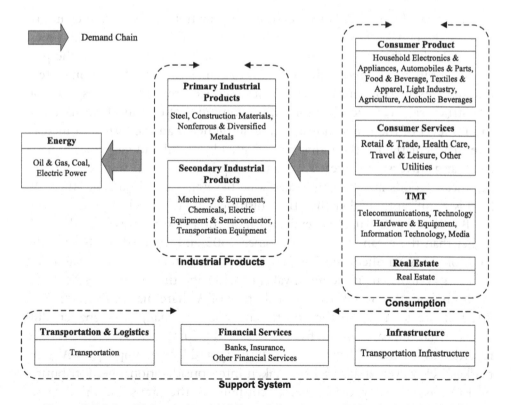

Figure 3.2.1.1   Xinhua industrial differentiation system of China's A-share market

and "secondary processing industrial product"; the "consumption" system is further divided into four industrial categories — "consumer goods", "consumer services", "TMT" (abbreviation of "telecommunications, media and technology"), and "real estate"; the "economic support system" is divided into three industrial categories — "transport and logistics", "financial services" and "infrastructure".

To keep the typicality and stability of the listed companies in the relevant industries, when making statistics, this book takes into consideration the stocks that meet the following conditions:

- Having been listed for more than one year (to reduce the influence exerted by the excessive fluctuation of stock price at the inception of being listed)
- More than RMB 100 million of the free float market capitalization (to guarantee the stocks under question are of certain scale and liquidity)
- Non-ST stock and non-PT stock
- Non-GEM stock (since GEM was launched not long ago, the valuation of non-GEM stocks is generally high, which may exert certain influence on the statistic results)

In terms of PB (TTM) to measure the valuation levels of various industries, by the end of 2010, PB of A-share market as a whole is about 3.9 times, slightly higher than the historical median value by 3.6 times. From the perspective of industry, among the 32 industries (including the "conglomerates" industry), except for banks, other financial services, real estate, transportation infrastructure, steel, electric utilities, telecommunications and light industry, the PB level of the other industries are all higher than the historical median level. Particularly, for the industries of agriculture, oil and gas, coal, nonferrous and diversified metals, electric equipment and semi-conductor, healthcare, foods and beverage, alcoholic beverages and insurance, their PB level is significantly higher than their historical median level.

By the end of 2010, the overall return on equity (ROE) was around 15.8%, higher than the mean value (10.1%) since 2005 and the median (10.6%); the ROE of Shanghai-Shenzhen 300 Index, Blue Chip stocks included, was about 17.1%, also higher than the mean value (14.1%) and the median (13.2%).

Seen from the overall ROE distribution of A-share market from 2005 to 2010, if the focus is on the constituent stock of Shanghai-Shenzhen 300 Index, what appeared most frequently is 13% (that is to say, 13% can be regarded as the overall level of ROE of the typical listed company on A-share market). However, if all market is taken into consideration, the distribution of ROE is relatively dispersive. According to the statistics, the interval between 7% and 14% is relatively the more frequently appeared interval.

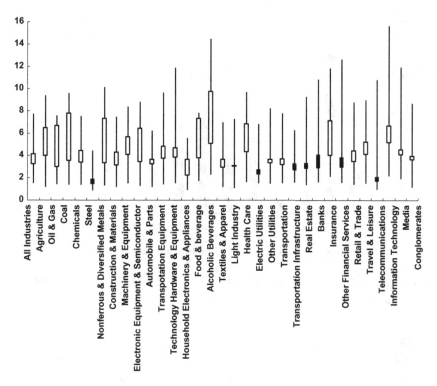

Figure 3.2.1.2 PB of different industries on A-share market by the end of 2010

("solid line" indicates that PB of the given industry was higher than the historical median by the end of 2010; "shade line" indicates that PB of the given industry was lower than the historical median by the end of 2010) (*Data source*: Xinhua Finance)

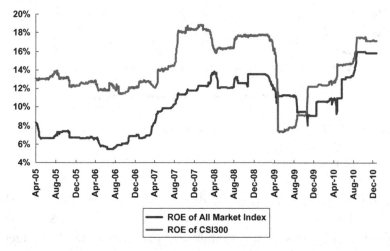

Figure 3.2.1.3 PB of different industries on A-share market by the end of 2010

(*Data source*: Xinhua Finance)

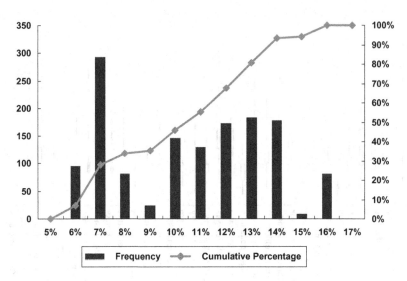

Figure 3.2.1.4　ROE distribution of all market index on A-share market from 2005 to 2010
(*Data source*: Xinhua Finance)

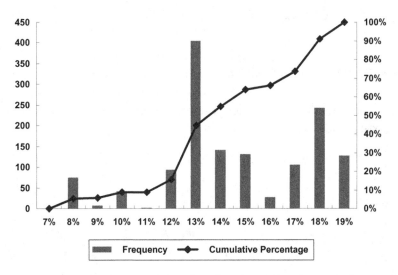

Figure 3.2.1.5　ROE distribution of Shanghai-Shenzhen 300 Index on A-share market from 2005 to 2010
(*Data source*: Xinhua Finance)

In terms of specific industries, by the end of 2010, whether from the per-spective of all market or the constituent stock of Shanghai-Shenzhen 300 Index, for the industries of automobile and parts, alcoholic beverages, coal, household electronics and appliances, machinery, and healthcare, their ROE were at the forefront.

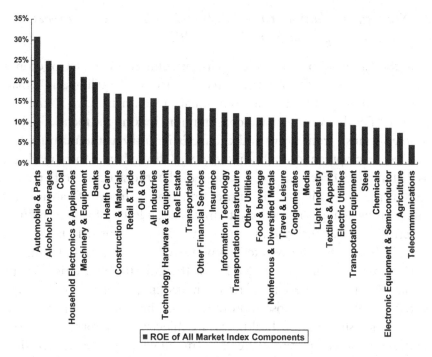

Figure 3.2.1.6 ROE distribution of various industries on A-share market by the end of 2010

(*Data source*: Xinhua Finance)

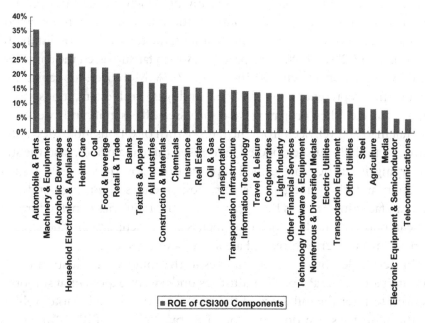

Figure 3.2.1.7 ROE distribution of the constituent stock of Shanghai-Shenzhen 300 Index by the end of 2010

(*Data source*: Xinhua Finance)

3.2.2 *Structural changes in the industries on A-share market during the period from 2005 to 2010*

In 2010, the Chinese government explicitly announced the policy of economic restructuring, the core of which can be reduced to two "equilibration": making the economic driving force transit from unitary investment drive to the equilibrated drive of both investment and consumption; making the focus of industrial development transit from heavy and chemicals industry as the mainstay to the equilibrated development of various industries. Reflected on A-share market, this means that in terms of return rate, it is embodied in the structural differentiation of the return rate of different industries and that in terms of valuation, it is embodied in the changes in the long-term valuation levels of various industries.

In terms of the annual rate of return, in "Xinhua Industrial Differentiation System of China's A Share Market", among the 32 industries, 16 industries achieved a positive return rate in 2011. For the industry of electric equipment and semiconductor, whose rate of return ranks first, its annual return rate of amounted to 49.1%. For those industries which benefited from the national industrial policy support like healthcare, machinery and information services, they also achieved a return rate above 25%, among which the yearly growth rates of healthcare and machinery were over 30%. In addition, with the rise in inflation expectation, for those industries which benefited from inflation like agriculture, nonferrous and diversified metals, and alcoholic beverages, also achieved a rate of return more than 19%, among which the growth rate of agriculture reached up to 23.2%. By contrast, the financial sector represented by banks and other financial services ranked among the top of the drop list in 2010, with a drop of 37.2% and 28.9% respectively, which far surpassed the annual drop range of Shanghai-Shenzhen 300 Index — 12.5%. Moreover, for capital-intensive industries represented by steel, oil and gas, real estate, transportation infrastructure, etc., their drop range also surpassed 20%, significantly weaker than the overall market level. Seen from the rates of turn of various industries in 2010, the investment theme was embodied in terms of three main lines: first, the strategic emerging industries that gained support from government policy, such as information and electronics, new energy equipment; second, high-end equipment manufacturing, such as healthcare; third, the industries benefited from the increase in bulk commodity (including metals and agricultural products), such as nonferrous metals, agriculture, and alcoholic beverages, etc.

In order to demonstrate the changes in the long-term valuation levels of various industries, the PB of the industries underwent exponential smoothing. Moreover, to filter the influence of the change in the overall market valuation upon the industries, we do not adopt PB, but "relative PB" (PBR, i.e. the ration between PB of a given industry and market PB). That is to say, we

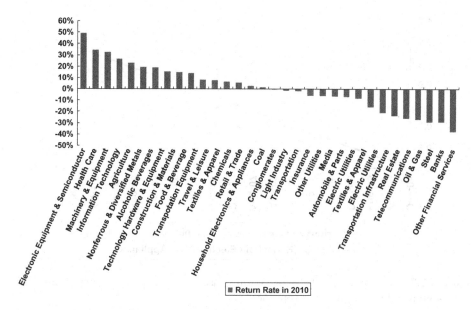

Figure 3.2.2.1 Annual return rate of various industries in 2010

(*Data source*: Xinhua Finance)

adopt the exponential smoothing value of relative PB of various industries to demonstrate the long-term variation tendency of their corresponding valuation levels.

From the linear regression of exponential smoothing values of PBR during the 2005–2010 period, three categories of industries can be distinguished, namely, industries with significant decline in valuation level, industries with significant increase in valuation level, and industries whose valuation level is basically in a cyclic change.

Included in the first category of industries are household electronics and appliances, agriculture, alcoholic beverages, machinery, healthcare, retail and trade. These 6 industries underwent a significant rise in their valuation levels during the period from 2005 to 2010. Their R^2 in the linear regression model is above 0.5, among which the first 5 industries is over 0.6, and the first three is above 0.8. Among these 6 industries, there are in total 5 industries belonging to the industry related to consumption or consumer service (the first three being consumption industry), while the elevation of valuation level mainly lies in its inclusion of a group of listed companies related to new energy and high-end equipment manufacturing. That is to say, although the policy of economic restructuring was officially put forward in 2010, in the long-term valuation of the securities market, the valuation advantages of consumer goods and high-end manufacturing have turned out in a subtle way.

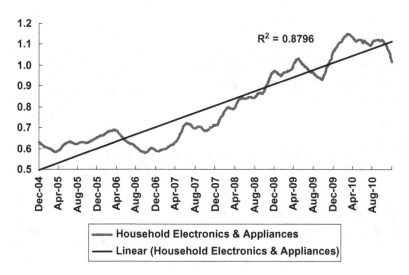

Figure 3.2.2.2-a Industry with significant increase in valuation level between 2005 and 2010 — household electronics and appliances

(*Data source*: Xinhua Finance)

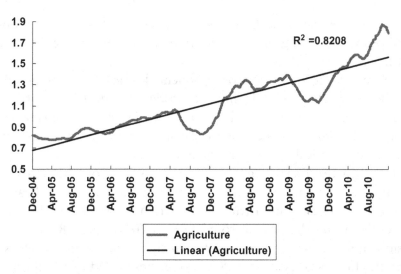

Figure 3.2.2.2-b Industry with significant increase in valuation level between 2005 and 2010 — agriculture

(*Data source*: Xinhua Finance)

Industries with significant decline in valuation level mainly include transportation infrastructure, banks and steel, the main feature of which is relevant to infrastructure and capital-intensive industries.

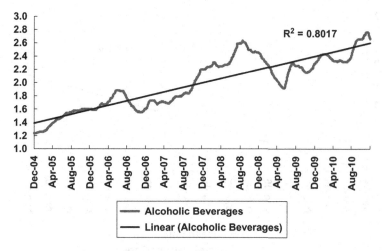

Figure 3.2.2.2-c Industry with significant increase in valuation level between 2005 and 2010 — alcoholic beverages

(*Data source*: Xinhua Finance)

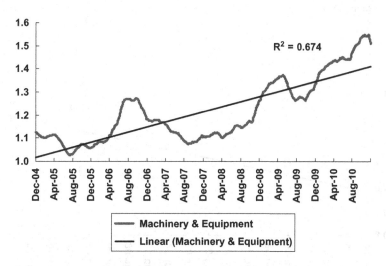

Figure 3.2.2.2-d Industry with significant increase in valuation level between 2005 and 2010 — machinery

(*Data source*: Xinhua Finance)

The characteristic of the third category is that the long-term tendency of valuation level is not so evident, which embodied in the linear regression model is that their R^2 is below 0.4, even below 0.3. However, their valuation levels appear in a kind of cyclic feature, especially the industry of nonferrous and diversified metals, mainly including coal, nonferrous and diversified metals, construction and materials, and automobile and parts.

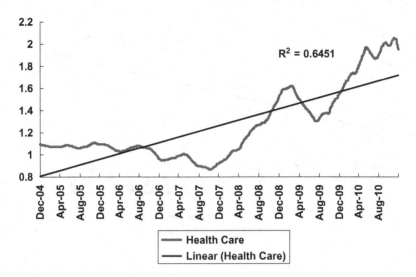

Figure 3.2.2.2-e   Industry with significant increase in valuation level between 2005 and 2010 — healthcare

(*Data source*: Xinhua Finance)

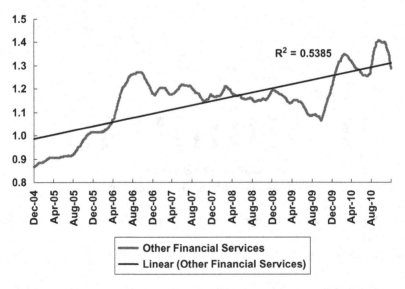

Figure 3.2.2.2-f   Industry with significant increase in valuation level between 2005 and 2010 — retail and trade

(*Data source*: Xinhua Finance)

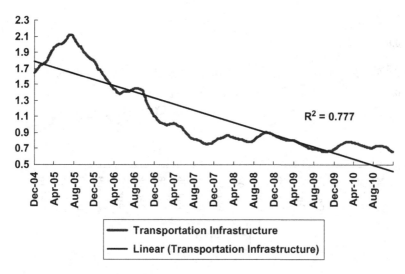

Figure 3.2.2.3-a Industry with significant decline in valuation level between 2005 and 2010 — transportation infrastructure

(*Data source*: Xinhua Finance)

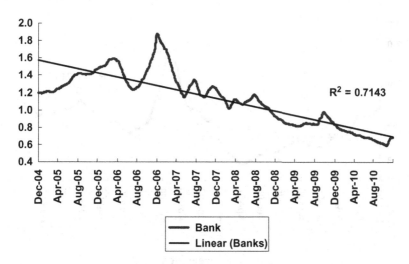

Figure 3.2.2.3-b Industry with significant decline in valuation level between 2005 and 2010 — banks

(*Data source*: Xinhua Finance)

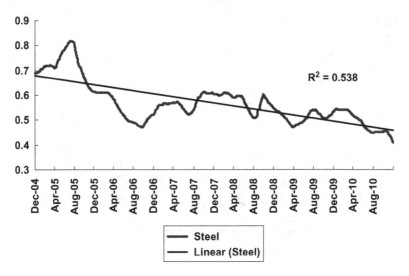

Figure 3.2.2.3-c   Industry with significant decline in valuation level between 2005 and 2010 — steel

(*Data source*: Xinhua Finance)

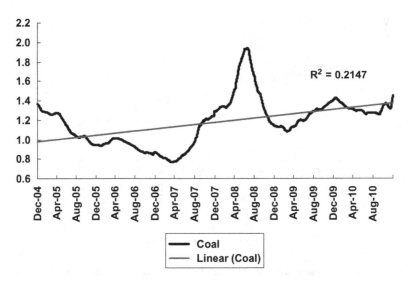

Figure 3.2.2.4-a   Industry with cyclic change in valuation level between 2005 and 2010 — coal

(*Data source*: Xinhua Finance)

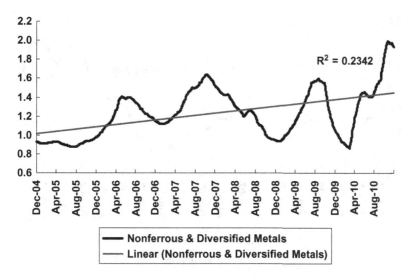

Figure 3.2.2.4-b Industry with cyclic change in valuation level between 2005 and 2010 — nonferrous and diversified metals

(*Data source*: Xinhua Finance)

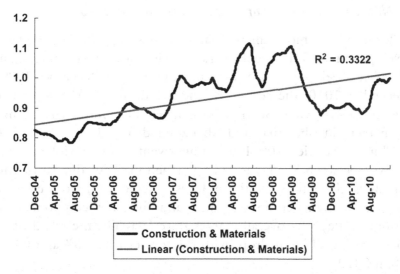

Figure 3.2.2.4-c Industry with cyclic change in valuation level between 2005 and 2010 — construction and materials

(*Data source*: Xinhua Finance)

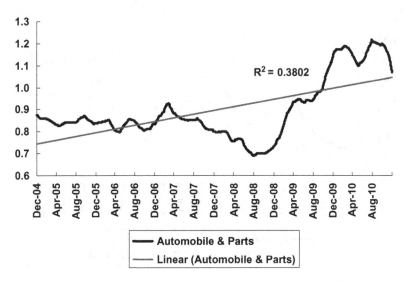

Figure 3.2.2.4-d   Industry with cyclic change in valuation level between 2005 and 2010 — automobile and parts

(*Data source*: Xinhua Finance)

3.2.3 *New characteristics of A-share market in 2010*

In 2010, one of the most salient characteristics of A-share market is that the development of SME stock market is significantly stronger than the overall maket development. For example, during 31th December 2009 and 31th December 2010, the composite index indicating SME stock had an increase of 28.4%, while Shanghai-Shenzhen 300 Index indicating the overall markets in Shanghai and Shenzhen dropped by 12.5%. What's more, China Securities 100 Index underwent a more violent drop of 19.3%. Even between Shanghai and Shenzhen markets, due to the differences in stock characteristics, the indexes differed a lot from each other. For instance, Shanghai composite index and Shenzhen component index, though both reflect the overall market state (actually, the trend of large-cap stock), had a different drop, with the former by 14.3% and the latter by 9.1% in 2010.

From the perspective of industries, in 2010, different industries were quite distinct from each other. For example, in the 32 industries within "Xinhua Finance Model of China's Macro Economic Status", steel ranked the 7th in terms of Shanghai-Shenzhen 300 Index constituent stock at the end of 2009, while droping to the 14th place at the end of 2010. On the contrary, healthcare industry elevated from the 16th place at the end of 2009 to the 10th place at the end of 2010.

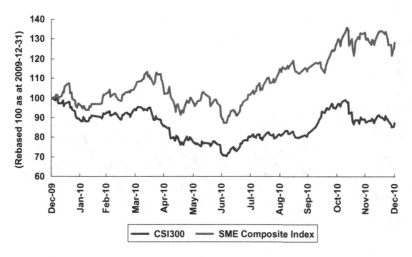

Figure 3.2.3.1   The SME trend was significant stronger than market trend in 2010
(*Data source*: China Securities Index Co Ltd, Shenzhen Stock Exchange)

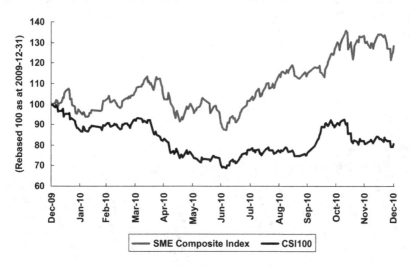

Figure 3.2.3.2   The SME trend was significant stronger than large-cap stock trend in 2010
(*Data source*: China Securities Index Co Ltd, Shenzhen Stock Exchange)

Seen from the change in the share of each industries in Shanghai-Shenzhen 300 constituent stock, although by the end of 2010 banks still ranked the first, its share had declined from 21.3% by the end of 2009 to 17.4%, with a drop of nearly 4%. Other industries that had relatively significant decline include steel, other financial services, real estate and coal, etc. By contrast, the industries that had a relatively significant rise in this share include nonferrous and diversified metals,

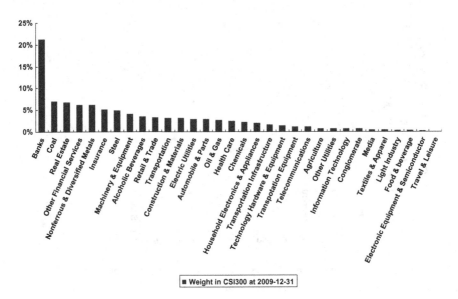

Figure 3.2.3.3 The industrial distribution of Shanghai-Shenzhen 300 Index constituent stock by the end of 2009

(*Data source*: Xinhua Finance)

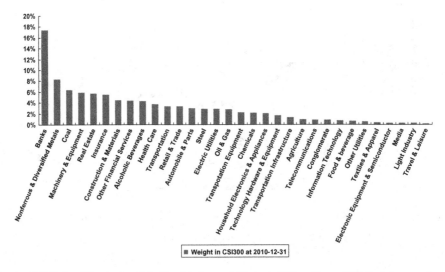

Figure 3.2.3.4 The industrial distribution of Shanghai-Shenzhen 300 Index constituent stock by the end of 2010

(*Data source*: Xinhua Finance)

machinery, construction and materials, healthcare, and non-automobile transportation equipment. Their share in Shanghai-Shenzhen 300 Index had an increase of over 1%, among which the share of nonferrous and diversified metals rose by 2.2%.

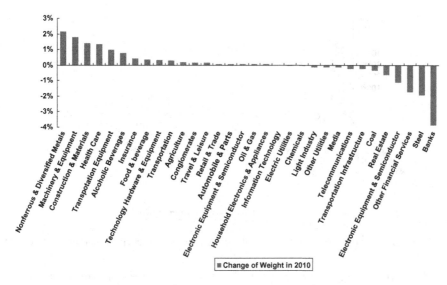

Figure 3.2.3.5   Change in the share of Shanghai-Shenzhen 300 Index constituent stock in 2010

(*Data source*: Xinhua Finance)

3.3 A-Share Market within Global Vision

3.3.1 *Comparison of the scales of A-share market and world's major securities markets*

According to the data by 2008, the total market capitalizations of Shanghai Stock Exchange and Shenzhen Stock Exchange accounted for 30.2% and 8.2% respectively in the GDP of the Chinese mainland, that is, the ratio of A-share market capitalization against the Chinese mainland GDP was about 38.4%. Compared with the developed markets, this ratio is still relatively low: the market capitalization of American NYSE Euronext and NASDAQ OMX accounted for 63.8% and 15.6% (79.4% in total) respectively in GDP; the market capitalization of London Stock Exchange accounted for 69.7%; the market capitalization of Tokyo Stock Exchange accounted for 63.4%; the market capitalization of Taiwan Stock Exchange Corporation accounted for 91.1%; and Hong Kong Exchanges accounted for a high of 617% in GDP of the Hong Kong Special Administrative Region.

In terms of the number of the listed companies, during the years 2001–2010, the numbers in Shanghai Stock Exchange and Shenzhen Stock Exchange increased from 646 to 894, and from 894 to 1169 respectively. Their average yearly compound growth rates were 3.7% and 9.7% respectively, ranking among the first of the world's major securities markets.

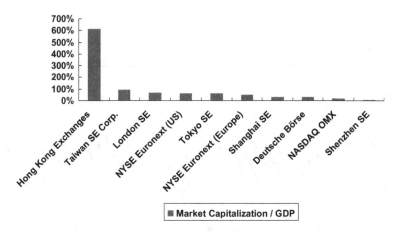

Figure 3.3.1.1   Ratio of the market capitalization of various securities markets against GDP in 2008

(*Note*: GDP on Hong Kong market adopts GDP of the Hong Kong Special Administrative Region)

(*Data source*: World Federation of Exchanges)

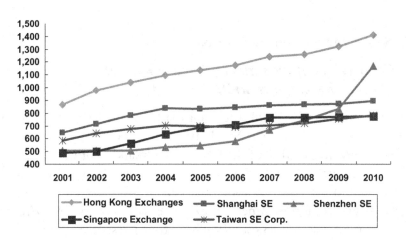

Figure 3.3.1.2   Comparison of the number of companies listed in the stock exchanges on A-share market and the emerging markets in the Asia-Pacific region

(*Data source*: World Federation of Exchanges)

From 2002 to 2009, the average yearly compound growth rates of the market capitalizations of Shanghai Stock Exchange and Shenzhen Stock Exchange reached up to 36.5% and 27.7% respectively, ranking the first among the world's major securities markets. Today the market capitalization of

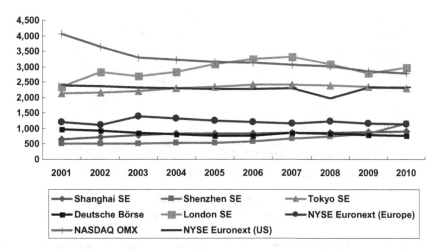

Figure 3.3.1.3   Comparison of the number of companies listed in the stock exchanges on A-share market and the developed markets

(*Data source*: World Federation of Exchanges)

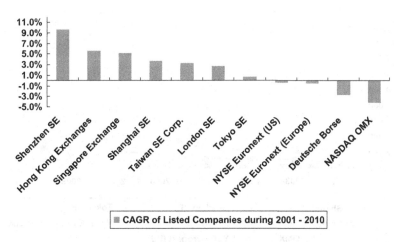

Figure 3.3.1.4   Comparison of the growth rates of the listed companies on A-share market and world's major securities markets in number

(*Data source*: World Federation of Exchanges)

Shanghai Stock Exchange is among the first of the exchanges on the emerging markets in the Asia-Pacific region, but still has a long way to go when compared with the absolute level of the market capitalization of the developed markets, American markets in particular. In 2009, Shanghai Stock Exchange ranked 6th among the world's top ten exchanges in market capitalization.

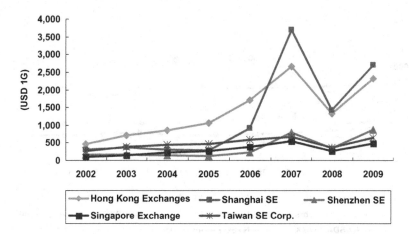

Figure 3.3.1.5   A comparison of the market capitalization of the exchanges on A-share and emerging markets in the Asia-Pacific region

(*Data source*: World Federation of Exchanges)

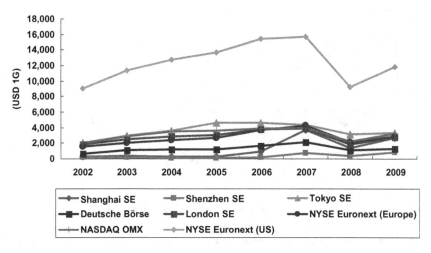

Figure 3.3.1.6   Comparison of the market capitalization of the exchanges on A-share markets and the developed markets

(*Data source*: World Federation of Exchanges)

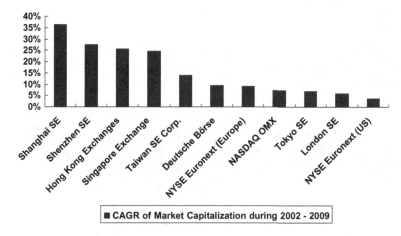

Figure 3.3.1.7 Comparison of the growth rates of the market capitalizations of A-share market and the world's major securities markets

(*Data source*: World Federation of Exchanges)

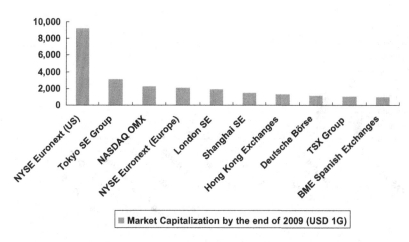

Figure 3.3.1.8 World's top ten securities markets in market capitalization in 2009

(*Data source*: World Federation of Exchanges)

3.3.2 Comparison of liquidity of A-share market and the world's major securities markets

Seen from trading volume of the year, in 2009, Shanghai Stock Exchange and Shenzhen Stock Exchange ranked among the first in the list of major exchanges in the Asia-Pacific region, with a trading volume of USD 5 trillion

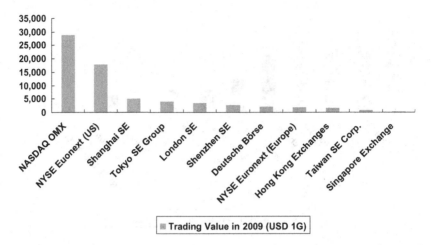

Figure 3.3.2.1 Comparison of the trading values of A-share market and the world's major securities markets in 2009

(*Data source*: World Federation of Exchanges)

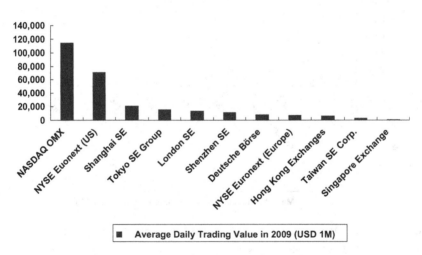

Figure 3.3.2.2 Comparison of average daily trading values of A-share market and the world's major securities markets in 2009

(*Data source*: World Federation of Exchanges)

and 2.8 trillion respectively. The year trading volume of Shanghai Stock Exchange surpassed that of Tokyo Stock Exchange. However, there is still a wide gap between the year trading volume of Shanghai Stock Exchange and that of NYSE and NASDAQ in America.

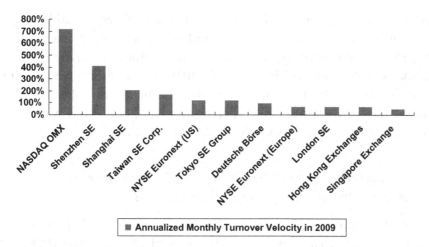

Figure 3.3.2.3 Comparison of annualized monthly turnover velocity of A-share market and the world's major securities markets in 2009

(*Data source*: World Federation of Exchanges)

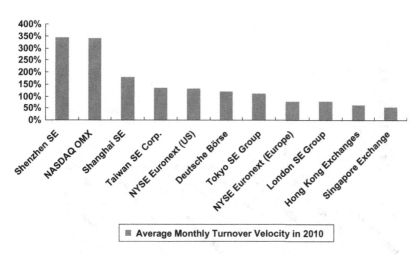

Figure 3.3.2.4 Comparison of average monthly turnover velocity of A-share market and the world's major securities markets in 2010

(*Data source*: World Federation of Exchanges)

In 2009, the daily trading volumes of the two exchanges had a similar situation: the daily trading volumes of Shanghai Stock Exchange and Shenzhen Stock Exchange were USD 20.7 billion and 11.4 billion respectively, which, though stayed at a relatively high level among the world's major securities markets, still largely fell behind American NYSE and NASDAQ.

In terms of turnover velocity, in 2009, the annualized monthly turnover velocity of Shanghai Stock Exchange and Shenzhen Stock Exchange was 207% and 208% respectively, above that of the majority of the major securities markets in the Asia-Pacific region. In 2010, the monthly average (simple average) turnover velocity of Shanghai Stock Exchange and Shenzhen Stock Exchange was 178% and 344% respectively, which, compared with world's major securities markets, was still at a relatively high level.

3.3.3 *Comparison of IPO financing on A-share market and the world's major securities markets*

In 2009, the number of IPO enterprises in Shanghai Stock Exchange and Shenzhen Stock Exchange was 9 and 90 respectively, and their IPO market capitalizations were USD 18.3 billion and 0.92 billion respectively, with their IPO financing amounts ranking among the first of the world's major securities markets.

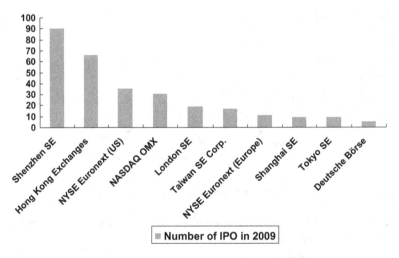

Figure 3.3.3.1   Comparison of the number of IPO companies on A-share market and the world's major securities markets in 2009

(*Data source*: World Federation of Exchanges)

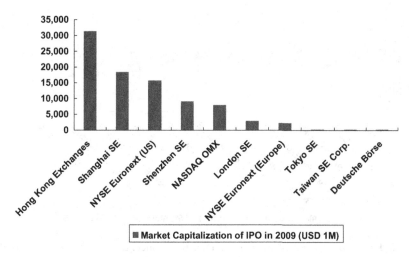

Figure 3.3.3.2 Comparison of the market capitalization of IPO companies on A-share market and the world's major securities markets in 2009

(*Data source*: World Federation of Exchanges)

3.3.4 *Comparison of market concentration of A-share market and the world's major securities markets*

Seen from the perspective of market capitalization concentration, in the year 2009, in Shanghai Stock Exchange, the listed companies of market capitalization of 5% most capitalized accounted for 62.8% of the total market capitalization, and the listed companies whose market capitalization was among the ten most capitalized accounted for 41.2%, while in Shenzhen Stock Exchange, these two ratios were 34.9% and 14.5% respectively. The comparison of the world's major securities markets and those in the Asia-Pacific region demonstrates that the market capitalization concentration of Shanghai Stock Exchange was similar to that of the world's major securities markets while that of Shenzhen Stock Exchange was relatively lower.

In terms of trading value concentration, in the year 2009, in Shanghai Stock Exchange, the stocks of a trading value share of 5% most traded accounted for 31.5% of the total trading value, and those of a trading value

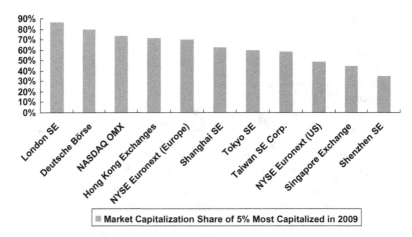

Figure 3.3.4.1 Comparison of market capitalization concentration of A-share market and the world's major securities markets in 2009 (1)

(*Data source*: World Federation of Exchanges)

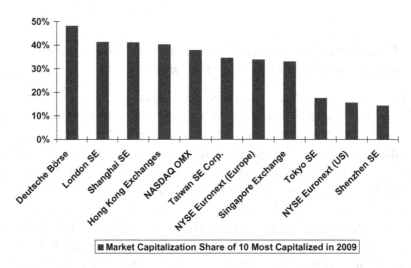

Figure 3.3.4.2 Comparison of market capitalization concentration of A-share market and the world's major securities markets in 2009 (2)

(*Data source*: World Federation of Exchanges)

share amongst the 10 most traded accounted for 31.5% of the total trading value; while in Shenzhen Stock Exchange, the above two ratios changed into 27.5% and 11.4% respectively, also lower than those of the major securities markets in the Asia-Pacific region, and its trading value concentration was similar to that of NASDAQ market.

Figure 3.3.4.3 Comparison of trading value concentration of A-share market and the world's major securities markets in 2009 (1)

(*Data source*: World Federation of Exchanges)

Figure 3.3.4.4 Comparison of trading value concentration of A-share market and the world's major securities markets in 2009 (2)

(*Data source*: World Federation of Exchanges)

3.3.5 *Change in correlation between A-share market and stock markets in Hong Kong and America*

The relation between China's economy and the global economy is increasingly close, which is also more or less embodied in the correlation between the Chinese capital market and overseas capital markets. From the correlation between A-share market and the stock markets in Hong Kong and America and the changes in the recent years, it can be seen that the correlation between the capital markets both at home and abroad is gradually enhanced.

According to monthly data, during 2005 and 2010, the monthly correlation between the indexes of A-share market in Shanghai and Shenzhen, namely, Shanghai Composite Index and Shenzhen Component Index, and the major indexes of Hong Kong markets reached above 0.5, displaying characteristics of the following two aspects:

(1) The correlation between A-share market and H-share index is higher than Red Chip Index and Hang Seng Index, reason largely being that a significant part of H-shares were listed on A-share market and Hong Kong market, thus its high correlation of changes in the stock prices.

(2) The correlation between A-share market and Hong Kong market (represented by Hang Seng Index) is significantly higher than American market (represented by S&P500 Index), the reason is also obvious: the correlation between the Chinese mainland economy and Hong Kong economy is much higher, the number of mainland enterprises listed on Hong Kong market much larger, and they account for a larger percentage on Hong Kong market.

Seen from the variation tendency of correlation, as more and more mainland enterprises were listed in Hong Kong, the correlation of China Capital Concept Indexes between A-share market and Hong Kong market (calculated by the fluctuation correlation coefficient within 36 months) demonstrated a trend of gradual rise. Moreover, the increase in correlation between A-share market and H-share Index was significant larger than Red

Table 3.3.5.1 Monthly correlation between A-share market and the American stock market (2005–2010)

	Shanghai Composite Index	Shenzhen Component Index
Hang Seng Index	0.60	0.53
Hang Seng China Enterprises Index (H-share Index)	0.68	0.62
Hang Seng China-Affiliated Corporations Index (Red Chip Index)	0.55	0.49
American S&P500 Index	0.41	0.38

(*Data source*: Xinhua Finance)

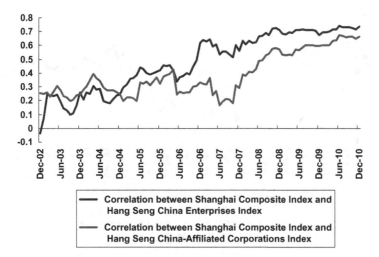

Figure 3.3.5.1 Monthly fluctuation correlation between Shanghai composite index and China capital concept index of Hong Kong market within 26 months (2005–2010)

(*Data source*: Xinhua Finance)

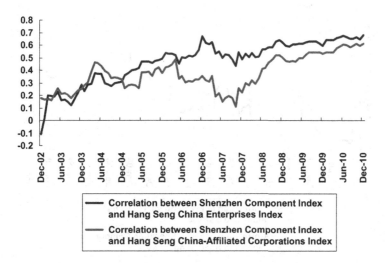

Figure 3.3.5.2 Monthly fluctuation correlation between Shenzhen component index and China capital concept index of Hong Kong market within 26 months (2005–2010)

(*Data source*: Xinhua Finance)

Chip Index. It is the same in terms of the overall market: during 2005 and 2010, the correlation between A-share market and the American market manifests a trend of gradual increase.

By the end of 2010, the fluctuation correlation between A-share market and Hong Kong market within 36 months has been above 0.6, and that

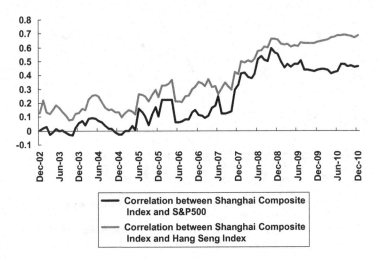

Figure 3.3.5.3   Monthly fluctuation correlation between Shanghai composite index and Hong Kong and the American markets within 36 months (2005–2010)

(*Data source*: Xinhua Finance)

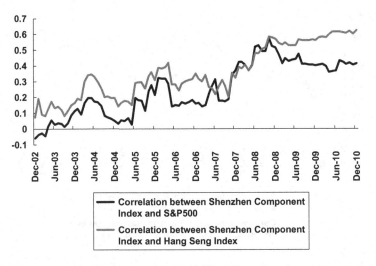

Figure 3.3.5.4   Monthly fluctuation correlation between Shenzhen component index and Hong Kong and American markets within 36 months (2005–2010)

(*Data source*: Xinhua Finance)

between A-share market and the American market kept above 0.4. Compared with 2005, the former increased from 0.1–0.2 to 0.6–0.7, while the latter increased from nearly 0 (namely, basically irrelevant) to 0.40–0.45, indicating a significant uptrend.

Table 3.3.5.2 Fluctuation correlation coefficient between A-share market and Hong Kong and the American markets within 36 months by the end of 2010

	Shanghai Composite Index	Shenzhen Component Index
Hang Seng Index	0.66	0.61
Hang Seng China Enterprises Index (H-share Index)	0.74	0.68
Hang Seng China-Affiliated Corporations Index (Red Chip Index)	0.66	0.46
American S&P500 Index	0.44	0.40

(*Data source*: Xinhua Finance)

Table 3.3.5.3 Weekly correlation between A-share market and Hong Kong and the American markets (2005–2010)

	Shanghai Composite Index	Shenzhen Component Index
Hang Seng Index	0.41	0.38
Hang Seng China Enterprises Index (H-share Index)	0.51	0.47
Hang Seng China-Affiliated Corporations Index (Red Chip Index)	0.42	0.39
American S&P500 Index	0.28	0.24

(*Data source*: Xinhua Finance)

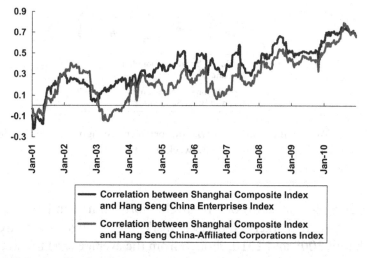

Figure 3.3.5.5 Weekly fluctuation correlation between Shanghai composite index and China capital concept index of Hong Kong market within 52 weeks (2005–2010)

(*Data source*: Xinhua Finance)

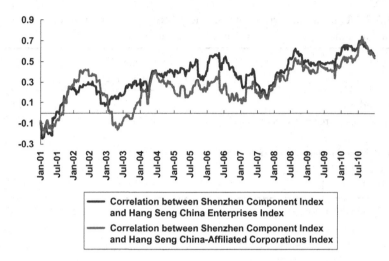

Figure 3.3.5.6   Weekly fluctuation correlation between Shenzhen component index and China capital concept index of Hong Kong market within 52 weeks (2005–2010)

(*Data source*: Xinhua Finance)

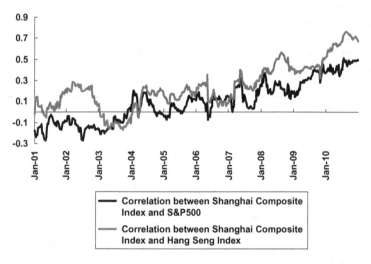

Figure 3.3.5.7   Weekly fluctuation correlation between Shanghai composite index and Hong Kong and American markets within 52 weeks (2005–2010)

(*Data source*: Xinhua Finance)

   In addition, even in terms of a relatively shorter time window, the correlation between A-share market and overseas market also manifests an uptrend. For example, during 2005 and 2010, though from the average level the weekly correlation between A-share market and Hong Kong market remained around 0.4 (the correlation between Shanghai Composite Index and H-share Index was the strongest, about 0.5), yet its weekly correlation with the American market was

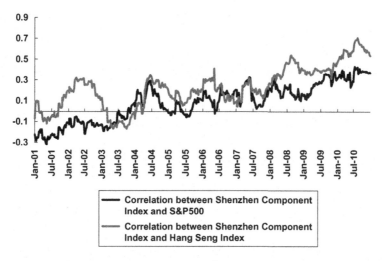

Figure 3.3.5.8 Weekly fluctuation correlation between Shenzhen component index and Hong Kong and American markets within 52 weeks (2005–2010)

(*Data source*: Xinhua Finance)

Table 3.3.5.4 Weekly fluctuation correlation coefficient between A-share market and Hong Kong and the American markets within 52 weeks by the end of 2010

	Shanghai Composite Index	Shenzhen Component Index
Hang Seng Index	0.67	0.53
Hang Seng China Enterprises Index (H-share Index)	0.67	0.55
Hang Seng China-Affiliated Corporations Index (Red Chip Index)	0.66	0.53
American S&P500 Index	0.49	0.37

(*Data source*: Xinhua Finance)

much lower, less than 0.3. However, seen from the fluctuation correlation coefficient within 52 weeks (namely one year), its uptrend was still quite marked.

Seen from the variation tendency, the weekly correlation coefficient between A-share market and Hong Kong market increased from basically 0 (i.e. almost irrelevant) in 2005 to around 0.6 by the end of 2010, and its weekly correlation with American market increased from negative correlation in 2005 to around 0.4–0.5 by the end of 2010, thus its more salient uptrend than that of its monthly correlation. Besides, it can also be found that the interaction circle between overseas markets and A-share market is shortening, and the information reflection between markets is speeding up.

Chapter 4

BOND MARKET

4.1 Overview of Bond Market

4.1.1 *Structure of bond market*

In terms of trading places, China's bond market can be divided into over-the-counter market (OTC market) and floor trading market. The former mainly refers to the inter-bank bond markets and over-the-counter trade in commercial banks; and the latter refers to exchange traded bond markets (including Shanghai Stock Exchange and Shenzhen Stock Exchange). Seen from trading volume, inter-bank bond market is the main trading place for China's bond market, and plays a leading role in China's bond market.

China's bond market mainly includes the following categories:

(1) Government bond: including book-entry Treasury bonds (T-bonds), saving bonds (certificate), and saving bonds (electronic).
(2) Central bank bond: namely central bank bill whose issuer is the People's Bank of China, and whose maturity ranges from 3 months to 3 years, mainly of the short-term (less than 1 year) bills.
(3) Financial bond: including policy financial bond, commercial banks bond, special financial bond, bond of non-bank financial institutions, securities bond, short-term note of secutiries. Among these, commercial banks bond include commercial banks junior bond and commercial banks general bond.
(4) Enterprise bond: including central enterprise bond and local enterprise bond.
(5) Short-term note: issued by non-financial enterprises qualified as a legal person within the Chinese territory.
(6) Asset backed securities.
(7) Non-bank financial bond: including bond of non-bank and financial institutions and short-term note of securities.
(8) International agency bond: bond issued by international agencies within the Chinese territory.
(9) Convertible bond.

Table 4.1.1.1   Distribution of the trading markets for the major bond categories

	Inter-bank bond market	Exchange bond market
Treasury bond	√	√
Enterprise bond	√	√
Central bank bill	√	
Financial bond	√	
Short-term note	√	
Corporate bill	√	
Financial junior bond	√	
Corporate bond		√
Convertible bond		√

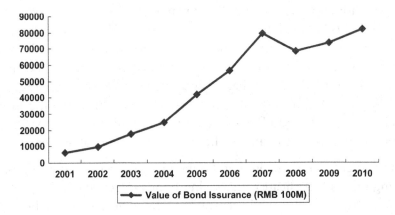

Figure 4.1.2.1   Steady increase in total value of issuance of bonds (2001–2010)

(*Data source*: China bond market information network)

The above bond categories are not necessarily traded on all the markets. By far, only the Treasury bond and enterprise bond admit trading in both the inter-bank bond market and the stock exchange; central bank bill, financial bond (and financial junior bond), short-term note and corporate bill can only be traded in the inter-bank market; enterprise bond and convertible bond can only be traded in the stock exchange.

4.1.2 *Development of bond market*

Since the beginning of this century, China's bond market has witnessed steady development. During the ten years from 2001 to 2010, the total value of issuance rose from RMB 0.6 trillion to over RMB 8 trillion, with an annual average compound growth rate close to 29.6%.

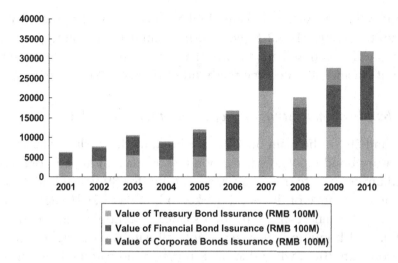

Figure 4.1.2.2 Treasury bond, financial bond and corporate bond are the major bonds on China's bond market

(*Data source*: China's bond market information network)

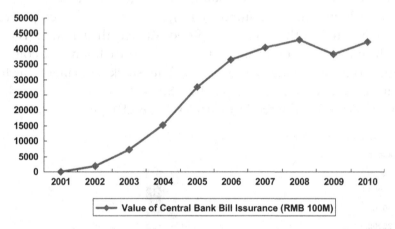

Figure 4.1.2.3 A rapid increase in the value of issuance of central bank bill

(*Data source*: China bond market information network)

On China's bond market, Treasury bond, financial bond and corporate bond take a significant place. According to data for 2010, the total value of issuance of these three bonds were RMB 1.4582 trillion, 1.3570 trillion and 0.3629 trillion respectively.

In recent years, central bank bond has increasingly become one important means of liquidity control by the central bank, and the issuance of central bank bill also increased year by year. During the 9 years from 2002 to 2010, the annual value of issuance of central bill increased from less than RMB 0.2 trillion up to over RMB 4.2 trillion, with an annual compound growth rate up to 40.9%. The central bank bill now has surpassed Treasury bond in terms of value of issuance and become the bond of largest issuance.

4.1.3 *Bond-category structure of bond market in 2010*

In 2009 and 2010, the main bonds of the bond market included central bank bill, Treasury bond (spot), financial bond, short-term note, corporate bond, and medium-term note, respectively accounting for 89.9% and 88.4% of the total value of issuance of the bond market in 2009 and 2010. Seen from the perspective of issuance, in 2010, the issuance of central bank bill, Treasury bond, financial bond and short-term note all witnessed a slight increase in comparison with 2009, while that of corporate bond and medium-term note slightly reduced. It is also the case when seen from the perspective of shares of each bond category: except for shares of corporate bond and medium-term note, the share of the other accumulated bonds all witnessed a slight rise.

Seen from the perspective of trading status since central bank bill, financial bond (including financial junior bond), short-term note, corporate bill, etc., are only listed in the Inter-Bank Bond Market, their trading is distributed on the inter-bank bond market. By contrast, since bonds like convertible bond and corporate bond are only listed in stock exchanges (including Shanghai Stock Exchange and Shenzhen Stock Exchange), the trading of these two bonds is distributed in the two stock exchanges.

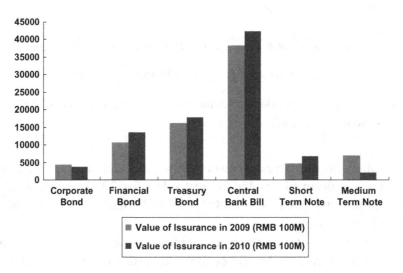

Figure 4.1.3.1   Value of issuance of the major bonds on bond markets (2009–2010)

(*Data source*: China bond market information network)

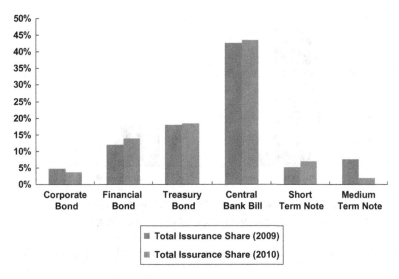

Figure 4.1.3.2   Issuance shares of the major bonds on bond markets (2009–2010)

(*Data source*: China bond market information network)

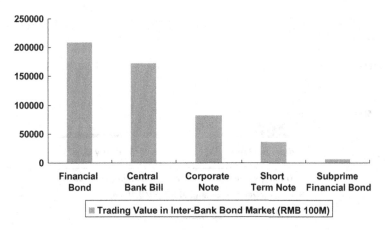

Figure 4.1.3.3   Trading value of the bonds that can only be traded in inter-bank bond market in 2010

(*Data source*: Xinhua Finance)

Among the bonds traded on the inter-bank bond market, financial bond ranked the first in trading value (about a total of RMB 21 trillion for 2010), immediately followed by central bank bill (a total of above RMB 17 trillion for 2010). Among the bonds traded in exchanges, the trading value of convertible bond is significantly higher than that of corporate bond, the former being over RMB 0.13 trillion while the latter less than RMB 0.05 trillion. Meanwhile, the trading value in Shanghai Stock Exchange is significantly larger than that in Shenzhen Stock Exchange.

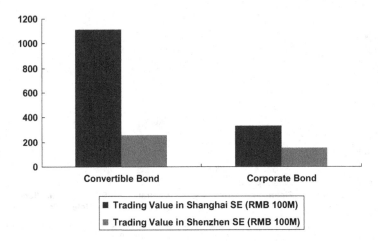

Figure 4.1.3.4   Trading value of the bonds that can only be traded in stock exchange in 2010

(*Data source*: Xinhua Finance)

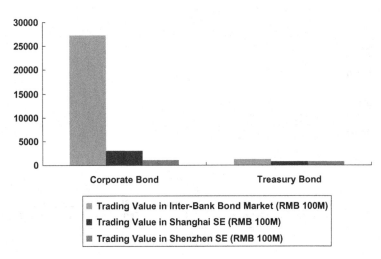

Figure 4.1.3.5   Trading value of the bonds that can be traded in both inter-bank bond market and stock exchange in 2010

(*Data source*: Xinhua Finance)

Among various bond categories, only corporate bond and Treasury bond can be traded both on inter-bank and exchange bond markets. For corporate bond, its trading value in inter-bank market is far higher than in stock exchange. For example, in 2010, the trading value of corporate bond in inter-bank market was about RMB 2.7 trillion, while that of the two exchanges in total was just around RMB 0.4 trillion. For Treasury bond, its trading values in the two exchanges were similar to each other.

4.1.4 *Credit structure of issuing companies*

Among more than 1000 issuing companies, 65% of companies' credit rate is above AA, among which companies of AAA credit rate and AA+ credit rate both account for 15.9%. Enterprises with credit rate below BBB+ account for 3.7%.

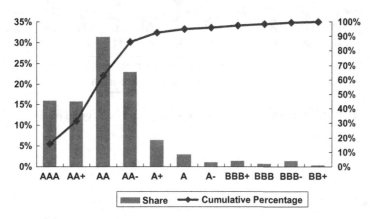

Figure 4.1.4.1 Share of issuing companies with different credit rates
(*Data source*: Xinhua Finance)

4.2 Inter-Bank Bond Market

4.2.1 *Issuance of treasury bonds in inter-bank bond market*

As a whole, in 2010, the value of issuance of Treasury bonds in inter-bank bond market (about RMB 1.4300 trillion) was slightly higher than in 2009 (about RMB 1.2147 trillion). Seen from the perspective of maturity structure, in 2010, the value of issuance of short-term Treasury bonds (e.g. three months, six months and nine months) was slightly lower than in 2009, while that of medium and long-term Treasury bonds (5 years and over) significantly surpassed that in 2009.

In terms of interest rate of issuance, among the Treasury bonds issued in 2010, although medium and long-term bonds witnessed a significant rise, three-month Treasury bonds' weighted average interest rate of issuance changed little, yet for short-term Treasury bonds of maturity below one year,

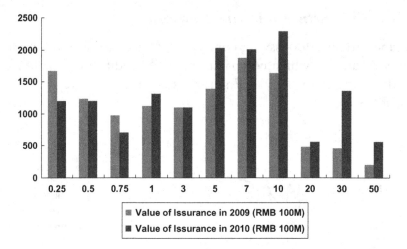

Figure 4.2.1.1   Value of issuance of Treasury bonds in inter-bank bond market (2009–2010)

(*Data source*: Xinhua Finance)

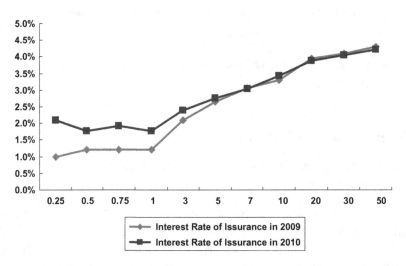

Figure 4.2.1.2   Maturity structure of interest rate of issuance for Treasury bonds in inter-bank bond market (2009–2010)

(*Data source*: Xinhua Finance)

their interest rate of issuance had a significant rise, among which the weighted average interest rate of issuance of the three-month Treasury bonds increased from 1% to 2.09%, semiannual bonds and nine-month bonds also rose from 1.2% to 1.77% and from 1.2% to 1.93% respectively.

4.2.2 *Issuance of corporate bonds in inter-bank bond market*

Different from the increase in the issue of Treasury bonds, in 2010, the value of issuance of corporate bonds in inter-bank bond market dropped from RMB 0.4247 trillion in 2009 to RMB 0.3629 trillion in 2010. In terms of maturity structure, either in 2009 or 2010, corporate bonds basically concentrated on seven-year maturity and 10-year maturity; from the perspective of credit structure, AAA bonds occupied the majority. Further division will

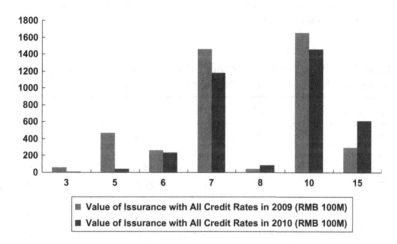

Figure 4.2.2.1 Value of issuance of corporate bonds (2009–2010) (1)

(*Data source*: Xinhua Finance)

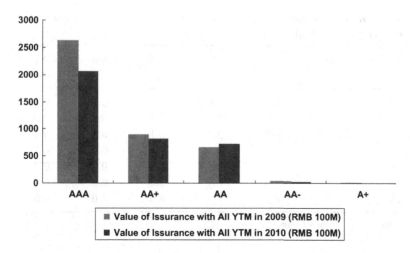

Figure 4.2.2.2 Value of issuance of corporate bonds (2009–2010) (2)

(*Data source*: Xinhua Finance)

Table 4.2.2.1   Issuance maturity of corporate bonds in inter-bank bond market and their credit rates in 2009 (RMB 100M)

Maturity (Year)	AAA	AA+	AA	AA−	A+
3	51	0	10	0	0
5	340	106	20	0	0
6	10	83	129.8	33	5
7	709	387.7	346	11.3	5
8	0	35	10	0	0
10	1214.88	292	148.5	0	0
15	300	0	0	0	0

(*Data source*: Xinhua Finance)

Table 4.2.2.2   Issuance maturity of corporate bonds in inter-bank bond market and their credit rates in 2010 (RMB 100M)

Maturity (Year)	AAA	AA+	AA	AA−	A+
3	8	0	0	0	0
5	35	0	6.3	0	0
6	45	90	83	18	0
7	246	437	494.5	5	0
8	0	52	35	0	0
10	1114.4	245	105	0	0
15	610	0	0	0	0

(*Data source*: Xinhua Finance)

Table 4.2.2.3   Issuance maturity of corporate bonds in inter-bank bond market and their credit rates in 2009 (share)

Maturity (Year)	AAA (%)	AA+ (%)	AA (%)	AA− (%)	A+ (%)
3	1.2	0.0	0.2	0.0	0.0
5	8.0	2.5	0.5	0.0	0.0
6	0.2	2.0	3.1	0.8	0.1
7	16.7	9.1	8.1	0.3	0.1
8	0.0	0.8	0.2	0.0	0.0
10	28.6	6.9	3.5	0.0	0.0
15	7.1	0.0	0.0	0.0	0.0

(*Data source*: Xinhua Finance)

Table 4.2.2.4 Issuance maturity of corporate bonds in inter-bank bond market and their credit rates in 2010 (share)

Maturity (Year)	AAA (%)	AA+ (%)	AA (%)	AA− (%)	A+ (%)
3	0.2	0.0	0.0	0.0	0.0
5	1.0	0.0	0.2	0.0	0.0
6	1.2	2.5	2.3	0.5	0.0
7	6.8	12.0	13.6	0.1	0.0
8	0.0	1.4	1.0	0.0	0.0
10	30.7	6.8	2.9	0.0	0.0
15	16.8	0.0	0.0	0.0	0.0

(*Data source*: Xinhua Finance)

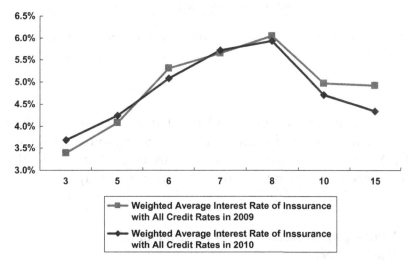

Figure 4.2.2.3 Interest rate of issuance of corporate bonds in inter-bank bond market (2009–2010) (1)

(*Data source*: Xinhua Finance)

show that the corporate bonds with the highest issuance share during the 2009–2010 period were all ten-year AAA bonds, followed by seven-year AAA bonds (for 2009) and fifteen-year AAA bonds (for 2010).

In terms of interest rate of issuance, seen from the perspective of maturity structure, the maturity curve of the weighted average interest rate of issuance in 2010 was similar to 2009 but with a drop at the end of long-term bond (mainly because among AAA bonds of low weighted average interest rate of issuance, a significant part of the bonds had a maturity of 15 years, and the share of 10-year AAA bonds also witnessed an increase). Seen from the

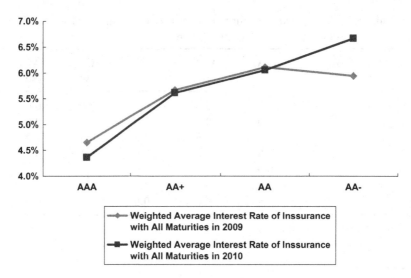

Figure 4.2.2.4   Interest rate of issuance of corporate bonds in inter-bank bond market (2009–2010) (2)

(*Data source*: Xinhua Finance)

perspective of credit rate, either in 2009 or 2010, the weighted average interest rate of issuance increased as the credit rates declined (in 2009, the interest rate of AA- bond was slightly lower than AA bond, but due to the low issuance volume of AA- bond, this disparity was not typical).

4.2.3 *Issuance of financial bonds in inter-bank bond market*

The characteristics of the issuance of financial bonds in inter-bank market in 2010 are as follows: the value of issuance of financial bonds with a maturity below 3 years (including 3 years) declined, while for those over 5 years (including 5 years), their issuance increased; meanwhile financial bonds with a maturity of 30 years were also issued. In terms of the interest rate of issuance, the weighted average of interest rate of issuance for the financial bond of a maturity below 7 years (including 7 years) slightly increased against that in 2009. What's more, the shorter the maturity, the greater the increase in the interest rate of issuance. For example, the interest rate of issuance for 6-month and one-year financial bonds increased by more than 0.9%, while for 3-year, 5-year and 7-year financial bonds this rate only rose by 0.3%.

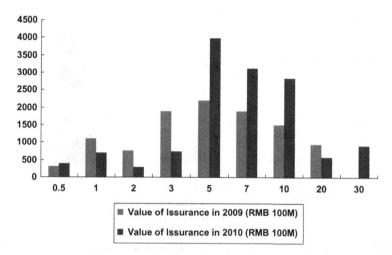

Figure 4.2.3.1   Value of issuance of financial bonds in inter-bank bond market (2009–2010)

(*Data source*: Xinhua Finance)

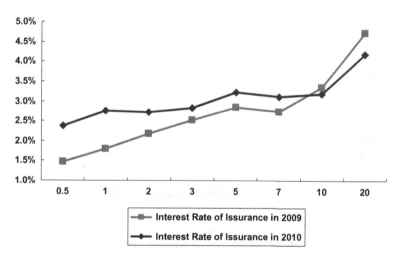

Figure 4.2.3.2   Interest rate of issuance of financial bonds in inter-bank bond market (2009–2010)

(*Data source*: Xinhua Finance)

4.2.4 *Issuance of short-term notes in inter-bank bond market*

One significant characteristic of the inter-bank market in 2010 is the large issuance volume of short-term notes (especially those of 1-year maturity). In terms of value of issuance, in 2010, the total value of issuance of 1-year short-term notes was RMB 0.6358 trillion, increasing by 83% against a total of

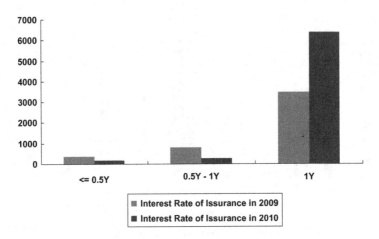

Fugure 4.2.4.1 Value of issuance of short-term notes in inter-bank bond market (2009–2010)

(*Data source*: Xinhua Finance)

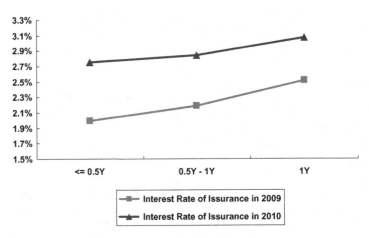

Figure 4.2.4.2 Interest rate of issuance of short-term notes in inter-bank bond market (2009–2010)

(*Data source*: Xinhua Finance)

RMB 0.3471 trillion in 2009. In the market of short-term notes, those of 1-year maturity became the main force, whose value of issuance accounted for 74.6% of the total in 2009. In 2010, this share was higher, up to 93.4%.

In 2010, the interest rates of issuance of short-term notes in all maturities were all higher than those in 2009, growth rate ranging from 0.56 to 0.76%. The basic tendency was that the shorter the maturity, the greater the increase in the interest rate of issuance.

4.3 Stock Exchange Bond Market

4.3.1 *Issuance of treasury bonds in stock exchange*

In 2010, the issuance scale of Treasury bonds in stock exchange (including Shanghai Stock Exchange and Shenzhen Stock Exchange) was larger than that in 2009: a rise from RMB 2.4853 trillion in 2009 to RMB 2.9163 trillion. Similar to the inter-bank bond market, in 2010 the

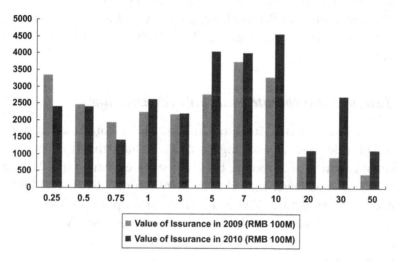

Figure 4.3.1.1 Value of issuance of Treasury bonds in stock exchange (2009–2010)

(*Data source*: Xinhua Finance)

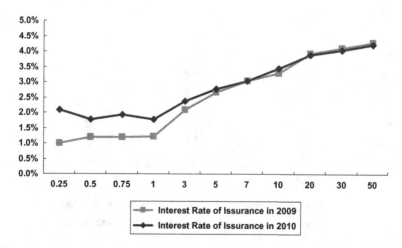

Figure 4.3.1.2 Maturity structure of the interest rate of issuance for Treasury bonds in stock exchange (2009–2010)

(*Data source*: Xinhua Finance)

issuance scale of short-term Treasury bonds with a maturity below 1 year was smaller than that in 2009, while for medium and long-term Treasury bonds of a maturity of 5 years and over, this scale was significantly larger than that in 2009.

In terms of the interest rate of issuance, among the Treasury bonds issued in stock exchange, their change in maturity structure is also similar to that in inter-bank bond market: the medium and long-term rate basically keep stable, and short-term rate significantly rises. For those of maturities of 3 months, 6 months and 9 months, their weighted average interest rate of issuance increased from 1%, 1.2%, 1.2% in 2009 to 2.09%, 1.77%, 1.93% respectively.

4.3.2 *Issuance of corporate bonds in stock exchange*

Although corporate bonds are listed in both inter-bank market and stock exchange, its scale in stock exchange is much smaller than that of the other. The value of issuance of corporate bonds in stock exchange in 2010 (around RMB 90 billion) was lower than that in 2009 (around RMB 120 billion). In terms of maturity structure, 7-year and 10-year corporate bonds had a relatively high value of issuance; while seen from the perspective of credit rate, the corporate bonds issued in stock exchange in 2010 mainly concentrated on AA+ rate and AA rate.

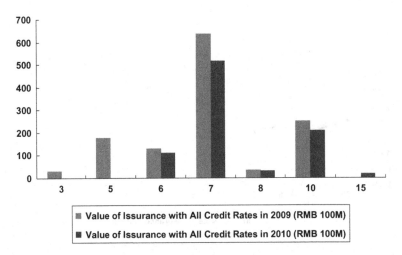

Figure 4.3.2.1   Value of issuance of corporate bonds in stock exchange (2009–2010) (1)

(*Data source*: Xinhua Finance)

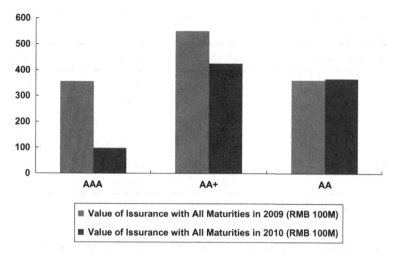

Figure 4.3.2.2 Value of issuance of corporate bonds in stock exchange (2009–2010) (2)
(*Data source*: Xinhua Finance)

Table 4.3.2.1 Issuance maturity of corporate bonds in stock exchange and their credit rates in 2009 (RMB 100M)

Maturity (Year)	AAA	AA+	AA
3	23	0	10
5	165.5	13	0
6	0	60	68.8
7	167	275	196
8	0	35	0
10	0	166	85.5
15	0	0	0

(*Data source*: Xinhua Finance)

Table 4.3.2.2 Issuance maturity of corporate bonds in stock exchange and their credit rates in 2010 (RMB 100M)

Maturity (Year)	AAA	AA+	AA
3	0	0	0
5	0	0	0
6	25	44	43
7	24	232.5	260
8	0	17	15
10	28.4	132	50
15	20	0	0

(*Data source*: Xinhua Finance)

Table 4.3.2.3   Issuance maturity of corporate bonds in stock exchange and their credit rates in 2009 (share)

Maturity (Year)	AAA	AA+	AA
3	1.8%	0.0%	0.8%
5	13.1%	1.0%	0.0%
6	0.0%	4.7%	5.4%
7	13.2%	21.7%	15.5%
8	0.0%	2.8%	0.0%
10	0.0%	13.1%	6.8%
15	0.0%	0.0%	0.0%

(*Data source*: Xinhua Finance)

Table 4.3.2.4   Issuance maturity of corporate bonds in stock exchange and their credit rates in 2010 (share)

Maturity (Year)	AAA	AA+	AA
3	0.0%	0.0%	0.0%
5	0.0%	0.0%	0.0%
6	2.8%	4.9%	4.8%
7	2.7%	26.1%	29.2%
8	0.0%	1.9%	1.7%
10	3.2%	14.8%	5.6%
15	2.2%	0.0%	0.0%

(*Data source*: Xinhua Finance)

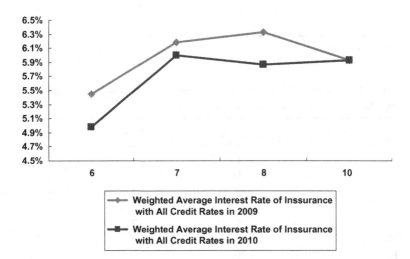

Figure 4.3.2.3   Interest rate of issuance for corporate bonds in stock exchange (2009–2010) (1)

(*Data source*: Xinhua Finance)

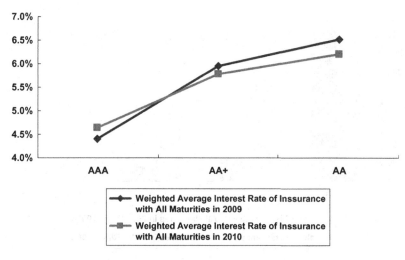

Figure 4.3.2.4 Interest rate of issuance for corporate bonds in stock exchange (2009–2010) (2)

(*Data source*: Xinhua Finance)

4.3.3 *Issuance of Corporate Bonds in Stock Exchange*

Since the number of corporate bonds is relatively low and they are only listed in stock exchange, their value of issuance is generally lower as well: in 2009, the yearly value of issuance being only RMB 74.6 billion and in 2010, much lower, about RMB 51.7 billion, mainly the 5-year and 10-year corporate bonds.

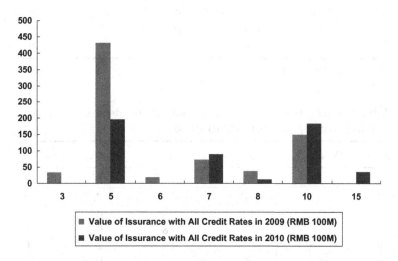

Figure 4.3.3.1 Value of issuance of corporate bonds in stock exchange (2009–2010) (1)

(*Data source*: Xinhua Finance)

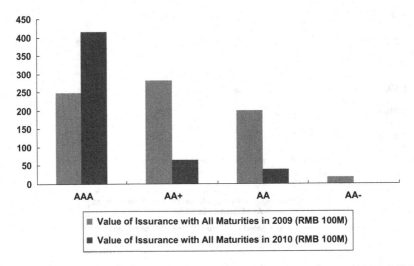

Figure 4.3.3.2   Value of issuance of corporate bonds in stock exchange (2009–2010) (2)

(*Data source*: Xinhua Finance)

Table 4.3.3.1   Issuance maturity of corporate bonds in stock exchange and their credit rates in 2009 (RMB 100M)

Maturity (Year)	AAA	AA+	AA	AA–
3	0	28.4	6	0
5	104	198.6	111.5	17.3
6	0	0	18.5	0
7	0	54	19	0
8	0	0	37.6	0
10	144	0	7	0
15	0	0	0	0

(*Data source*: Xinhua Finance)

Table 4.3.3.2   Issuance maturity of corporate bonds in stock exchange and their credit rates in 2010 (RMB 100M)

Maturity (Year)	AAA	AA+	AA	AA–
3	0	0	0	0
5	164	24.5	7.7	0
6	0	0	0	0
7	30	39.8	19.5	0
8	0	0	12	0
10	185	0	0	0
15	35	0	0	0

(*Data source*: Xinhua Finance)

Table 4.3.3.3 Issuance maturity of corporate bonds in stock exchange and their credit rates in 2009 (share)

Maturity (Year)	AAA (%)	AA+ (%)	AA (%)	AA– (%)
3	0.0	3.8	0.8	0.0
5	13.9	26.6	14.9	2.3
6	0.0	0.0	2.5	0.0
7	0.0	7.2	2.5	0.0
8	0.0	0.0	5.0	0.0
10	19.3	0.0	0.9	0.0
15	0.0	0.0	0.0	0.0

(*Data source*: Xinhua Finance)

Table 4.3.3.4 Issuance maturity of corporate bonds in stock exchange and their credit rates in 2010 (share)

Maturity (Year)	AAA (%)	AA+ (%)	AA (%)	AA– (%)
3	0.0	0.0	0.0	0.0
5	31.7	4.7	1.5	0.0
6	0.0	0.0	0.0	0.0
7	5.8	7.7	3.8	0.0
8	0.0	0.0	2.3	0.0
10	35.7	0.0	0.0	0.0
15	6.8	0.0	0.0	0.0

(*Data source*: Xinhua Finance)

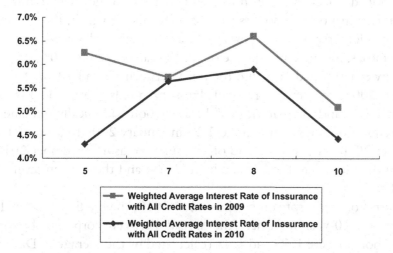

Figure 4.3.3.3 Interest rate of issuance for corporate bonds in stock exchange (2009–2010) (1)

(*Data source*: Xinhua Finance)

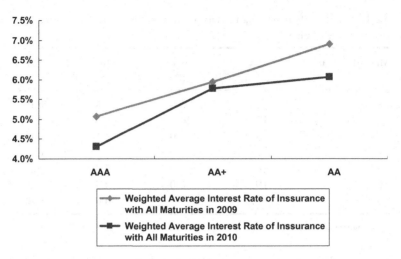

Figure 4.3.3.4 Interest rate of issuance for corporate bonds in stock exchange (2009–2010) (2)

(*Data source*: Xinhua Finance)

4.4 Maturity Structure of Interest Rate of Bond Market and Credit Spread Analysis

Similar to the bond markets in America and other countries, the change in the maturity structure of the interest rate for China's bond market can be generally described in terms of the following three factors: level, slope and curvature. Adopting China Securities Treasury bond yield curve, the principal component analysis of the daily data from May 2008 to December 2010 shows that the explanatory adequacy of these three factors specific to the change in the yield curve of Treasury bond amounts to over 99%, among which, the explanatory adequacy of level reaches up to over 80% (according to relevant references, for most countries, the influence degree of the first factor is above 70%, the second factor between 10% and 15%, and the third between 5% and 10%).

Since 2009, the term spread of Treasury bonds (based on the spread between 1-year and 10-year yield of Treasury bonds) basically remained at a down trend, dropping from average 2.2% in January 2009 to average 1.0% in December 2010. The term spread of Treasury bonds in December 2010 was significantly lower than the average level (1.6%) and the median level (1.7%) since May 2008.

In terms of credit spread, by the end of 2010, the credit spread of 1-year maturity and 10-year maturity (the spread between corporate bonds and Treasury bonds) were 1.5% and 1.6% (calculated by the average of December) respectively, at the same level with the mean value since May 2008 (respectively

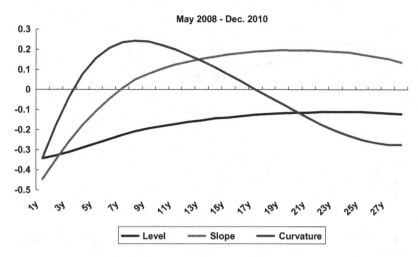

Figure 4.4.1 Factorization of the maturity structure of the yield of Treasury bonds (2008.5–2010.12)

(*Data source*: Xinhua Finance)

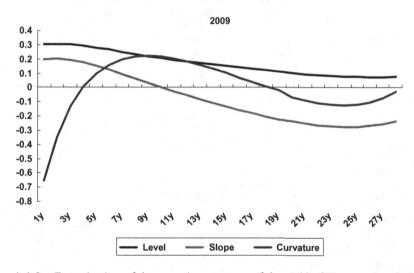

Figure 4.4.2 Factorization of the maturity structure of the yield of Treasury bonds (2009)

(*Data source*: Xinhua Finance)

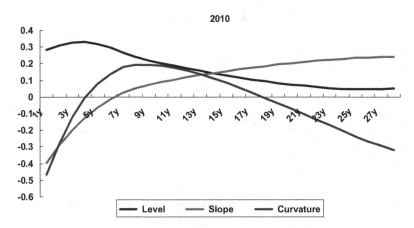

Figure 4.4.3 Factorization of the maturity structure of the yield of Treasury bonds (2010)

(*Data source*: Xinhua Finance)

Table 4.4.1 Explanatory adequacy of three factors specific to the change in the yield curve of Treasury bonds

	Level factor (Level) (%)	Slope factor (Slope) (%)	Curvature factor (Curvature) (%)	Sum (%)
2008.5–2010.12	88.6	9.5	1.6	99.7
2009	92.9	5.1	1.3	99.3
2010	79.0	15.5	4.9	99.3

(*Data source*: Xinhua Finance)

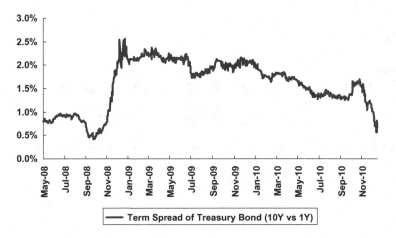

Figure 4.4.4 Term spread of Treasury bonds

(*Data source*: Xinhua Finance)

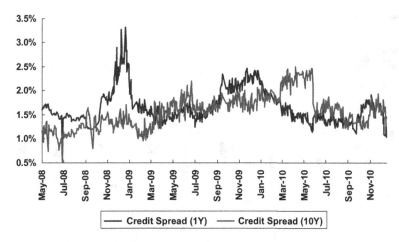

Figure 4.4.5 Term spread of Treasury Bonds (10Y vs 1Y)

(*Data source*: Xinhua Finance)

1.7% and 1.6%, their medians both being 1.6%). According to the tendency of credit spread in recent years, the credit spread remains at the level of below 2% in the latest two years except that under the impact of the global financial crisis (from October 2008 to the end of January 2009), the credit spread of 1-year maturity surpassed 2% (the highest level being 3.3%).

4.5 Comparison of Stock Exchange Bond Market and Major Bond Markets in the Asia-Pacific Region

4.5.1 *Comparison of stock exchange bond market scale*

Since China's bond market is divided into stock exchange bond market and inter-bank bonds market, and bonds of most categories are traded in inter-bank market, the scale of stock exchange bond market in the Chinese mainland is relatively smaller when compared to the major bond markets in the Asia-Pacific region.

For example, by the end of 2009, the total values of bonds listed in Shanghai Stock Exchange and Shenzhen Stock Exchange were USD 267.3 billion and USD 10.2 billion, which were not only far less than the Japanese bond market in the Asia-Pacific region, but also significantly lower than Korean and Indian bond markets.

In terms of the number of bond issuers, in 2009 the number of bond issuers in Shanghai Stock Exchange was 225, similar to the Indian bond market.

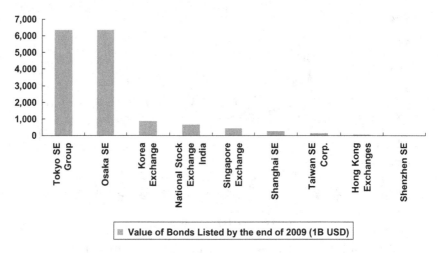

Figure 4.5.1.1   Comparison of the value of bonds listed stock exchange and in the major bond markets in the Asia–Pacific region in 2009

(*Data source*: World Federation of Exchanges)

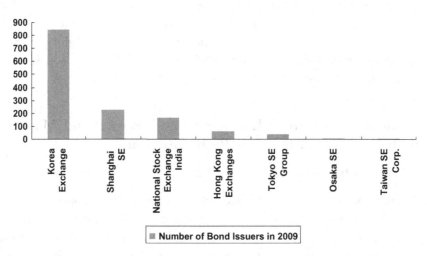

Figure 4.5.1.2   Comparison of the number of bond issuers in stock exchange and the major bond markets in the Asia-Pacific region in 2009

(*Data source*: World Federation of Exchanges)

By the end of 2009, there were in total 352 and 224 bonds listed respectively in Shanghai Stock Exchange and Shenzhen Stock Exchange, remaining at the medium level among the bond markets in the Asia-Pacific region. Among these bonds, those newly listed in 2009 were 198 and 164 respectively, also at the medium level in this region.

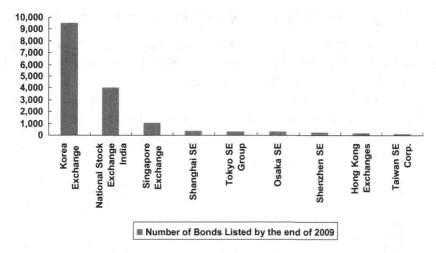

Figure 4.5.1.3 Comparison of the number of bonds listed in stock exchange and the major bond markets in the Asia-Pacific region by the end of 2009

(*Data source*: World Federation of Exchanges)

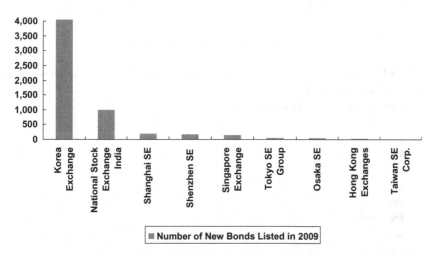

Figure 4.5.1.4 Comparison of the number of bonds newly listed in stock exchange and the major bond markets in the Asia-Pacific region in 2009

(*Data source*: World Federation of Exchanges)

4.5.2 *Comparison of liquidity of stock exchange bond market*

In 2009, the bond trading values in Shanghai Stock Exchange and Shenzhen Stock Exchange were USD 56.7 billion and USD 11.5 billion, lower than the Korean and Indian bond markets in the Asia-Pacific region. The investment flow (including newly-listed bonds and the capital flowing into the bonds already listed) into Shanghai Stock Exchange and Shenzhen Stock Exchange in 2009 was USD 237 billion and USD 252 billion respectively.

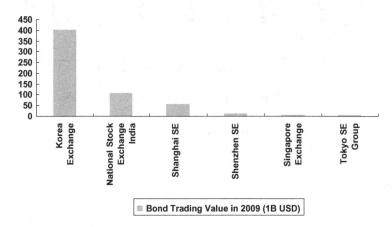

Figure 4.5.2.1   Comparison of trading value of stock exchange and the major bond markets in the Asia-Pacific region in 2009

(*Data source*: World Federation of Exchanges)

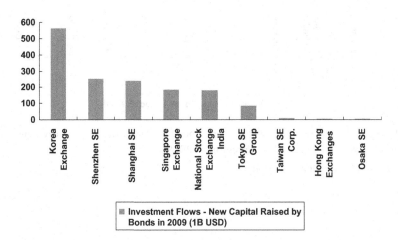

Figure 4.5.2.2   Comparison of investment flow into stock exchange and the major bond markets in the Asia-Pacific region in 2009

(*Data source*: World Federation of Exchanges)

Chapter 5

OTHER FINANCIAL MARKETS

The capital market, comprised of stock market and bond market, has become the main actor in the current Chinese financial market. Besides, the money market represented by the inter-bank lending market and the commodity futures market have also witnessed significant developments in recent years. The main characteristic is that market trading is increasingly active and the trading volume boasts a steady increase. In addition, along with the active trade, the reflection by various financial markets of the economic fundamentals has also been more and more rapid and accurate.

5.1 Inter-Bank Lending Market

The maturities of the inter-bank lending market are mainly divided into 11 levels: 1 day (namely "overnight inter-bank lending", 7 days, 14 days, 20 days, 30 days (namely 1 month), 60 days (namely 2 months), 90 days (namely 3 months), 120 days (namely 4 months), 6 months, 9 months and 1 year, among which, most inter-bank lending belongs to overnight lending, and inter-bank lending above 14 days rarely takes place.

5.1.1 *Overall situation of inter-bank lending market*

A comprehensive view of the inter-bank lending market in 2010 shows that as a whole it followed the trend of 2009 — a synchronous increase in trading value and average interest rate: the total trading value in 2009 increased from RMB 0.0627 trillion in January to RMB 2.1715 trillion in December; the total trading value in 2010 rose from RMB 1.7467 trillion in January to RMB 2.6830 trillion in December. Though funds in January 2010 appeared to be loose and the average interest rate dropped to 1.16%, in December it rose back to 2.92% and December became the month of the highest weighted average interest rate in 2010.

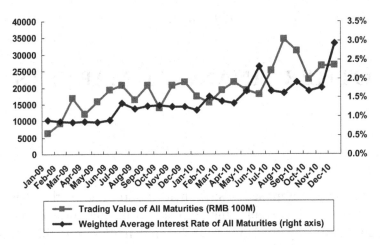

Figure 5.1.1.1 Change in the trading value and average interest rate of inter-bank lending market (2009–2010)

(*Data source*: People's Bank of China)

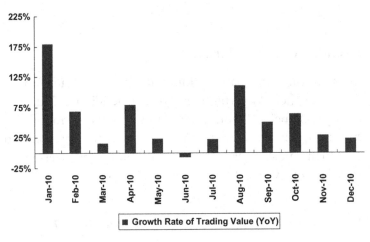

Figure 5.1.1.2 Growth rate of trading value of the inter-bank lending market (YoY) in 2010

(*Data source*: People's Bank of China)

According to the year-on-year data, the trading value of each month in 2010 basically witnessed a rise in comparison to the last year (except that there appeared to a reduction in June, possibly due to its excessive interest rate); in January the growth rate ranked the first, by about 178%. Corresponding to the trading value, the inter-bank lending rate for 2010 also appeared to be in an uptrend, with the highest growth rate in December, by 1.66%. Even for January — the month of lowest growth rate,

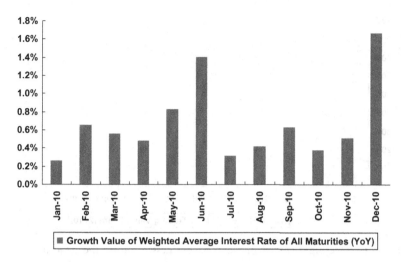

Figure 5.1.1.3 Growth value of weighted average interest rate of the inter-bank lending market (YoY) in 2010

(*Data source*: People's Bank of China)

its interest rate also rose by 0.26% compared with the previous year. Contrary to the loose funds under the influence of the economic stimulus plan in 2009, the funds in the inter-bank lending market in 2010 appeared to be relatively tight.

5.1.2 *Analysis of inter-bank lending of different maturities*

In the inter-bank lending market, although there are in total 11 levels of maturities ranging from 1 day to 1 year, yet in reality, the business of overnight inter-bank lending occupies the majority. According to data from 2009 to 2010, the trading value of overnight inter-bank lending accounted for 83.5% of the total in 2009, which rose to 87.9% in 2010. In addition, 7-day and 14-day inter-bank lending also have a certain part to play: their trading value respectively accounted for 11.0% and 3.1% of the total in 2009, and for 8.7% and 1.8% respectively in 2010. Generally speaking, the businesses of 1-day, 7-day and 14-day inter-bank lending in total had a share of 97.7% in 2009 and 98.4% in 2010.

Since overnight inter-bank lending is the major business in the inter-bank lending market, its interest rate becomes, in a sense, the symbolic interest rate of the inter-bank lending market. The interest rate variation curve of the overnight inter-bank lending in each month from 2009 to 2010 shows that the interest rate curve of overnight inter-bank lending in

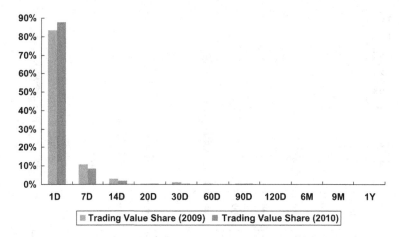

Figure 5.1.2.1   Overnight inter-bank lending business occupies the majority in the total inter-bank lending market

(*Data source*: People's Bank of China)

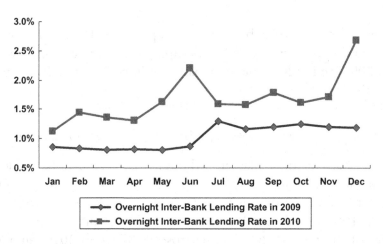

Figure 5.1.2.2   Interest rate of overnight inter-bank lending in 2010 significantly higher than in 2009 on a year-on-year basis

(*Data source*: People's Bank of China)

2010 was significantly higher than that in 2009. Statistics demonstrate that the average interest rate of overnight inter-bank lending within the 12 months of 2010 was significantly higher than that of 2009 by 0.65% (namely, 65 bases), and the median level of 2010 was higher than that of 2009 by 0.59%.

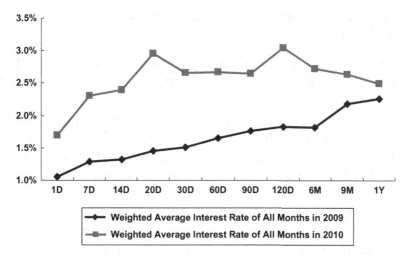

Figure 5.1.2.3 Maturity structure curve of inter-bank lending rate in 2010 significantly higher than in 2009

(*Data source*: People's Bank of China)

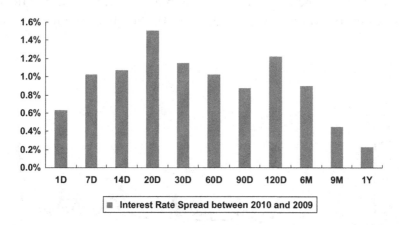

Figure 5.1.2.4 Spread of the inter-bank lending rate between 2010 and 2009

(*Data source*: People's Bank of China)

Seen from the perspective of maturity structure curve of weighted average inter-bank lending rate of all months, the curve in 2010 was significantly higher than in 2009. In terms of spread, the spread of the 20th day was the largest, up to 1.5% (however, the inter-bank lending businesses within 20 days only accounted for 0.5% and 0.2% of the annual trading value respectively in 2009 and 2010, hence not representative).

5.1.3 *Tendency of inter-bank lending rate during 2009 and 2010*

To more meticulously observe the variation tendency of inter-bank lending rate during 2009 and 2010, we make a statistic of "Shanghai Inter-Bank Offered Rate" (namely SHIBOR) within this time interval.

Wholly speaking, within this interval, the inter-bank lending rate demonstrates an uptrend, which is more obviously reflected in SHIBOR of longer maturity, such as SHIBOR of 9-month and 1-year maturities. However, for medium and short maturities, since the beginning of the second half of 2010, as market funds became tighter, SHIBOR witnessed a significant rise. For example, overnight SHIBOR and 1-week SHIBOR that best reflected the short-maturity funds, rose respectively from 1.12% and 1.42% at the beginning of the year to 4.52% and 6.39% at the end of the year.

In terms of interest rate maturity structure, the maturity structure curve at the beginning of 2010 basically coincides with that at the beginning of 2009, indicating an inconspicuous change in interest rate of SHIBOR within the year 2009. However, by the end of 2010, this curve significantly moves

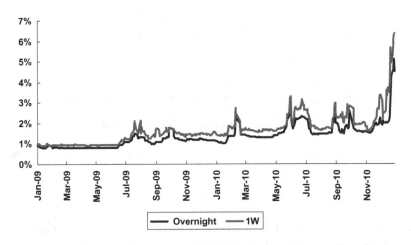

Figure 5.1.3.1   Tendency of SHIBOR during 2009 and 2010 (1)

up, especially the inter-bank lending rate of a maturity below 1 month (including 1 month) rising by 3%–5%. Comparatively speaking, the growth rate for a maturity below 1 month (including 1 month) is relatively low, around 1% to 2%.

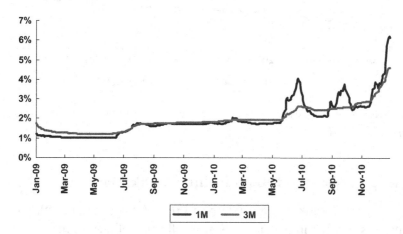

Figure 5.1.3.2   Tendency of SHIBOR during 2009 and 2010 (2)

(*Data source*: www.shibor.org)

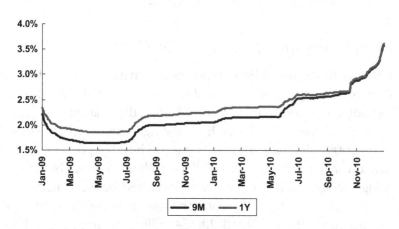

Figure 5.1.3.3   Tendency of SHIBOR during 2009 and 2010 (3)

(*Data source*: www.shibor.org)

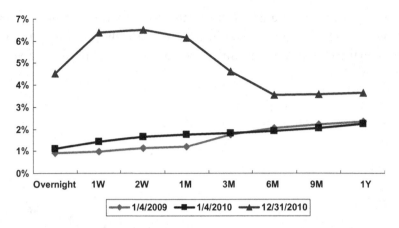

Figure 5.1.3.4   Comparison of maturity structure of SHIBOR during 2009 and 2010
(*Data source*: www.shibor.org)

5.2 Pledge-Style Bond Repo in Inter-Bank Market

The trade of inter-bank pledge-style bond repo (abbreviated as "bond repo" hereinafter) is another important indicator reflective of market funds. Similar to inter-bank lending market, the maturities of bond repo are mainly divided into 11 levels: 1 day (namely "overnight repo"), 7 days, 14 days, 21 days, 1 month, 2 months, 3 months, 4 months, 6 months, 9 months and 1 year, among which the overnight repo takes the majority of repo trade.

5.2.1 *Overall situation of pledge-style bond repo*

In 2009, the trading value of bond repo trading market witnessed a tendency in which there was a gradual increase during the first half of the year and a basically steady course during the second half of the year. However, in 2010 both the trading value and the weighted average interest rate underwent an uptrend. In 2009, the total trading value of bond repo rose from RMB 3.5917 trillion in January to RMB 7.2914 trillion in June, but the trading value during the second half of the year fluctuated between RMB 5 trillion and RMB 6 trillion; in 2010, the total trading value rose month by month from RMB 5.7465 trillion to RMB 9.8154 trillion in August and then gradually declined during the rest of the months. As the monetary policy became tight step by step, the weighted average interest rate in all maturities correspondingly increased: 0.9% in January 2009, up to 1.26% in December 2009; in January 2010 the average interest rate slightly dropped to 1.19% but rose back to a year high of 3.12% in December 2010.

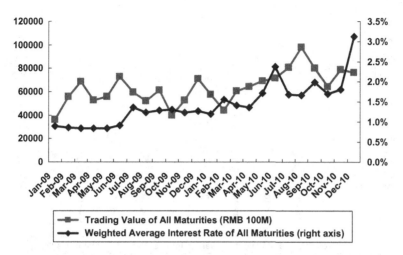

Figure 5.2.1.1 Change in trading value of pledge-style bond repo and average interest rate during 2009 and 2010

(*Data source*: People's Bank of China)

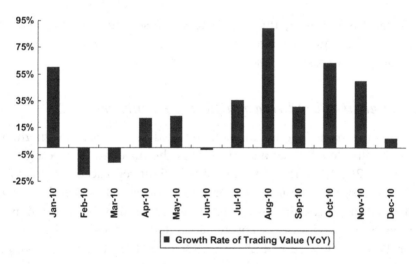

Figure 5.2.1.2 Growth rate of trading value of pledge-style bond repo in 2010 (YoY)

(*Data source*: People's Bank of China)

Seen from the perspective of YoY data, during the 12 months of 2010, the trading value of most months witnessed a rise when compared with the previous year (only in February and March were there a significant decline, and in June the trading value remained basically the same with the previous year), among which August had a highest growth rate of 88.9%. During the

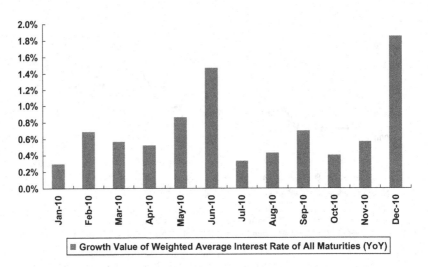

Figure 5.2.1.3 Growth value of weighted average interest rate of pledge-style bond repo in 2010 (YoY)

(*Data source*: People's Bank of China)

first 10 months of 2010, the repo rate witnessed an uptrend. December boasted a highest growth rate of 1.87%; even for January of the lowest growth rate, its interest rate also rose by 0.3% (YoY).

5.2.2 *Analysis of bond repo of different maturities*

Similar to inter-bank lending market, in bond repo trade, overnight repo (namely repo trade of 1-day maturity) takes the majority. According to data for 2009 and 2010, the trading value of overnight repo accounted for 77.8% of the total trading value for the year 2009, and in 2010 this share slightly rose to 80%. The 7-day and 14-day repo businesses also had a certain part to play: their trading values respectively accounted for 15.4% and 4.8% of the total for the year 2009, and 14.2% and 3.4% for 2010. Generally speaking, the businesses of 1-day, 7-day and 14-day maturities as a whole had a share of 98.0% in 2009 and 97.6% in 2010. Compared with inter-bank lending businesses, in bond repo trading, businesses of 7-day and 14-day maturities have a relatively higher share, but those of 1-day, 7-day and 14-day maturities have a share of 98% around, similar to one another.

The analysis of the interest rate variation of overnight repo that dominates the bond repo trade demonstrates that: seen from the perspective of interest rate variation curve of overnight inter-bank lending of all months from 2009 to 2010, the interest rate curve for 2010 is significantly higher than that for

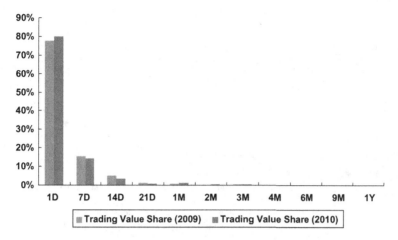

Figure 5.2.2.1 Overnight repo accounts for the majority in pledge-style bond repo trading

(*Data source*: People's Bank of China)

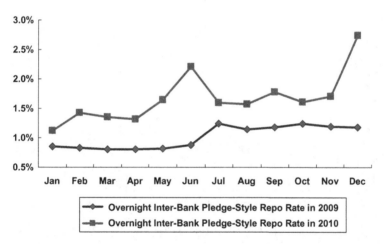

Figure 5.2.2.2 Overnight inter-bank pledge-style repo rate in 2010 significantly higher than that in 2009 (YoY)

(*Data source*: People's Bank of China)

2009. Statistics show that the average overnight inter-bank pledge-style repo rate of all months in 2010 was higher than that in 2009 by 0.66% (YoY) (namely 66 bases), and its median higher than the latter by 0.59%.

Seen from the perspective of maturity structure curve of weighted average repo rate of all months, the curve for 2010 is significantly higher than that for 2009. In terms of spread, the spread of 4-month maturity is the highest, up to 1.46% (but the 4-month maturity share of repo trading value is quite low, and thus not representative).

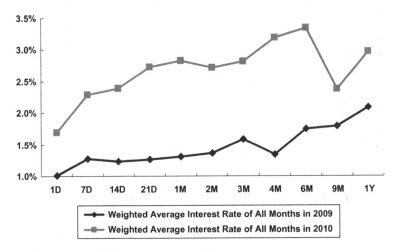

Figure 5.2.2.3   Maturity structure curve of inter-bank lending interest rate in 2010 significantly higher than in 2009

(*Data source*: People's Bank of China)

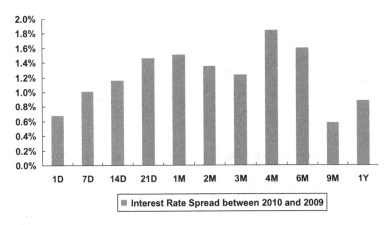

Figure 5.2.2.4   Inter-bank lending interest rate spread between 2010 and 2009

(*Data source*: People's Bank of China)

5.3 Interest-Rate Swap Market

According to different reference interest rates, in interest-rate swap market, the swap agreement in trading can be classified into four categories: interest-rate swap based on 7-day repo rate (FR007), based on SHIBOR (SHIBOR_O/N), based on 3-month SHIBOR (SHIBOR_3M), and based on 1-year time deposit rate (1-year time deposit). Since the maturity of inter-est-rate swap for 1-year time deposit rate is relatively short, this book mainly focuses on the analysis of FR007 and SHIBOR_O/N.

5.3.1 *Analysis of FR007 interest-rate swap*

During the years 2009 and 2010, the total nominal principal of FR007 interest-rate swap appeared to be on an uptrend, rising from RMB 14.5 billion in January 2009 to about RMB 60 billion in December 2010. Along with the gradually tightened monetary policy, the weighted average interest rate of all maturities also rose step by step, from 1.06% in January 2009 to 2.48% in December 2009, and in December 2010 reached up a year high of 3.35%.

In terms of year-on-year data, the nominal principal value of the 12 months in 2010 saw a rise, among which, May and November had the highest growth rate, up to about 380%. For most months of 2010, their repo interest rates also witnessed an uptrend, with that of January having the highest growth rate, about 1.52%, and only in August there was a YoY reduction of 0.03% in its weighted average interest rate.

In terms of nominal principal of all maturities, both in 2009 and 2010, the nominal principal shares of 1-year and 2-year maturities were relatively high, 31.8% and 22.6% in 2009, and 26.7% and 21.0% in 2010 respectively. For 7-year maturity, its share approximated to zero.

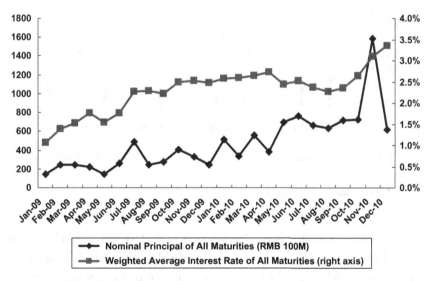

Figure 5.3.1.1   Change in nominal principal and average interest rate of FR007 interest-rate swap during 2009 and 2010

(*Data source*: National Interbank Lending Center)

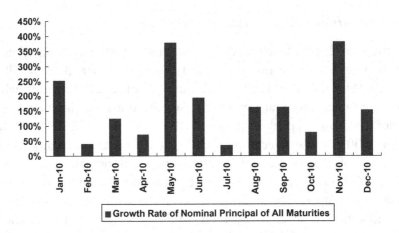

Figure 5.3.1.2   Growth rate of nominal principal of FR007 interest-rate swap in 2010 (YoY)

(*Data source*: National Interbank Lending Center)

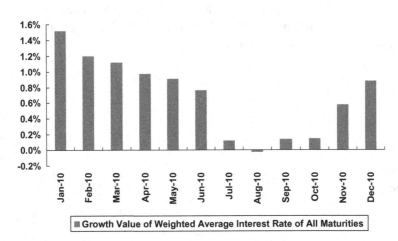

Figure 5.3.1.3   Growth value of weighted average interest rate of FR007 interest-rate swap in 2010

(*Data source*: National Interbank Lending Center)

In terms of weighted average interest rate of all months, 2010 was significantly higher than 2009. The average monthly share of all maturities for 2010 was 0.62%, among which the share of 3-month maturity ranked the highest, up to 0.81%, while that of 5-year maturity was relatively low, about 0.41%.

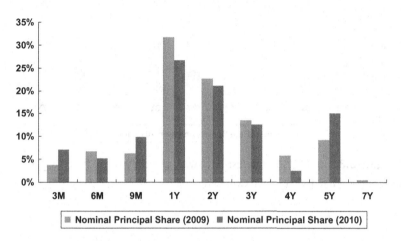

Figure 5.3.1.4 Nominal principal share of FR007 interest-rate swap of all maturities during 2009 and 2010

(*Data source*: National Interbank Lending Center)

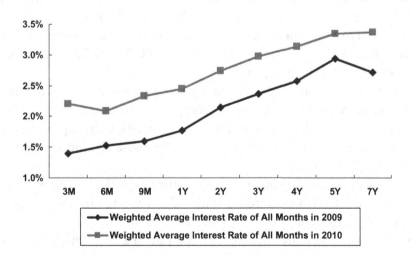

Figure 5.3.1.5 Weighted average interest rate of FR007 interest-rate swap in 2010 significantly higher than in 2009

(*Data source*: National Interbank Lending Center)

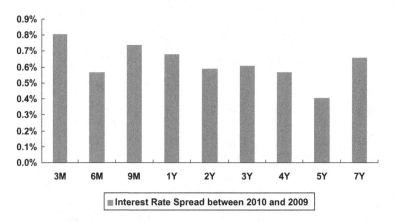

Figure 5.3.1.6   FR007 interest-rate swap spread between 2010 and 2009

(*Data source*: National Interbank Lending Center)

5.3.2 *Analysis of SHIBOR interest-rate swap*

During 2009 and 2010, the total nominal principal of SHIBOR interest-rate swap also remained on an uptrend: for 2009, the nominal principal of all months fluctuated around RMB 10 billion, while during the first three quarters of 2010, it rose up to over RMB 50 billion. With the gradual tightening of the monetary policy, the weighted average interest rate of all maturities also gradually increased, from 0.91% in January 2009 to 1.78% in December 2009, and up to 2.45% in December 2010.

In terms of year-on-year data, during the 12 months in 2010, the total nominal principal witnessed a rise, in comparison to 2009, with a relatively higher growth rate in January and December. In 2010, the repo interest rate of all months also kept an uptrend, with the most significant increase in January, March, June and October.

In terms of nominal principal of all maturities, either in 2009 or 2010, overnight-based SHIBOR interest rate of 7-day maturity was relatively higher, 62.3% in 2009 and 68.3% in 2010.

In terms of the weighted average interest rate of all months, 2010 was significantly higher than 2009, and the average monthly spread of all maturities was 0.92%: the highest spread in 3-month based SHIBOR interest rate of 1-year maturity, up to 1.34%, and overnight-based SHIBOR interest rate of 1-year maturity relatively lower, about 0.61%.

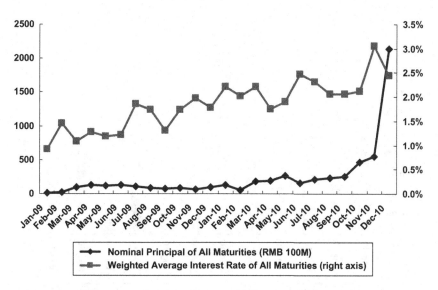

Figure 5.3.2.1 Change in total nominal principal of SHIBOR interest-rate swap and average interest rate during 2009 and 2010

(*Data source*: National Interbank Lending Center)

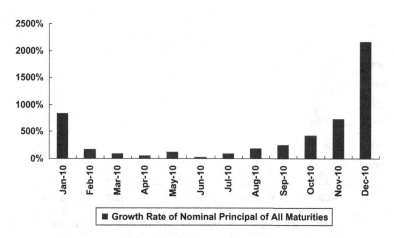

Figure 5.3.2.2 Growth rate of nominal principal of SHIBOR interest-rate swap in 2010 (YoY)

(*Data source*: National Interbank Lending Center)

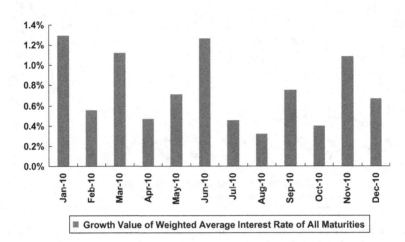

Figure 5.3.2.3 Growth value of weighted average of SHIBOR interest-rate swap in 2010 (YoY)

(*Data source*: National Interbank Lending Center)

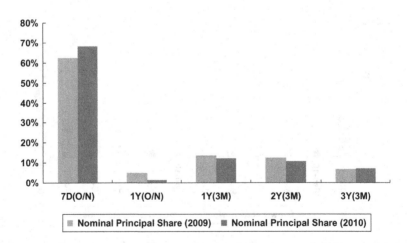

Figure 5.3.2.4 Nominal principal share of SHIBOR interest-rate swap of all maturities during 2009 and 2010

(*Data source*: National Interbank Lending Center)

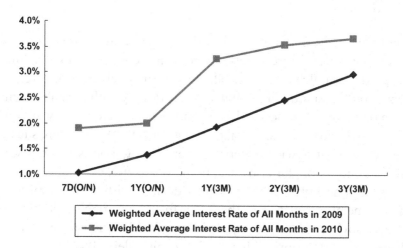

Figure 5.3.2.5 Weighted average of SHIBOR interest-rate swap in 2010 significantly higher than in 2009

(*Data source*: National Interbank Lending Center)

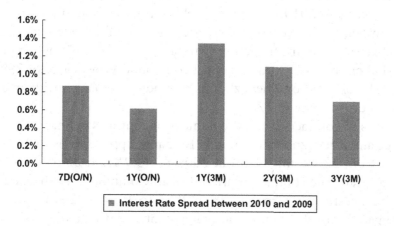

Figure 5.3.2.6 SHIBOR interest-rate swap spread between 2010 and 2009

(*Data source*: National Interbank Lending Center)

5.4 Commodity Futures Market

5.4.1 *Development of commodity futures market*

In the Chinese mainland, the commodity futures market includes three futures exchanges:

- Shanghai Futures Exchange: mainly dealing with raw materials and energy futures; the major futures contracts including copper cathode, aluminum, zinc, gold, natural rubber, fuel oil, steel rebar, steel wire rod, etc.;
- Zhengzhou Commodity Exchange: mainly dealing with agricultural futures; the major futures contracts including hard wheat (hard white winter wheat) (WT), strong gluten wheat (quality gluten wheat) (WS), cotton, sugar, PTA (Pure Terephthalic Acid, material for producing Polyester), rapeseed oil, early long-grain nonglutinous rice, mung bean, etc.;
- Dalian Commodity Exchange: mainly dealing with agricultural products and non-metal raw materials; the major futures contracts including yellow soybean, soybean meal, corn, soybean oil, LLDPE (linear low-density Polyethylene), Polyvinyl Chloride, RBD palm olein, PVC, etc.;

Since 2005, commodity futures has seen rapid development. In terms of the number of contracts, the annual trading value of the above three exchanges in total has increased from 320 million contracts in 2005 to 3.04 billion contracts in 2010, with an annual average compound growth rate of 56.6%. Among the three exchanges, the number of contracts in Shanghai Futures Exchange has the highest growth rate, rising from 67 million in 2005 to 1.24 billion in 2010, with an annual compound growth rate of 79%; it is immediately followed by Zhengzhou Commodity Exchange, with an annual compound growth rate of 77%. .

In terms of contracts share, the number of contracts in Shanghai Futures Exchange and Zhengzhou Commodity Exchange appears to rise, whose share increased from 20.9% and 17.6% in 2005 to 40.9% and 32.6% respectively. On the contrary, the contracts share of Dalian Commodity Exchange undergoes a decline, dropping from 61.4% in 2005 to 26.5% in 2010.

Compared with the number of trading contracts, the trading value of the futures market witnesses a more rapid rise. During the period from 2005 to 2010, the annual trading value of the three exchanges in total rose from RMB 13.6 trillion to RMB 227 trillion, with an annual average compound rate of 75.6%. Among them, the trading value in Zhengzhou Commodity Exchange ranked the first, rising from RMB 2.2 trillion in 2005 to RMB 61.8 trillion in 2010, with an annual average compound rate of 95.5%; the growth rate in

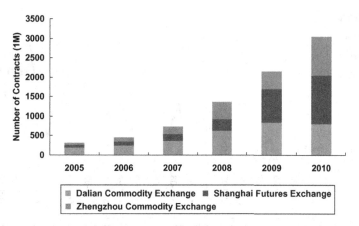

Figure 5.4.1.1 Number of contracts of commodity futures in each exchange
(*Data source*: China's Securities Regulatory Commission)

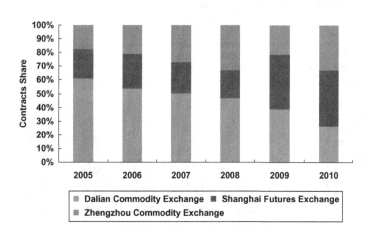

Figure 5.4.1.2 Contracts share of commodity futures for each exchange
(*Data source*: China's Securities Regulatory Commission)

Shanghai Futures Exchange ranked the second, with annual average compound rate of 79.1%.

Seen from the perspective of trading value share, during 2005 and 2010, the trading value share of Shanghai Futures Exchange basically fluctuated within the 50%–60% interval. In 2008, impacted by the recession in bulk metal products resulting from the global financial crisis, the trading value share reduced to 40.1% (but still ranked the first in trading value), and then

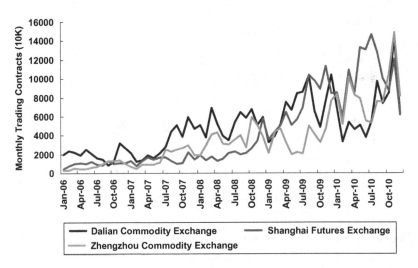

Figure 5.4.1.3   Monthly trading contracts of commodity futures in each exchange

(*Data source*: China's Securities Regulatory Commission)

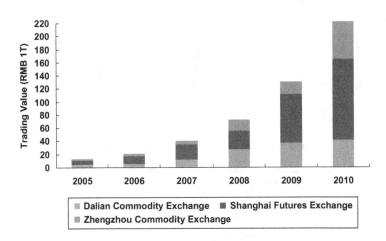

Figure 5.4.1.4   Trading value of commodity futures in each exchange

(*Data source*: China's Securities Regulatory Commission)

during 2009 and 2010 this share rose back to the interval around 55%. For Zhengzhou Commodity Exchange, the trading value share had a significant increase: during 2005 and 2007, it fluctuated within the 15%–16% interval, and then rose to a high of 27.2% in 2010. By comparison, the trading value share of Dalian Commodity Exchange dropped from approximately 30% during 2005 and 2007 to 18.4% in 2010.

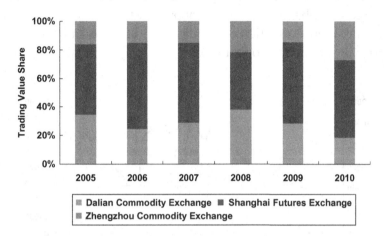

Figure 5.4.1.5 Trading value share of commodity futures in each exchange
(*Data source*: China's Securities Regulatory Commission)

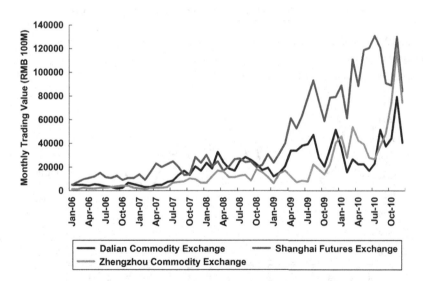

Figure 5.4.1.6 Monthly trading value of commodity futures in each exchange
(*Data source*: China's Securities Regulatory Commission)

5.4.2 *Price trend of major bulk commodity specific to commodity futures market price*

Recently, as China's economy is increasingly integrated into the global market, "China's demand" has become an influential factor of great importance in the change of global bulk commodity price, which, in a sense, elevates the correlation between domestic commodity futures price and the commodity futures price in the international market.

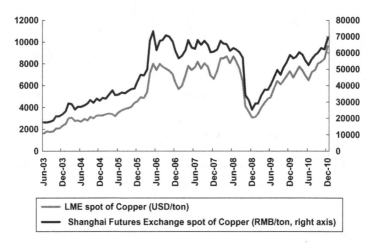

Figure 5.4.2.1   Relatively strong correlation between domestic copper cathode price trend and the international trend

(*Data source*: Shanghai Futures Exchange, Xinhua Finance)

Figure 5.4.2.2   Relatively weak correlation between domestic aluminum price trend and the international trend

(*Data source*: Shanghai Futures Exchange, Xinhua Finance)

For instance, since 2003 there has been a strong uniformity in the price trends of copper cathode in Shanghai Futures Exchange and London Merchandise Exchange (LME). The analysis of the monthly yield finds that the correlation between the two amounts to 0.87. This reflects to some extent the importance of China's demand in influencing copper cathode price.

Compared with copper cathode, the price trends of another important base metal — aluminum in domestic market and the international market have relatively weaker correlations. Analyzing the monthly yield of aluminum prices in Shanghai Futures Exchange and LME shows that, during 2003 and 2010 the monthly yield correlation between the two was only 0.52, significantly weaker than that of copper cathode.

However, on the other hand, the analysis of fluctuation correlation finds that in recent years, aluminum price witnessed an increasing strong correlation between domestic market and oversea market. For example, ever since 2003, the fluctuation correlation of the monthly yield of aluminum prices (adopting the fluctuation correlation within 36 months) in Shanghai Futures Exchange and LME has gradually rose from 0.43 to 0.65, indicating an escalation trend in correlation.

Even when daily trading price is taken into consideration, the uniformity in base metal price trends in the domestic market and the international market also shows a gradually strengthening tendency. The comparison between domestic base metal prices, after being converted to USD price in accordance with RMB/USD exchange rate, and the international market price can further indicate the correlation of metal prices. For example, during April

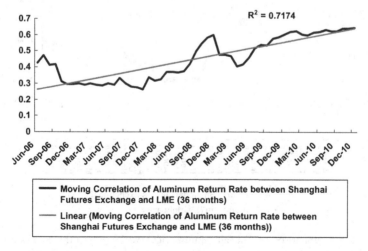

Figure 5.4.2.3 Escalation in the correlation between domestic aluminum price trend and the international trend

(*Data source*: Shanghai Futures Exchange, Xinhua Finance)

2007 and December 2010, after the futures prices in 3 months (daily prices) of three base metals (copper cathode, aluminum and zinc) in Shanghai Futures Exchange are converted to USD, the average price ratio between the converted USD prices and those in LME are 1.15, 1.06 and 1.18 respectively. Among the three, the ratio fluctuations for copper cathode and zinc are rather low, while that for aluminum is relatively high.

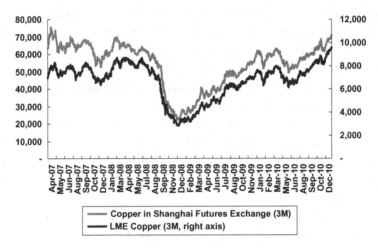

Figure 5.4.2.4   Comparison of daily copper cathode prices (within 3 months) in Shanghai Futures Exchange and LME

(*Data source*: Shanghai Futures Exchange, Xinhua Finance)

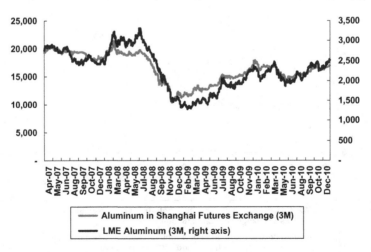

Figure 5.4.2.5   Comparison of daily aluminum prices (within 3 months) in Shanghai Futures Exchange and LME

(*Data source*: Shanghai Futures Exchange, Xinhua Finance)

Further analysis demonstrates that the standard deviations of the price ratio of these three metals are 4%, 11% and 7% respectively, indicating that the correlation between domestic and international market for copper cathode is comparatively stable, immediately followed by zinc, and the stability of aluminum's correlation is comparatively weak.

Compared with base metals, for agricultural products, the correlation of their price trend between domestic and international market is relatively

Figure 5.4.2.6 Comparison of daily zinc prices (within 3 months) in Shanghai Futures Exchange and LME

(*Data source*: Shanghai Futures Exchange, Xinhua Finance)

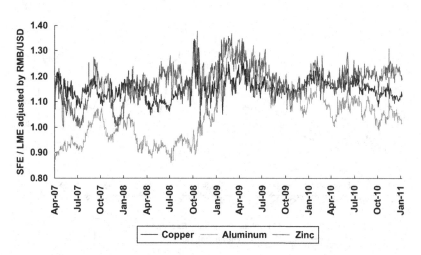

Figure 5.4.2.7 Price ratio between domestic and international prices of major metals in consideration of RMB/USD exchange rate

(*Data source*: Shanghai Futures Exchange, Xinhua Finance)

weaker. For example, during the end of 2004 and the end of 2010, the futures traded in Dalian Commodity Exchange — "No. 1 soybean" and "No. 2 soybean" had a monthly yield correlation of 0.53 and 0.5 respectively with CBOT soybean price (the monthly yield correlation between soybean 1 and

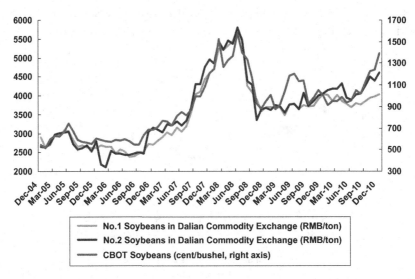

Figure 5.4.2.8   Certain correlation between soybean price in Dalian Commodity Exchange and in overseas market

(*Data source*: Dalian Commodity Exchange, Xinhua Finance)

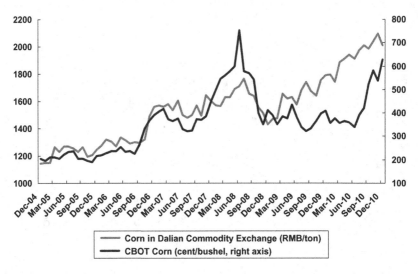

Figure 5.4.2.9   Relatively weak correlation between corn price in Dalian Commodity Exchange and in overseas market

(*Data source*: Dalian Commodity Exchange, Xinhua Finance)

soybean 2 was 0.6). Such correlation for corn was much weaker: the monthly yield correlation between corn price in Dalian Commodity Exchange and CBOT corn price was only 0.15.

For the agricultural products traded in Zhengzhou Commodity Exchange, their correlation between markets at home and abroad is also not strong. For

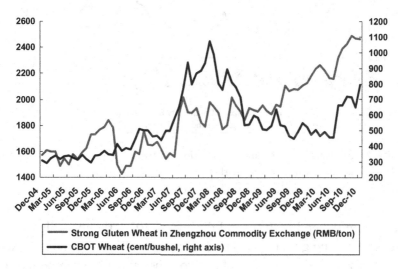

Figure 5.4.2.10 Relatively weak correlation between wheat price in Zhengzhou Commodity Exchange and in overseas market

(*Data source*: Zhengzhou Commodity Exchange, Xinhua Finance)

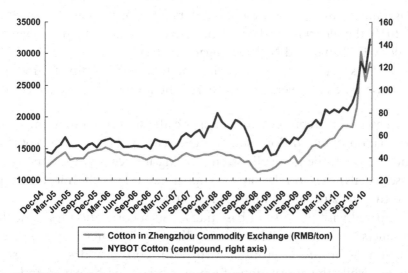

Figure 5.4.2.11 Relatively strong correlation between cotton price in Zhengzhou Commodity Exchange and in overseas market

(*Data source*: Zhengzhou Commodity Exchange, Xinhua Finance)

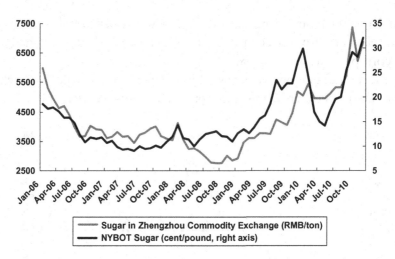

Figure 5.4.2.12 Relatively strong correlation between sugar price in Zhengzhou Commodity Exchange and in overseas market

(*Data source*: Zhengzhou Commodity Exchange, Xinhua Finance)

instance, during the end of 2004 and the end of 2010, the monthly yield correlation between strong gluten wheat traded in Zhengzhou Commodity Exchange and CBOT wheat was only 0.155. For two other agricultural products, cotton and sugar, their correlation between domestic and overseas market is relatively stronger. For example, during the end of 2004 and the end of 2010, the monthly yield correlation between cotton traded in Zhengzhou Commodity Exchange and NYBOT cotton was 0.54; during the beginning of 2006 and the end of 2010, the monthly yield correlation between sugar traded in Zhengzhou Commodity Exchange and NYBOT sugar was 0.51.

Generally speaking, the correlation of bulk commodity futures prices between domestic and oversea markets has the following two characteristics:

(1) For base metals represented by copper cathode, zinc, aluminum, etc., the correlation between domestic and overseas markets is relatively strong, and appears to be gradually strengthening in recent years. Among these base metals, the correlation for copper cathode is the most significant and that for zinc and aluminum is relatively weaker.

(2) Compared with the case of base metals, such correlation for agricultural products is relatively weaker. Among these agricultural products, the correlation of non-food crops like soybean, cotton and sugar is slightly higher, while the correlation of grains represented by wheat and corn is rather weak, reflecting to some extent the results of the price intervention policies in China and foreign countries towards different grains.

5.4.3 *Trading volume and position of main products in commodity futures market*

In terms of trading volume, trading value and position within each year, the main products in Dalian Commodity Exchange are soybean meal and soybean oil (since 2009 the trading value of RBD palm olein has a significant rise); the main products in Shanghai Futures Exchange are copper cathode, zinc and natural rubber (since 2009 the trading value of steel rebar has a

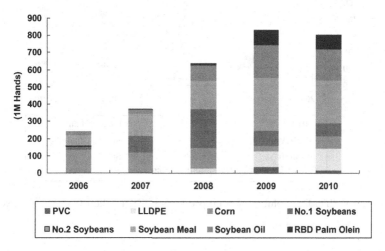

Figure 5.4.3.1 Trading volume of main products in Dalian Commodity Exchange
(*Data source*: China Futures Association)

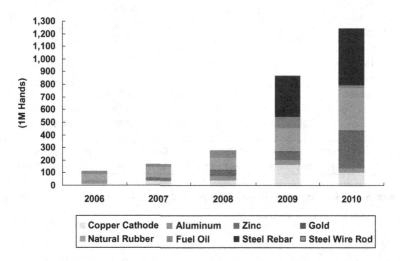

Figure 5.4.3.2 Trading volume of main products in Shanghai Futures Exchange
(*Data source*: China Futures Association)

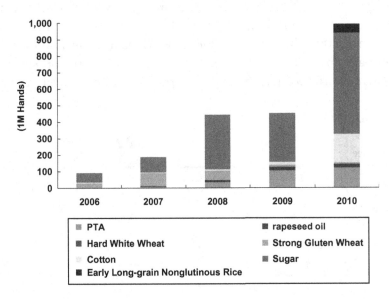

Figure 5.4.3.3   Trading volume of main products in Zhengzhou Commodity Exchange
(*Data source*: China Futures Association)

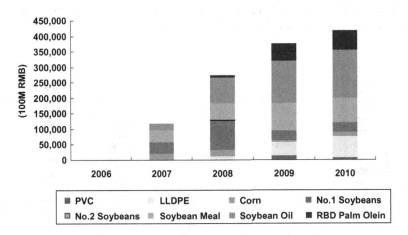

Figure 5.4.3.4   Trading value of main products in Dalian Commodity Exchange
(*Data source*: China Futures Association)

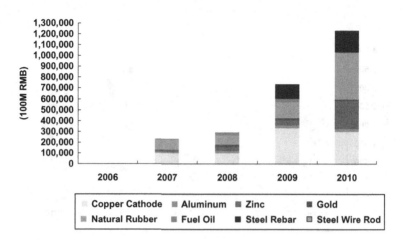

Figure 5.4.3.5 Trading value of main products in Shanghai Futures Exchange
(*Data source*: China Futures Association)

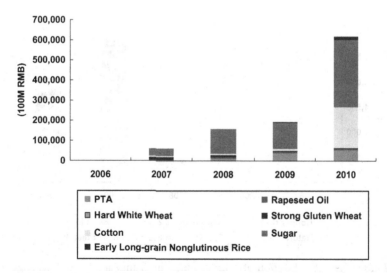

Figure 5.4.3.6 Trading value of main products in Zhengzhou Commodity Exchange
(*Data source*: China Futures Association)

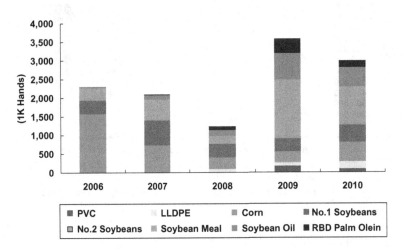

Figure 5.4.3.7 Position of main products in Dalian Commodity Exchange

(*Data source*: China Futures Association)

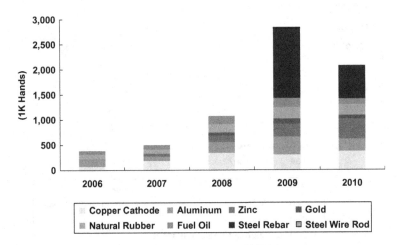

Figure 5.4.3.8 Position of main products in Shanghai Futures Exchange

(*Data source*: China Futures Association)

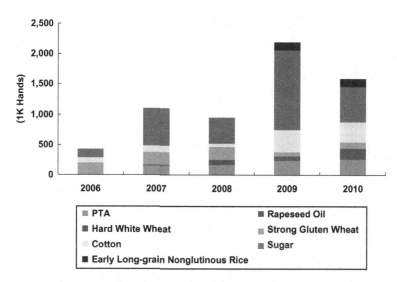

Figure 5.4.3.9 Position of main products in Zhengzhou Commodity Exchange (*Data source*: China Futures Association)

significant rise); the main products in Zhengzhou Commodity Exchange are sugar and cotton. Combined with the above-mentioned analysis of correlation of bulk commodity prices between domestic and overseas markets, it will show that among the aforesaid main products, such correlation for most products is relatively strong.

Chapter 6

BANKING

6.1 Development of Banking

6.1.1 *Framework of banking in present China*

China's banking industry is comprised of large commercial banks, joint-stock commercial banks, city commercial banks and other financial institutions. "Other financial institutions" include policy banks and China development banks (CDB), rural commercial banks, rural cooperative banks, urban credit cooperatives, rural credit cooperatives, postal savings banks, foreign banks and non-bank financial institutions. By 31st December, 2010, the total assets of China's financial institutions have surpassed RMB 94 trillion, and total liabilities have surpassed RMB 88 trillion.

(1) Large commercial banks: including Industrial and Commercial Bank of China, Agricultural Bank of China, Bank of China, Construction Bank and Bank of Communications. In the system of China's commercial banks, large commercial banks have an important role to play and are the significant financing source for enterprises, institutions and individual accounts. By the end of 2010, the total asset of these five major commercial banks accounts for about 50% of the total asset of China's banking.

(2) Joint-stock commercial banks: by the end of 2009, there are in total 12 joint-stock commercial banks within the Chinese territory. All of them have obtained permission to operate commercial bank business. By the end of 2010, the total asset of the above 12 joint-stock commercial banks accounts for 12% of the total asset of China's banking.

(3) City commercial banks: usually operating various commercial banking within the region licensed to do business. By far, several city commercial banks have obtained the permission to do cross-region business beyond their locations. Besides, Bank of Beijing Co., Ltd., Bank of Nanjing Co., Ltd., and Bank of Ningbo Co., Ltd. have issued A-share and are also

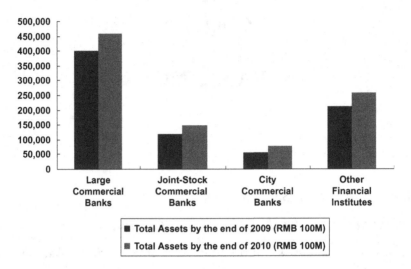

Figure 6.1.1.1   Total assets of various financial institutions by the end of 2009 and 2010
(*Data source*: China Banking Regulatory Commission)

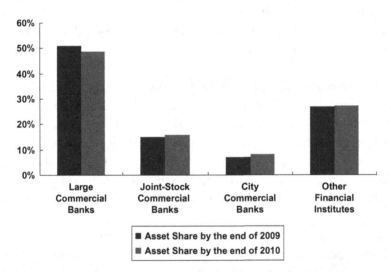

Figure 6.1.1.2   Total asset share of various financial institutions by the end of 2009 and 2010
(*Note*: The relevant share data was acquired by directly calculating the original data, thus slightly inconsistent with the share data published on the China Banking Regulatory Commission website)
(*Data source*: China Banking Regulatory Commission)

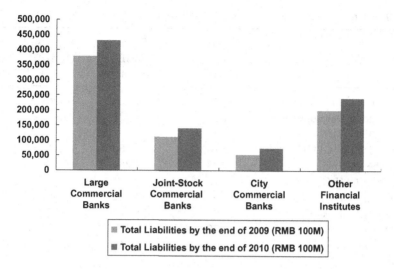

Figure 6.1.1.3 Total liabilities of various financial institutions by the end of 2009 and 2010

(*Data source*: China Banking Regulatory Commission)

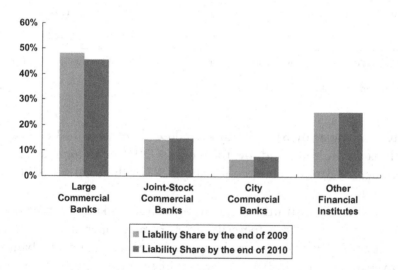

Figure 6.1.1.4 Total liability share of various financial institutions by the end of 2009 and 2010

(*Note*: The relevant share data was acquired by directly calculating the original data, thus slightly inconsistent with the share data published on the China Banking Regulatory Commission website)

(*Data source*: China Banking Regulatory Commission)

Table 6.1.1.1   Scale of joint-stock commercial banks by the end of 2009

	Number of domestic institutions	Assets (RMB 100M)	Deposits (RMB 100M)	Loans (RMB 100M)
China Merchants Bank (CMB)	738	20,679	16,081	11,858
Shanghai Pudong Development Bank (SPDB)	565	16,227	12,953	9,289
China CITIC Bank (CITIC)	616	17,750	13,419	10,656
China Minsheng Banking Corp., Ltd. (CMBC)	433	14,264	11,279	8,830
Industrial Bank (IB)	504	13,322	9,009	7,016
China Everbright Bank (CEB)	483	11,977	8,077	6,490
Hua Xia Bank	350	8,455	5,817	4,302
Guangdong Development Bank (GDDB)	518	6,665	5,439	3,809
Shenzhen Development Bank (SZDB)	301	5,878	4,546	3,595
Evergrowing Bank	95	2,138	1,387	9,373
China Zheshang Bank	46	1,634	1,211	874
Bohai Bank	41	1,175	1,016	697
TOTAL		**120,164**	**90,234**	**76,789**

Note: Data about the total assets was collected according to data published in various bank annual reports.

(*Data source*: Various bank annual reports)

listed in China. By 31st December, 2009, there were 143 city commercial banks in total and by the end of 2010 the total asset of city commercial banks accounted for about 8% of the total assets of China's banking.

(4) Other financial institutions: including policy banks and China development banks, rural commercial banks, rural cooperative banks, urban credit cooperatives, rural credit cooperatives, postal savings banks, foreign banks and non-bank financial institutions. By 31st December, 2009, among other financial banks, there were in total 2 policy banks and CDB, 43 rural commercial banks, 196 rural cooperative banks, 11 rural credit cooperatives, 3,056 rural credit cooperatives, and 1 postal savings bank, 37 foreign banks, 174 non-bank financial institutions including finance cooperatives of enterprise groups, trust companies, financial leasing companies, etc. By the end of 2010, the total asset of other financial institutions accounted for 27% of the total assets of China's banking.

6.1.2 *Asset size and development of banking*

In recent years, China's banking industry is witnessing a rapid development. In terms of asset size, this development goes as follows: during 2006 and 2010, the total asset size of banking increased from RMB 39 trillion to RMB 94 trillion, and the total liability rose from RMB 37 trillion to RMB 88 trillion, with an annual average compound growth rate of 21%.

In terms of year-on-year growth of asset size, from 2006 to 2010, the average quarterly growth rate was 20.6% (the median being 19.7%); for the second quarter of 2009, the growth rate reached the highest, up to 27.7%; the growth rate of the third quarter of 2006 ranked the lowest, yet still amounting to 17.0%.

In terms of different categories of commercial banks, the growth rate of asset size for joint-stock commercial banks and city commercial banks is comparatively higher than that for state-owned commercial banks. According to

Table 6.1.1.2   Number of financial institutions and their staff in China's banking industry by the end of 2009

Institutions/Items	Number of Staff	Number of Banks
Policy Banks and CDB	57,673	3
Large Commercial Banks	1,506,424	5
Joint-Stock Commercial Banks	197,657	12
City Commercial Banks	177,765	143
Urban Credit Cooperatives	2,956	11
Rural Credit Cooperatives	570,366	3,056
Rural Commercial Banks	66,317	43
Rural Cooperative Banks	74,776	196
Village and Township Banks	3,586	148
Lending Companies	75	8
Rural Mutual Cooperatives	96	16
Finance Cooperatives of Enterprise Groups	5,276	91
Trust Companies	5,464	58
Financial Leasing Companies	852	12
Auto Finance Companies	1,620	10
Money Brokerage Firms	173	3
Postal Savings Bank	132,536	1
Financial Asset Management Companies	8,589	4
Foreign Banks	32,502	37
Banking Institutions in Total	**2,844,703**	**3,857**

(*Data source*: China Banking Regulatory Commission)

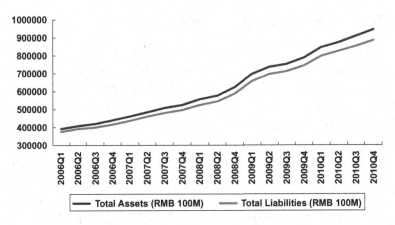

Figure 6.1.2.1 Growth rate of assets of banking institutions in China (1)
(*Data source*: China Banking Regulatory Commission)

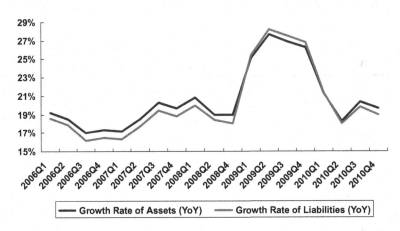

Figure 6.1.2.2 Growth rate of assets of banking institutions in China (2)
(*Data source*: China Banking Regulatory Commission)

statistics, from the first quarter of 2006 to the fourth quarter of 2010, the average quarterly growth rate (YoY) of assets for large commercial banks was 17.3%, while for joint-stock commercial banks this growth rate was 27.7%; for city commercial banks this rate was much higher, up to 30.1%. After 2009, the growth rate surpassed 32%, even above 36%. Within 2010, for large commercial banks, the growth rate of all quarters was all below 20%, while for joint-stock commercial banks it ranged between 25% and 28%, and for city commercial banks, it remained below 33%.

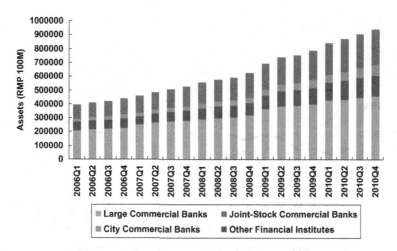

Figure 6.1.2.3 Growth of total assets of various financial institutions

(*Data source*: China Banking Regulatory Commission)

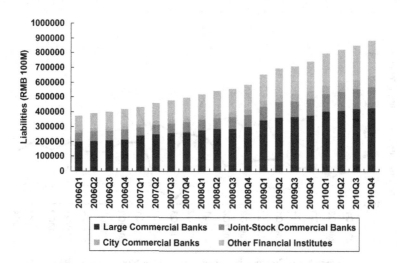

Figure 6.1.2.4 Growth of total liabilities of various financial institutions

(*Data source*: China Banking Regulatory Commission)

Corresponding to the asset size growth of city commercial banks is that their share in bank financial institutions is increasingly elevated. For example, for the first quarter of 2006, the ratio between large commercial banks, joint-stock commercial banks, city commercial banks and other financial institutions was 53.1 : 15.5 : 5.3 : 26.1, and by the end of the fourth quarter of 2010 it changed to 48.7 : 15.8 : 8.3 : 27.2, with city commercial banks boasting the most significant asset growth rate.

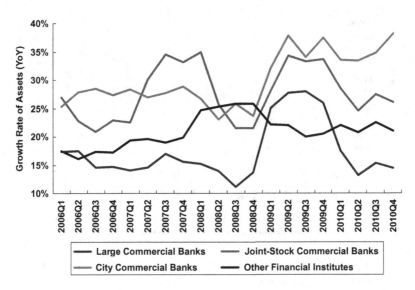

Figure 6.1.2.5   Growth rate of total assets of various financial institutions

(*Data source*: China Banking Regulatory Commission)

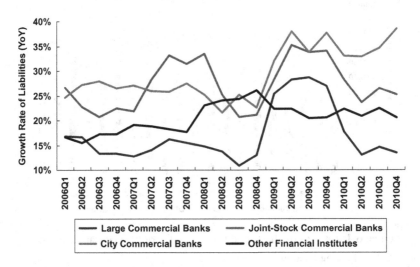

Figure 6.1.2.6   Growth rate of total liabilities of various financial institutions

(*Data source*: China Banking Regulatory Commission)

Similarly, from 2006 to 2010, the equity share of city commercial banks in bank financial institutions witnessed a steady increase. For the first quarter of 2006, this share was 4.8% (the share of large commercial banks and joint-stock commercial bank was 53.1% and 13.1% respectively, and share for other

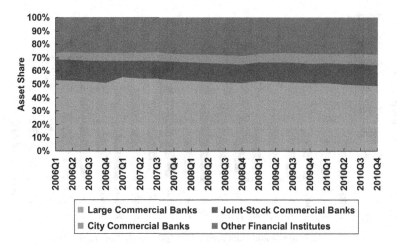

Figure 6.1.2.7   Total asset share of various financial institutions

(*Data source*: China Banking Regulatory Commission)

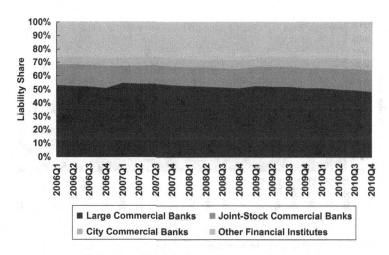

Figure 6.1.2.8   Total liability share of various financial institutions

(*Data source*: China Banking Regulatory Commission)

financial institutions was 28.4%). But when it comes to the fourth quarter of 2010, this share for city commercial banks rose to 8.3%, while for large commercial banks, it dropped down to 49.0%; the share for joint-stock commercial banks slightly increased and share for other financial institutions remained stable, about 28.7%.

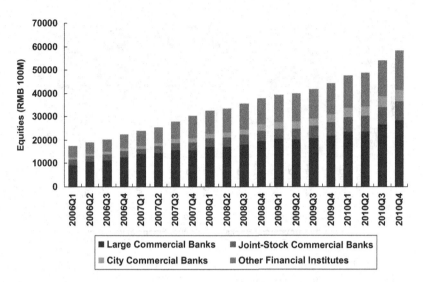

Figure 6.1.2.9   Equity growth of various financial institutions

(*Data source*: China Banking Regulatory Commission)

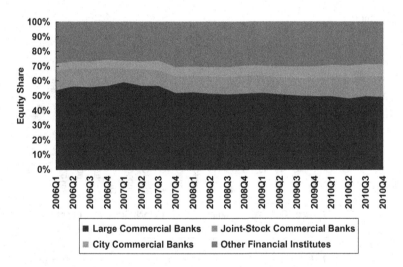

Figure 6.1.2.10   Equity share of various financial institutions

(*Data source*: China Banking Regulatory Commission)

6.1.3 *Overall anti-risk capability of banking*

Since 2006, for commercial banks the ratio between non-performing loan (NPL) balance and non-performing loan (NPL) basically stayed at a downward trend, among which, non-performing loan balance reduced from RMB 1.3

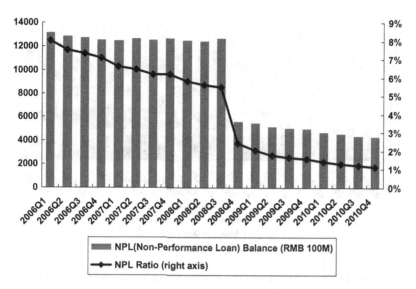

Figure 6.1.3.1 NPL balance and NPL ratio for commercial banks
(*Data source*: China Banking Regulatory Commission)

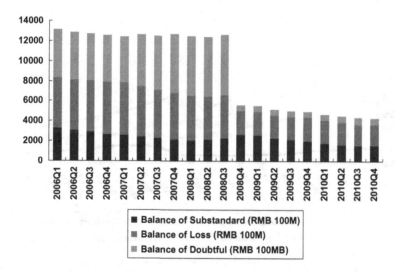

Figure 6.1.3.2 NPL balance of the five kinds of loans for commercial banks
(*Data source*: China Banking Regulatory Commission)

trillion in the first quarter of 2006 to RMB 0.4 trillion in the fourth quarter of 2010, and NPL ratio reduced from 8% in the first quarter of 2006 to 1.14% in the fourth quarter of 2010.

Within the 5-grade loan classification system, share of substandard, share of doubtful and share of loss also undergo a gradual change, among which

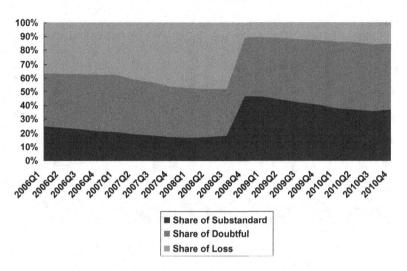

Figure 6.1.3.3   NPL ratio of the five kinds of loans for commercial banks

(*Data source*: China Banking Regulatory Commission)

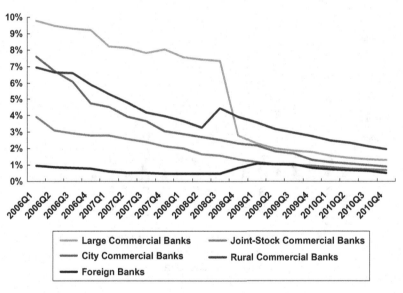

Figure 6.1.3.4   NLP ratio variation of various commercial banks

(*Data source*: China Banking Regulatory Commission)

share of loss decreased from 36.6% in the first quarter of 2006 to 15.3% in the fourth quarter of 2010, while share of substandard and share of doubtful rose from 25.0% and 38.4% to 37.1% and 47.6% respectively.

Among the four general categories of financial institutions, in the case of large commercial banks, the NPL ratio witnessed a rapid decrease, dropping

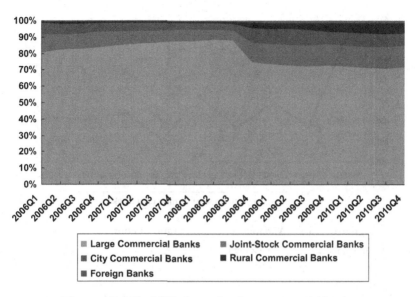

Figure 6.1.3.5   NLP share of various commercial banks

(*Data source*: China Banking Regulatory Commission)

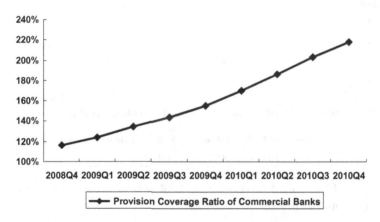

Figure 6.1.3.6   Variation in provision coverage ratio of commercial banks

(*Data source*: China Banking Regulatory Commission)

from 9.78% (ranked the first among commercial banks) in early 2006 to 1.31% in the fourth quarter of 2010; the decline in NPL ratio for city commercial banks was also significant, from 7.59% in the first quarter of 2006 down to 0.91% in the fourth quarter of 2010. Joint-stock commercial banks and foreign banks kept a relatively lower NPL ratio, with that of the former dropping from 3.92% in early 2006 to 0.70% in the fourth quarter of 2010 and that of the latter remaining below 1% (in the fourth quarter of 2010 the

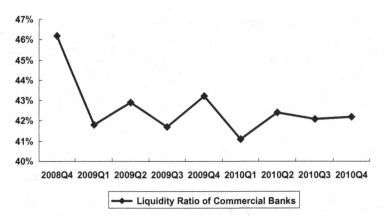

Figure 6.1.3.7   Variation in liquidity ratio of commercial banks

(*Data source*: China Banking Regulatory Commission)

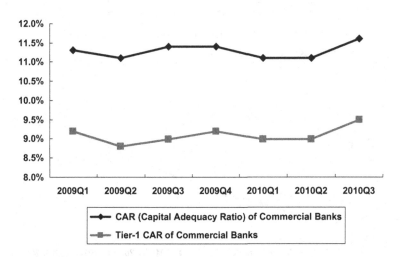

Figure 6.1.3.8   Variation in CAR of commercial banks

(*Data source*: China Banking Regulatory Commission)

NPL ratio of foreign banks was 0.53%, the lowest among the various financial institutions). By contrast, although the NLP ratio of rural commercial banks slightly reduced (from 6.96% in 2006 to 1.95% in the fourth quarter of 2010), it still presently ranks the first among the various bank financial institutions.

Corresponding to the above-mentioned NLP ratio variation is the share variation of NLP in commercial banks in the total NLP. From 2006 to the fourth quarter of 2010, NLP in large commercial banks had a significant drop

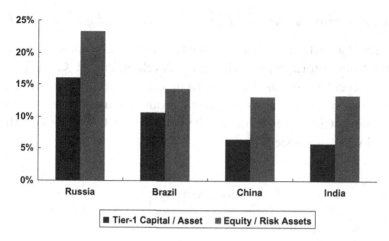

Figure 6.1.3.9   Comparison of CAR in "BRIC"

(*Data source*: thebankerdatabase.com)

in its share in total NLP (from 80.67% down to 71.77%), while for joint-stock commercial banks and city commercial banks, the NLP share was not obvious (respectively rising from 11.28% and 6.56% to 13.16% and 7.58%). The most significant increase in NLP share was that of rural commercial banks, from 1.2% to 6.35%.

During 2009 and 2010, the provision coverage ratio of commercial banks also witnessed a constant increase, rising from 116.4% by the end of the fourth quarter of 2008 to 218.3% in the fourth quarter of 2010.

During 2009 and 2010, liquidity ratio of commercial banks basically remained between 41% and 43%: in 2009, the quarterly average liquidity ratio was 42.4% and in 2010 this ratio changed into 42.0%.

During 2009 and 2010, capital adequacy ratio (CAR) of commercial banks remained above 11% (the quarterly average CARs for the first three quarters of 2009 and 2010 were both 11.3%), and the tier-1 CAR kept above 9% (the quarterly average tier-1 CARs for the first three quarters of 2009 and 2010 were 9.1% and 9.2% respectively).

However, from the perspective of global horizontal comparison, CAR of China's banking industry (especially tier-1 CAR) is not that high. For example, by the end of 2009, among "BRIC" (namely Brazil, Russia, India and China), both tier-1 CAR and CAR (equity/risk assets) for Russia and Brazil are higher than those for China; tier-1 CAR for China is only slightly higher than that for India but India's CAR is slightly higher than China's CAR.

6.1.4 *Comparison between China's banking and global banking*

With the rapid growth of China's economy and the development opportunity benefiting from reform in banking, the development of China's banking industry in recent years has obtained significant achievement. Among 2009 global top ten banks in terms of pretax profit, Industrial and Commercial Bank of China, China Construction Bank, Bank of China ranked the first, second and seventh respectively.

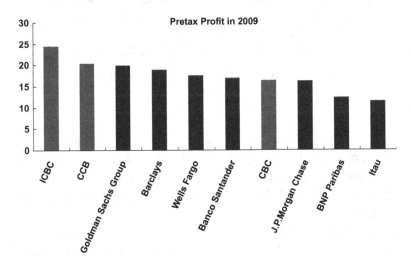

Figure 6.1.4.1   2009 Global top ten banks in terms of pretax profit

(*Data source*: The Banker)

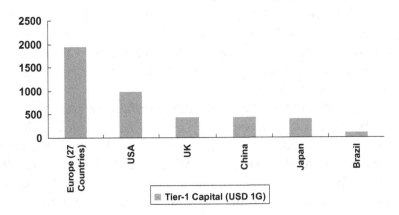

Figure 6.1.4.2   Global comparison of tier-1 asset of China's banking in 2009

(*Data source*: thebankerdatabase.com)

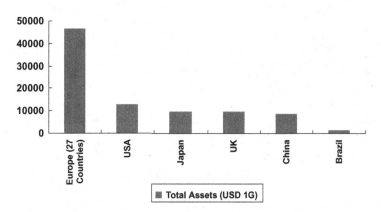

Figure 6.1.4.3　Global comparison of total assets of China's banking in 2009

(*Data source*: thebankerdatabase.com)

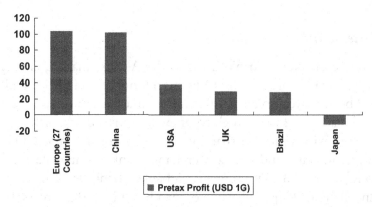

Figure 6.1.4.4　Global comparison of pretax profit of China's banking in 2009

(*Data source*: thebankerdatabase.com)

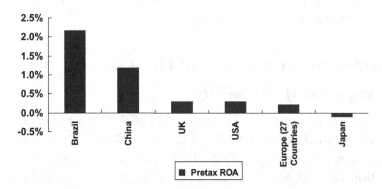

Figure 6.1.4.5　Global comparison of pretax ROA (return on assets) of China's banking in 2009

(*Data source*: thebankerdatabase.com, Xinhua Finance)

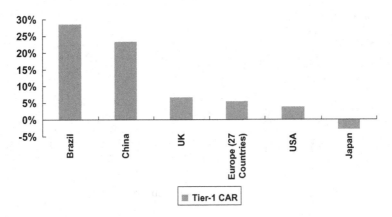

Figure 6.1.4.6   Global comparison of pretax tier-1 ROA of China's banking in 2009
(*Data source*: thebankerdatabase.com, Xinhua Finance)

6.1.5 *Listed banks*

By far there are in total 16 banks listed in the A-share market, among which half (namely 8 banks) are also listed in the Hong Kong market, and 5 large commercial banks have also been listed at the same time in A-share market and Hong Kong market; 12 joint-stock commercial banks, 8 of which are listed in A-share market, with a number share of 67%, 3 of which (China CITIC Bank, China Minsheng Bank and China Merchants Bank) meanwhile are listed in Hong Kong market; 3 city commercial banks (Bank of Nanjing, Bank of Ningbo and Bank of Beijing) have also been listed in A-share market.

Since all the main commercial banks (including large commercial banks and joint-stock commercial banks) in China's banking industry have been basically listed, we can know about the main status of China's banking through the analysis of the listed banks.

6.2 Comparison of Profitability of Listed Banks

6.2.1 *Comparison of profitability*

The average Rate of Return on Equity (ROE) of the 16 listed banks in 2009 was 18.82% (its median was 19.13%); the average ROE of large commercial banks was above the average of the 16 listed banks. Among them, China Construction Bank, Agricultural Bank of China, Industrial and Commercial Bank of China, Bank of Communications and Bank of China ranked 5, 6, 7, 8 and 11 respectively. For the first half of 2010, the average ROE of the listed banks was 11.40%, and the median was 12.03%.

Table 6.1.5.1 Codes and categories of listed banks

Name	A-share market code	Hong Kong market code	Large commercial banks	Categories Joint-stock commercial banks	City commercial banks
Industrial and Commercial Bank of China	601398	01398	✓		
Agricultural Bank of China	601288	01288	✓		
Bank of China	601988	03988	✓		
China Construction Bank	601939	00939	✓		
Bank of Communications	601328	03328	✓		
China CITIC Bank	601998	00998		✓	
China Minsheng Bank	600016	01988		✓	
China Merchants Bank	600036	03968		✓	
China Everbright Bank	601818			✓	
Shanghai Pudong Development Bank	600000			✓	
Industrial Bank	601166			✓	
Hua Xia Bank	600015			✓	
Shenzhen Development Bank A	600000			✓	
Bank of Nanjing	601009				✓
Bank of Ningbo	002142				✓
Bank of Beijing	601169				✓

(*Data source:* Xinhua Finance)

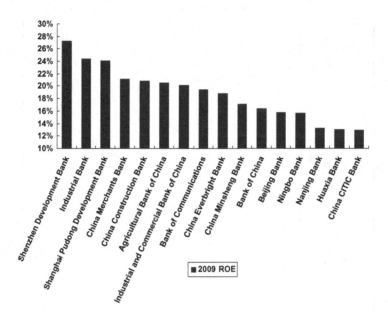

Figure 6.2.1.1   ROE of listed banks in A-share market in 2009

(*Data source*: Financial reports of each listed bank)

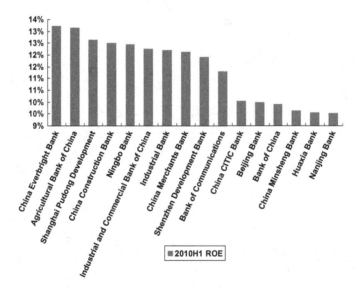

Figure 6.2.1.2   ROE of listed banks in A-share market for the first half of 2010

(*Data source*: Financial reports of each listed bank)

In terms of ROA, the average ROA of the 16 listed banks in 2009 was 1% (its median was 1.01%); for the first half of 2010 the average ROA was 0.58% with a median of 0.58%.

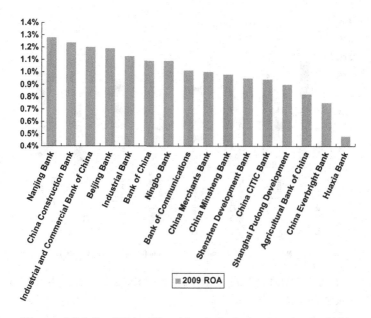

Figure 6.2.1.3   ROA of listed banks in A-share market in 2009

(*Data source*: Financial reports of each listed bank)

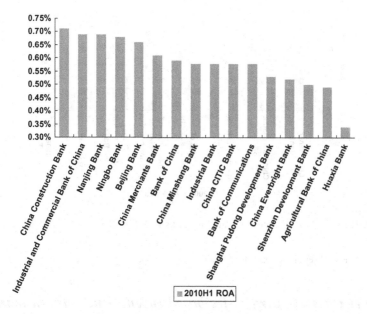

Figure 6.2.1.4   ROA of listed banks in A-share for the first half of 2010

(*Data source*: Financial reports of each listed bank)

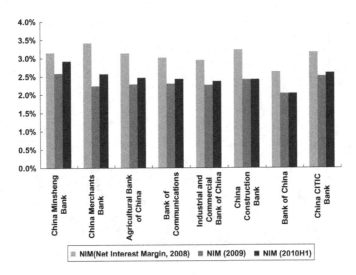

Figure 6.2.2.1   NIM of banks listed in Hong Kong during 2008 and 2010

(*Data source*: Financial reports of each listed bank)

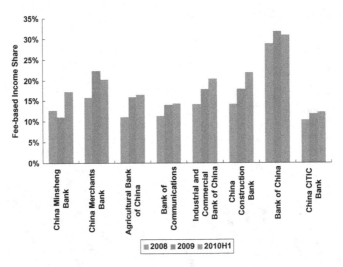

Figure 6.2.2.2   Fee-based income share of banks listed in Hong Kong market during 2008 and 2010

(*Data source*: Financial reports of each listed bank)

6.2.2 *Net interest margin, fee-based income and foreign loans*

Since by now deposit and loan spread are still the main sources of profits for China's banking industry, net interest margin (= net interest income/average interest-earning assets; net interest income = interest income — interest

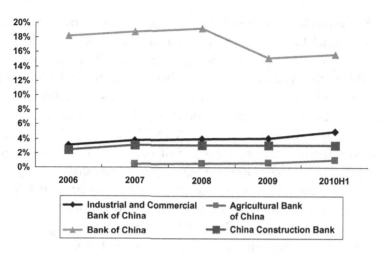

Figure 6.2.2.3   Foreign loan share of large commercial banks
(*Data source: Security Market Weekly*, 2011-1-8, p. 37)

expense) is one significant indicator to measure profitability of commercial banks. From 2008 to the first half of 2010, as the monetary policy changed from loosening to tightening, and then from tightening to loosening, the NIM of main commercial banks underwent a trend from high to low and then from low to high (due to the problem of data acquisition, the commercial banks analyzed in this present section are banks listed in Hong Kong market). The average NIM of the 8 commercial banks listed in Hong Kong market (including all large commercial banks and 3 joint-stock commercial banks) dropped from 3.09% in 2008 to 2.33% in 2009 and then rose back to 2.48% for the first half of 2010 (the medians were 3.13%, 2.30% and 2.47% respectively). For 2009, the average NIM (2.44%) of the three joint-stock commercial banks — China Minsheng Bank, China Merchants Bank and China CITIC Bank was slightly higher than that of 5 large commercial banks (2.26%). It was basically the same case for the first half of 2010: the average NIM of the 3 joint-stock commercial banks was 2.69%, higher than that of 5 large commercial banks — 2.34%.

Moreover, the fee-based income business in China's banking industry also gained an increasingly strengthening trend, which reflected in fee-based income share during 2008 and 2010 demonstrates that the average fee-based income share of the 8 commercial banks listed in Hong Kong market rose from 14.84% in 2008 to 17.80% in 2009, and then rose further to 19.24% in 2010 (the medians for the above 3 years were 14.19%, 17.80% and 19.24% respectively). In terms of fee-based income share, the share of large commercial banks listed in Hong Kong market was higher than that of joint-stock commercial banks listed in Hong Kong market: for 2009, the average fee-based income share of the 5 large commercial banks was 19.45%, higher than that of the 3 joint-stock commercial banks — 15.05%; for the first half of 2010, the average fee-based income share of the 5 large commercial banks rose to 20.82%, significantly higher than that of the 3 joint-stock commercial banks — 16.60%.

In terms of foreign loan share, for Industrial and Commercial Bank of China, Agricultural Bank of China, Bank of China and China Construction Bank, due to historical reason, the share of Bank of China always remained relatively high, above 15%. However, since 2009, this share has significantly declined. By contrast, the foreign loan share for Industrial and Commercial Bank of China keeps rising year by year since 2006, from 3.1% in 2006 to 4.1% in 2009 (5% for the first half of 2010). The share for Agricultural Bank of China is rather low but still increases step by step. For China Construction Bank, the share remains relatively stable, basically around 3%.

6.3 Comparison of Anti-Risk Capability of Listed Banks

In terms of approaches to disposing risk, risk management can be divided into 4 aspects:

(1) Avoiding risk events: for commercial banks, this means that through industry and business analysis they determine which enterprise or project is worth granting loans or should avoid granting loans.
(2) Reducing risk event probability: for commercial banks, this means that through loan tracking they spot as early as possible problems that may impact the credit quality of the enterprise or project occurring in their operation and take timely measures. One important indicator of measuring risk event probability is non-performing loan.
(3) Reducing loss caused by the occurrence of risk event: for commercial banks, this means that by means of collecting collateral or pledge, etc. to withdraw part or all principal and interest through auction of collateral or pledge in case the loan default loss occurs.
(4) Accepting risk loss and avoiding, by one way or another, further expansion of single or partial risk loss: for commercial banks, to elevate CAR and tier-1 CAR and make risk diversification are highly important in this risk management approach.

6.3.1 *Comparison between CAR and tier-1 CAR*

From 2009 to the first half of 2010, the average CAR of the 16 banks listed in A-share market reduced from 11.14% to 11%, but the median of CAR rose

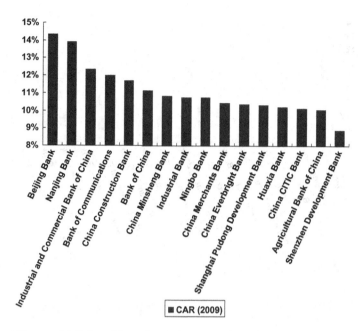

Figure 6.3.1.1   CAR of banks listed in A-share market in 2009

(*Data source*: Financial reports of each listed bank)

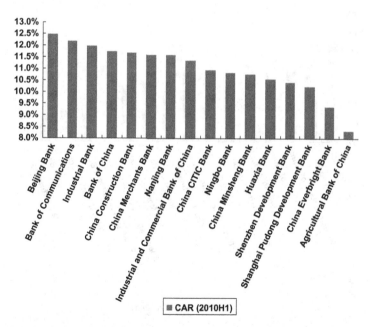

Figure 6.3.1.2   CAR of banks listed in A-share market for the first half of 2010

(*Data source*: Financial reports of each listed bank)

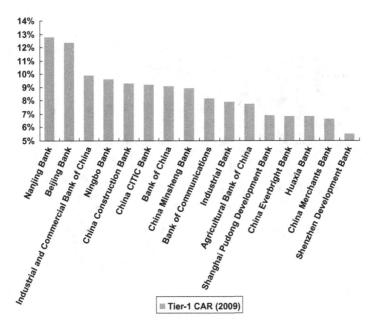

Figure 6.3.1.3 Tier-1 CAR of banks listed in A-share market for 2009

(*Data source*: Financial reports of each listed bank)

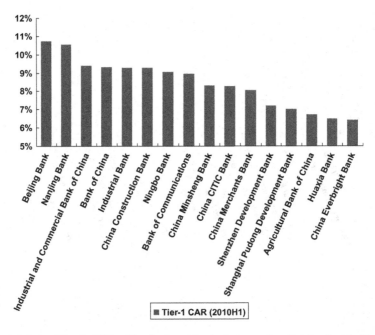

Figure 6.3.1.4 Tier-1 CAR of banks listed in A-share market for the first half of 2010

(*Data source*: Financial reports of each listed bank)

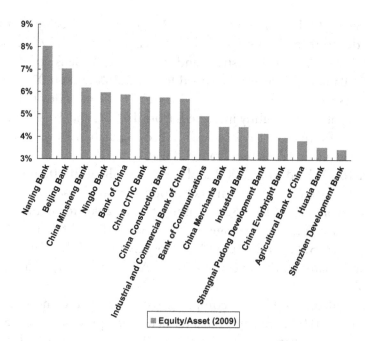

Figure 6.3.1.5 Equity/asset rate for banks listed in A-share market for 2009

(*Data source*: Financial reports of each listed bank)

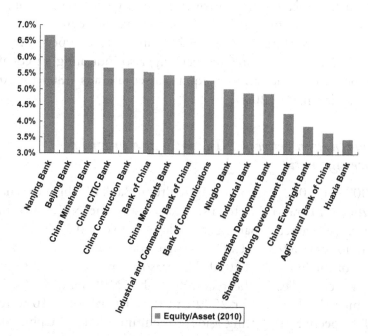

Figure 6.3.1.6 Equity/asset rate for banks listed in A-share market for the first half of 2010

(*Data source*: Financial reports of each listed bank)

from 10.75% to 11.15%, among which, CAR of Bank of Beijing and Bank of Nanjing reduced from 14.35% and 13.9% to 12.47% and 11.59% respectively, by about 2%; CAR of Industrial and Commercial Bank of China and Agricultural Bank of China also dropped from 12.36% and 10.07% to 11.34% and 8.31% respectively, both by more than 1%; CAR of Industrial Bank and China Merchants Bank slightly increased, from 10.75% and 10.45% to 11.96% and 11.6%, by more than 1%. Besides, CAR of Shenzhen Development Bank A also enjoyed a significant rise, from 8.88% to 10.41%.

Similar to CAR, during 2009 and the first half of 2010, average tier-1 CAR of banks listed in A-share market dropped from 8.6% to 8.44%, but its median rose from 8.54% to 8.63%. Among these banks, for Bank of Nanjing and Bank of Beijing, the average tier-1 CAR reduced from 12.77% and 12.38% to 10.53% and 10.75% respectively, while for Shenzhen Development Bank A, this average tier-1 CAR significantly increased from 5.52% to 7.2%.

Either CAR or tier-1 CAR, compared with that by the end of 2009, for the first half of 2010, there appeared a tendency of equalization for each listed bank. According to statistics, for the 16 listed banks, the standard deviations of CAR and tier-1 CAR were 1.43% and 1.99% respectively for 2009 but 1.08% and 1.37% respectively for the first half of 2010, significantly lower than the former, indicating the narrowing gap in CAR between banks.

For 2009 and the first half of 2010, the average equity/asset rate for banks listed in A-share market were 5.21% and 5.12% respectively, and the medians were 5.33% and 5.36% respectively, also indicating an equalization tendency: the standard deviation of equity/asset rate was 1.30% for 2009 and 0.92% for the first half of 2010.

6.3.2 *Comparison between NPL ratio and provision coverage ratio*

During 2009 and 2010, except for Agricultural Bank of China that had a relatively higher NPL ratio due to historical reason, the NPL ratio for banks listed in A-share market remained at the level between 0.5% and 1.5%: average NPL ratio for 2009 was 1.20% (median was 1.12%) and 0.99% (median was 0.88%) for the first half of 2010. The reason why average was significantly higher than median lies in the relatively higher NPL ratio for Agricultural Bank of China (NPL ratios for 2009 and the first half of 2010 were 2.91% and 2.32% respectively). Putting aside Agricultural Bank of China, the average NPL ratio for banks listed in A-share market was 1.09% for 2009 and 0.90% for the first half of 2010.

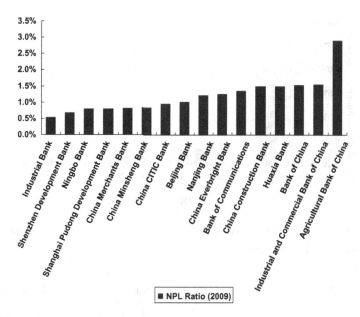

Figure 6.3.2.1 NPL ratio for banks listed in A-share market for 2009

(*Data source*: Financial reports of each listed bank)

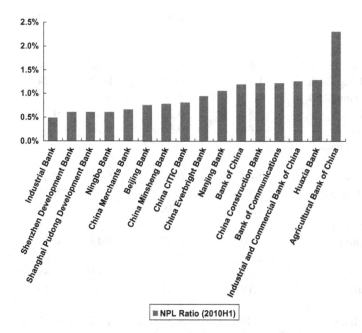

Figure 6.3.2.2 NPL ratio for banks listed in A-share market for the first half of 2010

(*Data source*: Financial reports of each listed bank)

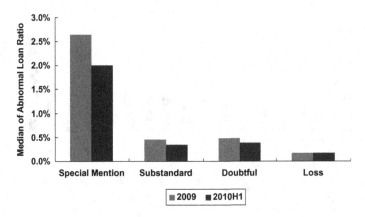

Figure 6.3.2.3   Abnormal loan ratio for banks listed in A-share market

(*Data source*: Financial reports of each listed bank)

Table 6.3.2.1   Abnormal loan ratio for banks listed in A-share market for 2009

	Special mention (%)	Substandard (%)	Doubtful (%)	Loss (%)	Abnormal loan ratio (%)
Shenzhen Development Bank A	0.38	0.41	0.15	0.12	1.06
Shanghai Pudong Development Bank	0.79	0.45	0.21	0.14	1.59
Hua Xia Bank	2.92	0.79	0.48	0.23	4.42
China Minsheng Bank	1.46	0.28	0.32	0.24	2.30
China Merchants Bank	1.19	0.25	0.24	0.34	2.01
Bank of China	2.83	0.73	0.53	0.26	4.35
Industrial and Commercial Bank of China	4.00	0.56	0.76	0.23	5.54
Industrial Bank	1.07	0.20	0.28	0.06	1.60
China CITIC Bank	0.77	0.30	0.49	0.16	1.73
Bank of Communications	2.73	0.58	0.62	0.15	4.09
Bank of Ningbo	2.60	0.47	0.14	0.18	3.39
Bank of Nanjing	2.58	0.67	0.51	0.04	3.80
Bank of Beijing	2.68	0.09	0.35	0.58	3.70
China Construction Bank	4.17	0.45	0.89	0.16	5.66
Agricultural Bank of China	7.85	1.27	1.52	0.12	10.75
China Everbright Bank	2.71	0.16	0.54	0.55	3.96

(*Data source*: Financial reports of each listed bank)

Table 6.3.2.2 Abnormal loan ratio for banks listed in A-share market for the first half of 2010

	Special mention (%)	Substandard (%)	Doubtful (%)	Loss (%)	Abnormal loan ratio (%)
Shenzhen Development Bank A	0.25	0.35	0.16	0.11	0.86
Shanghai Pudong Development Bank	0.70	0.27	0.23	0.11	1.31
Hua Xia Bank	1.88	0.47	0.53	0.28	3.17
China Minsheng Bank	1.29	0.34	0.23	0.22	2.07
China Merchants Bank	1.06	0.15	0.22	0.29	1.72
Bank of China	2.71	0.52	0.44	0.24	3.91
Industrial and Commercial Bank of China	3.67	0.41	0.66	0.19	4.93
Industrial Bank	0.89	0.16	0.28	0.05	1.38
China CITIC Bank	0.67	0.25	0.44	0.13	1.49
Bank of Communications	2.40	0.58	0.51	0.13	3.62
Bank of Ningbo	2.12	0.29	0.17	0.16	2.73
Bank of Nanjing	2.79	0.62	0.38	0.05	3.84
Bank of Beijing	2.20	0.09	0.15	0.53	2.96
China Construction Bank	3.92	0.35	0.69	0.18	5.14
Agricultural Bank of China	6.75	0.89	1.29	0.14	9.07
China Everbright Bank	1.86	0.11	0.40	0.45	2.81

(*Data source*: Financial reports of each listed bank)

In terms of abnormal loan ratio (i.e. including special mention, substandard, doubtful and loss), for banks listed in A-share market, the ratio for the first half of 2010 witnesses a slight drop in comparison with that for 2009. Among these four categories of loans, the special mentioned loan ratio dropped from 2.64% to 2%; substandard dropped from 0.45% to 0.34%; doubtful dropped from 0.48% to 0.39% and loss remained basically the same (0.17%). Basically speaking, all the listed banks have witnessed a drop in their own NPL ratio for each category.

Normally, "special mentioned" loan is not counted. However, comparing NPL ratio and special mentioned loan ratio for each bank concerned will show that there exists certain correlation between the two ratios, in that for banks with higher special mentioned loan ratio their NPL loan ratio also

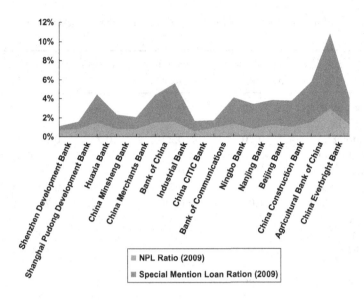

Figure 6.3.2.4   Comparison between NPL ratio and special mentioned loan ratio for banks listed in A-share market for 2009

(*Data source*: Financial reports of each listed bank)

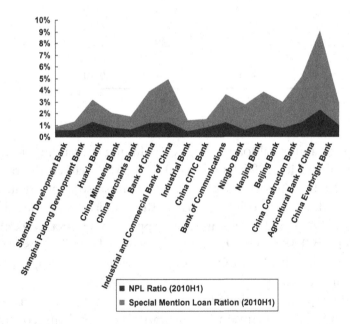

Figure 6.3.2.5   Comparison between NPL ratio and special mentioned loan ratio for banks listed in A-share market for the first half of 2010

(*Data source*: Financial reports of each listed bank)

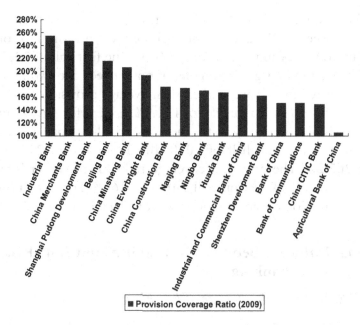

Figure 6.3.2.6   Provision coverage ratio for banks listed in A-share market for 2009

(*Data source*: Financial reports of each listed bank)

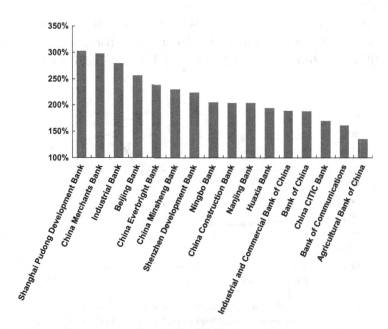

Figure 6.3.2.7   Provision coverage ratio for banks listed in A-share market for the first half of 2010

(*Data source*: Financial reports of each listed bank)

tends to be relatively high. Actually, statistics also demonstrate that the correlation between NPL ratio and special mentioned loan ratio for the 16 banks was up to 94.0% and 90.6% for 2009 and the first half of 2010 respectively, indicating a quite significant correlation between the two ratios.

For banks listed in A-share market, their average provision coverage ratio for 2009 was 183.3% with a median of 171.9%. Except for Agricultural Bank of China, provision coverage ratio for the rest of the listed banks was basically above 150%. For the first half of 2010, this ratio rose to 217.4% with a median of 205.2%. The provision coverage ratio for the other listed banks except Agricultural Bank of China all surpassed 160%. For Agricultural Bank of China, its provision coverage ratio rose from 105.4% for 2009 to 136.1%.

6.4 Mutual Influence between Profitability and Anti-Risk Capability of Banking

6.4.1 *ROE, ROA and leverage of banking*

Since 2005 with the push-on of the reform in state-owned commercial banks, the profitability of China's banking industry has enjoyed a rise to some extent. In terms of banks listed in A-share market, their average ROE was 14.5% in 2005 but rose to above 17% during 2008 and 2009, higher than the average ROE for Shanghai-Shenzhen 300 Index constituent stock in A-share market since 2005; for banks listed in Hong Kong market, the average ROE during 2005 and 2007 fluctuated between 12% and 13%, then rose to the

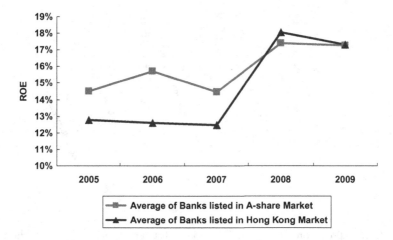

Figure 6.4.1.1   Average ROE for listed banks (Average of all listed banks)

(*Data source*: Financial reports of each listed bank)

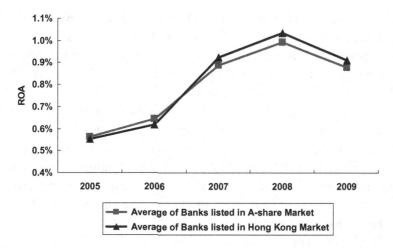

Figure 6.4.1.2   Average ROA of listed banks (Average of all listed banks)
(*Data source*: Financial reports of each listed bank)

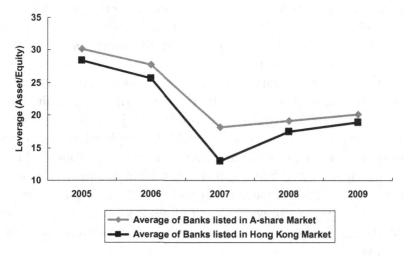

Figure 6.4.1.3   Average leverage (asset/equity) (average of all listed banks)
(*Data source*: Financial reports of each listed bank)

range between 17% and 18%. In terms of ROE data, the profitability of China's banking industry has really boasted a relatively significant elevation.

We can also use another indicator — ROA to measure the profitability of banking. During 2005 and 2006, the average ROA for banks listed in A-share market and Hong Kong market altogether was within the 0.5%–0.6% interval; after 2007, the ROA elevated; by 2009, ROA for banks listed in A-share market was 0.88% and 0.91% for banks listed in Hong Kong market.

In the case of a given ROA, the main influential factor over ROE is leverage (asset/equity). The analysis of historical data shows that the leverage of the listed banks was relatively high during 2005 and 2006: the average leverage for banks listed in A-share market was 30.11 and 27.76 respectively, while for banks listed in Hong Kong market was 28.36 and 25.64 respectively. After 2007, however, leverage of listed banks underwent a relatively significant reduction, down to the lowest in 2007 when the average leverage for banks listed in A-share market and Hong Kong market reached 18.15 and 12.93 respectively. During 2008 and 2009, with credit expansion due to the economic stimulus plan, leverage witnessed a rise, with an average leverage of 20.16 for the banks listed in A-share market during the year 2009 (for banks listed in Hong Kong market it was 18.95).

The level of leverage, whether high or low, is closely related to economic structure, bank credit and profit structure of the banking industry. When the leverage of banking industry is relatively high, this reflects expectation in two aspects: first, the rapid growth of China's economy that is able to back up the high leverage of banks; second, the government credit that is hidden behind banks. However, another fairly important impetus is the profit model of China's banks. For one thing, the major source of profit for commercial banks still lies in their deposit and loan spread; for another, deposit and loan interest rate is under government control. This leads to total bank profit having to rely on the expansion of asset (credit) size, and hence goes the circle: to acquire more profits, the listed banks have to possess more assets (loans), and more assets lead to higher leverage; while the regulation of asset adequacy requires banks to have more capital, the acquisition of which for listed banks can only be from the financing of capital market; moreover, the precondition for smooth financing is more profits. When economic growth slows down and liquidity contracts, such a model of solving the profitability problem through asset expansion will meet with impediments.

6.4.2 *Influence of credit migration on anti-risk capability of commercial banks*

In inspecting the anti-risk capability of commercial banks, one indicator liable to be ignored yet relatively important is "migration ratio". Migration ratio is defined as "the probability of loan of a certain credit rate migrating to a much lower credit rate". For example, the migration ratio for normal loans refers to the probability of normal loans' migration to special mentioned loans or non-performance loans (substandard, doubtful, loss);

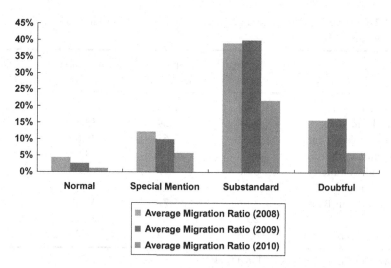

Figure 6.4.2.1   Average migration ratio for banks listed in Hong Kong market during 2008 and the first half of 2010 (Average of all listed banks)

(*Data source*: Financial reports of each listed bank)

migration ratio for special mentioned loans is the probability of doubtful loans' migration to loans of loss.

During 2008 and the first half of 2010, the migration ratio of normal loans for banks listed in Hong Kong market and special mentioned loans witnessed a downtrend, but substandard and doubtful loans remained basically stable (the data for the first half of 2010 is unable to support the conclusion that migration ratio underwent a significant reduction). During this period, the average migration ratio for normal loans is 2.62%, special mentioned loans is 9.34%, while substandard and doubtful loans amounts to 33.62% and 12.89% respectively.

The migration ratio exerts a certain influence over the anti-risk capability of commercial banks. If we estimate future migration ratio on the basis of the average migration ratio of the 8 banks listed in Hong Kong market during the period from 2008 to during the first half of 2010, and then take into consideration the migration of special mentioned loans to NPL, the average NPL ratio for these 8 banks during this period will rise from 1.19% to 1.43% (the growth rate surpasses 20%) while the average provision coverage ratio for the first half of 2010 will drop from 197.15% to 166.96%.

For banks of a relatively high share for special mentioned loans (e.g. Agricultural Bank of China), or banks of a relatively high migration ratio for

Table 6.4.2.1   Yearly average migration ratio for banks listed in Hong Kong market during 2008 and the first half of 2010

	Normal (%)	Special mention (%)	Substandard (%)	Doubtful (%)
China Minsheng Bank	1.92	12.94	43.49	32.57
China Merchants Bank	1.97	7.24	33.26	14.46
Agricultural Bank of China	6.43	7.65	35.89	8.17
Bank of Communications	1.75	20.53	33.96	8.09
Industrial and Commercial Bank of China	3.37	7.27	28.30	10.93
China Construction Bank	2.50	5.77	43.48	11.15
Bank of China	2.30	7.08	24.25	7.93
China CITIC Bank	0.75	6.22	26.32	9.78

(*Data source*: Financial reports of each listed bank)

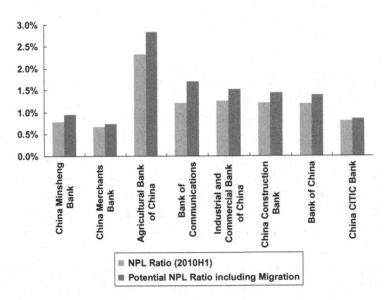

Figure 6.4.2.2   Potential NPL ratio including migration of special mentioned loans for banks listed in Hong Kong market

(*Data source*: Financial reports of each listed bank, Xinhua Finance)

special mentioned loans (e.g. Bank of Communications), this potential risk is much more significant. For example, calculated according to the above method, the provision coverage ratios for Agricultural Bank of China and Bank of Communications during the first half of 2010 rose from 136.11% and 161.17% to 111.32% and 114.79%.

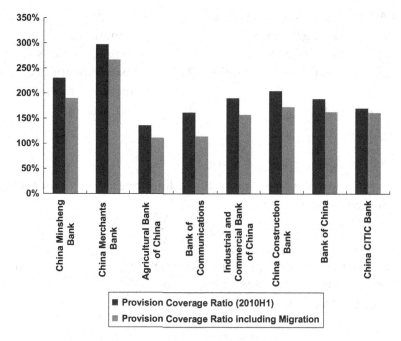

Figure 6.4.2.3 Provision coverage ratio including migration of special mentioned loans for banks listed in Hong Kong market

(*Data source*: Financial reports of each listed bank, Xinhua Finance)

6.4.3 *Balance between security and profitability — case of provision coverage ratio*

When the migration ratio for special mentioned loans is included, banks' "potential provision coverage ratio" will reduce. In this case, to elevate "potential provision coverage ratio", it needs to elevate "real" provision coverage ratio. But since the provision will offset bank profits, a balance between security and profitability is thus formed: the elevation of provision coverage ratio will improve asset security of banks while reducing their profitability (at least in terms of book value).

We can use a simple formula deduction to analyze the migration ratio including migration for special mentioned loans and resultantly elevate provision coverage, thus the influence over banks' profitability.

Definition:

P   — Currently-withdrawn reserves D   — Current NPL balance
       for bad debts

ΔP — Added reserves for bad debts including migration of special mentioned loans

ΔD — Added NPL caused by the migration of special mentioned loans

L_S — Special mentioned loan ratio

M — Special mentioned loans migration ratio

A — Total assets

E — Net earnings

Then:

(1) Current provision coverage ratio: $C_p = \frac{P}{D}$

(2) New provision coverage ratio (including migration ratio for special mentioned loans):

$$C'_P = \frac{P + \Delta P}{D + \Delta D}$$

(3) To ensure that the new provision coverage ratio is at least equal to the current provision coverage ratio, then $\frac{P+\Delta P}{D+\Delta P} = \frac{P}{D}$, thus the added reserves for bad debts:

$$\Delta P = P \times \frac{\Delta D}{D} = C_P \times \Delta D$$

(4) Define the current NPL ratio as $d = \frac{D}{A}$, hence the added NPL ratio including migration of special mentioned loans:

$$\Delta d = \frac{\Delta D}{A} = \frac{L_S \times A \times M}{A} = L_S \times M,$$

thus the added reserves for bad debts:

$$\Delta P = C_P \times (\Delta d \times A) = C_P \times L_S \times M \times A$$

(5) Thence the ratio between added reserves for bad debts and net earnings:

$$\frac{\Delta P}{E} = C_P \times L_S \times M \times \frac{A}{E} = \frac{C_P \times L_S \times M}{ROA}$$

The above discussion is a simplified version, say, the formula assumes that asset is a constant, but in reality total bank assets are always expanding (especially under the environment of China's current economy and finance). However, certain laws can still be discerned from the above formula:

(1) A quite apparent law is that the higher the aimed provision coverage ratio, the more influence exerted by newly provided reserves for bad debts upon profits;

(2) The higher the special mentioned loans migration ratio (namely the higher probability of special mentioned loans migrated to NPL), the more influence exerted by newly provided reserves for bad debts upon profits;

(3) The higher the special mentioned loans share, the more influence exerted by newly provided reserves for bad debts upon profits. Therefore, in analyzing bank security, except NPL ratio, special mentioned loan ratio is also an indicator of significance;

(4) The lower ROA, the more influence exerted by newly provided reserves for bad debts upon profits. Though not quite significant, this law can be understood as: if special mentioned loan ratio and migration ratio are decided (namely asset risk is decided), the lower the asset profitability, the more influence exerted by potential loss caused by risk upon profit expectation. According to this viewpoint, under the precondition of risk control, the elevation of ROA is also a pretty important indicator.

We can make the analysis according to the real data for banks listed in Hong Kong market for the year 2009: for the 8 banks listed in Hong Kong market, the average provision coverage ratio was 168.73%, and the average special mentioned loan ratio was 3.13%. Based on the data about the average migration ratio for each bank showed in the above section, the average special

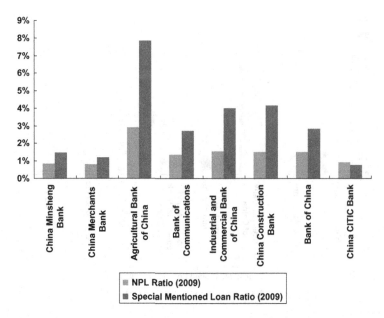

Figure 6.4.3.1   NPL ratio and special mentioned loan ratio for banks listed in Hong Kong market for 2009

(*Data source*: Financial reports of each listed bank)

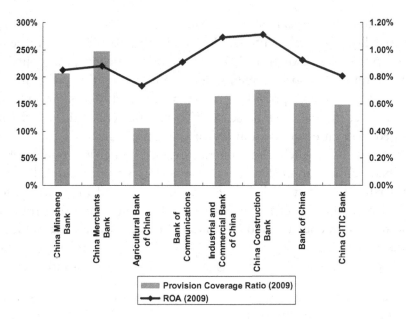

Figure 6.4.3.2   Provision coverage ratio and ROA for banks listed in Hong Kong market for 2009

(*Data source*: Financial reports of each listed bank)

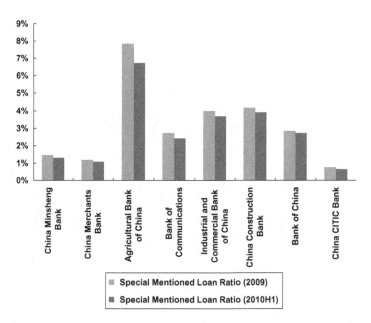

Figure 6.4.3.3   Special mentioned loan ratio variation for banks listed in Hong Kong market during 2009 and 2010

(*Data source*: Financial reports of each listed bank)

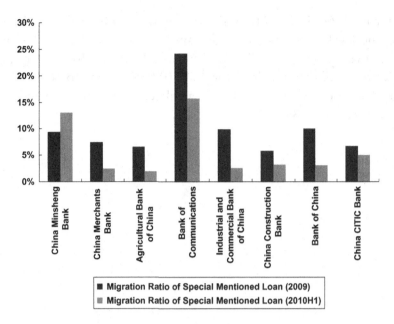

Figure 6.4.3.4 Special mentioned loans migration ratio variation for banks listed in Hong Kong market during 2009 and 2010

(*Data source*: Financial reports of each listed bank)

mentioned loans migration ratio for these 8 banks can be calculated as 9.34%. Hence the potential NPL including migration of special mentioned loans was 0.29%. The ROA for banks listed in Hong Kong market for 2009 was 0.91%. According to the above formula, if we elevate potential provision coverage ratio to a real provision coverage ratio of 168.73%, then the share of potential provided reserves for bad debts in net profits for 2009 amounted to 53.95%.

Of course, during the reduction of the above formula, we have made many simplified assumptions, but we can still recognize the importance of a balance between asset security and profitability. It is because of this we find out from the financial reports in 2010 that for many banks, both their special mentioned loan ratio and special mentioned loans migration ratio have witnessed declines. For example, for the 8 banks listed in Hong Kong market, special mentioned loan ratio during the first half of 2010 was lower than that for 2009, and average special mentioned loans ratio also dropped from 3.13% in 2009 to 2.81% for the first half of 2010, by 0.32%. Except for China Minsheng Bank, the other 7 banks all witnessed a drop in special mentioned loans migration ratio: average migration ratio for special mentioned loans reduced from 9.99% in 2009 to 5.87% during the first half of 2010, by 4.13%. Suppose the level would be kept constant for 2010, and given the average provision coverage ratio of 197.15% for banks listed in Hong Kong market, even if ROA was at the same level for 2009 (0.91%), the ratio between potential provided reserves for bad debts calculated/net profits (based on our model) will reduce to 39.69%.

Chapter 7

INSURANCE

7.1 Overview of Insurance Sector Development

7.1.1 *Development of insurance sector in China*

According to incomplete statistics, by 2010 there are in all 137 insurance financial institutions operating in the Chinese mainland. Among which, 4 insurance companies are listed in Hong Kong market, i.e. China Life Insurance Company Co., Ltd., Ping An Insurance (Group) Company of China, China Pacific Insurance (Group) Co., Ltd., Peoples Insurance Company of China, with the first three also listed in A-share market. With Chinese economic growth, the insurance sector in China enjoyed a significant advance in recent years: during the 11 years from 1999 to 2010, the annual premium income increased from RMB 139.3 billion to RMB 1.4528 trillion, with an average annual compound growth rate of 23.8%. Besides, during the same period, indemnity increased from RMB 51 billion to RMB 320 billion, with an average annual compound growth rate of 18.2%.

During 1999 and 2010, property insurance premium rose from RMB 52.1 billion to RMB 389.5 billion, with an annual compound growth rate of 20.1%; life insurance premium increased from RMB 87.2 billion to RMB 1.0632 trillion, with an annual compound growth rate of 25.5%, significantly higher than that for property insurance. In terms of share, life insurance premium share rose from 62.6% in 2009 to 73.2% in 2010, during which, from 2001 to 2003, life insurance enjoyed a relatively rapid development, with its share rising from above 60% in 2009 to above 70% in 2010, and remaining basically around 75% in the following years.

In the case of life insurance, life insurance premium dominates: during the 11 years from 1999 to 2010, its share was between 85% and 90%, and its premium rose from RMB 76.8 billion in 1999 to RMB 967.9 billion in 2010, with an annual compound growth rate of 25.9%. Immediately following is health insurance: health insurance boasts the rapidest development among the various types of life insurance, rising from RMB 3.65 billion to RMB

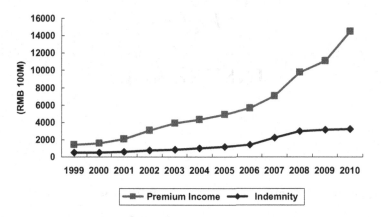

Figure 7.1.1.1 Premium income and indemnity for China's insurance sector

(*Data source*: Chinese Protecting and Supervising Association)

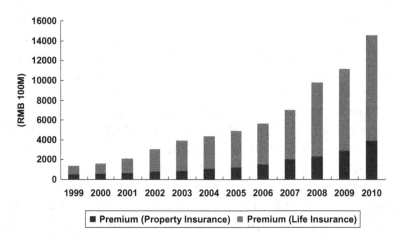

Figure 7.1.1.2 Property insurance premium and life insurance premium increase year by year

(*Data source*: Chinese Protecting and Supervising Association)

67.7 billion, with an annual compound growth rate up to 30.4%, and its share also increased from 4.2% in 1999 to 6.4% in 2010 and even once amounted to 9% (in 2006). The share of accidental injury insurance stayed at the bottom, with an average of 4.3% during the past 11 years: the premium rose from RMB 6.7 billion to RMB 27.5 billion, with an annual compound growth rate of 13.7%. Due to its relatively lower growth rate, the share of health insurance declined from 7.7% in 1999 to 2.6% in 2010.

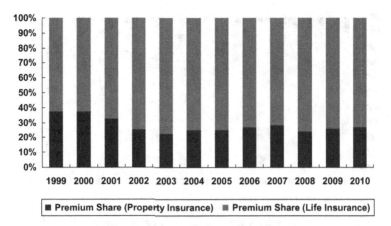

Figure 7.1.1.3   Property insurance premium share and life insurance premium share
(*Data source*: Chinese Protecting and Supervising Association)

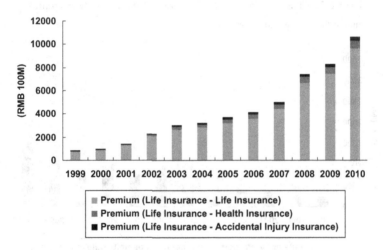

Figure 7.1.1.4   Premium growth of various types of life insurance
(*Data source*: Chinese Protecting and Supervising Association)

In terms of distinct insurance types, the indemnity of property insurance rose from RMB 28 billion in 1999 to RMB 176.5 billion, with an annual compound growth rate of 18.2%; the indemnity of life insurance rose from RMB 23 billion in 1999 to RMB 144.4 billion in 2010, with an annual compound growth rate of 18.2%.

Different from the case of premium, in terms of indemnity share, the share for property insurance is higher than that for life insurance: during these 11 years, average indemnity for property insurance was around 54% while that for life insurance was 46%. In other words, though premium share for property insurance is relatively lower, yet its indemnity share is relatively higher.

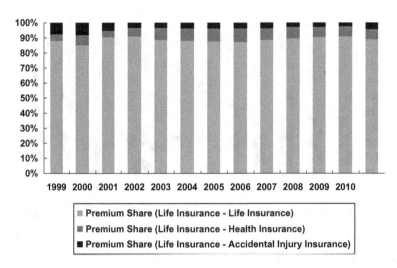

Figure 7.1.1.5   Premium share for various types of life insurance

(*Data source*: Chinese Protecting and Supervising Association)

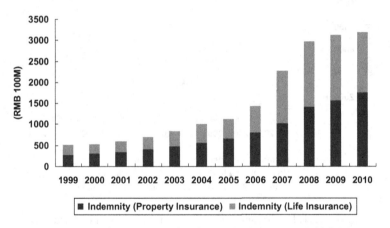

Figure 7.1.1.6   Indemnity growth of property insurance and life insurance

(*Data source*: Chinese Protecting and Supervising Association)

Similar to the premium income structure, in the case of life insurance, life insurance has the highest indemnity share, with an average about 77% during the past 11 years. Its indemnity rose from RMB 19.2 billion in 1999 to RMB 110.8 billion, with an annual compound growth rate of 17.3%; health insurance enjoys the highest indemnity growth rate, with indemnity increasing from RMB 1.1 billion in 1999 to RMB 26.4 billion and an annual compound growth rate of 33.5%. Besides, its share also rose from 4.8% in 1999 to 18.3% in 2010. Accidental injury insurance has the lowest indemnity share, reducing from 11.6% in 1999 to 4.9% in 2010, and the indemnity rose from RMB 2.67 billion in 1999 to RMB 7.14 billion, with an annual compound growth rate of 9.3%.

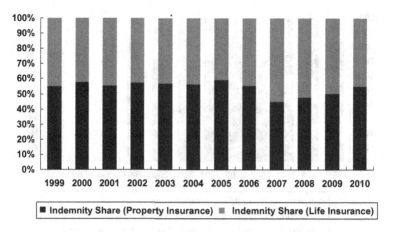

Figure 7.1.1.7 Indemnity share for property insurance and life insurance
(*Data source*: Chinese Protecting and Supervising Association)

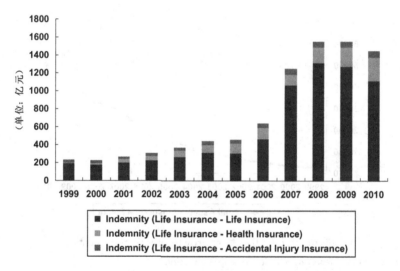

Figure 7.1.1.8 Indemnity growth for various types of life insurance
(*Data source*: Chinese Protecting and Supervising Association)

Another indicator of the development of the insurance sector lies in the asset growth of insurance. During 1999 and 2010, the total assets of the insurance sector increased from RMB 260.4 billion up to more than RMB 5 trillion, with an annual compound growth rate of 30.9%.

In correspondence to the total assets growth is the adjustment of asset structure of the insurance sector. One of the most remarkable characteristic lies in a gradual elevation of investment with a relative reduction of bank deposits. During the above-mentioned 11 years, investment rose from

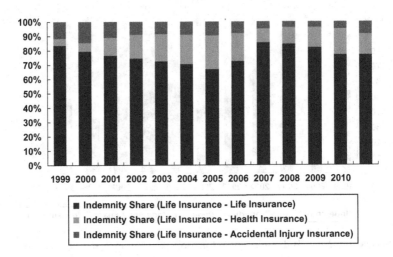

Figure 7.1.1.9   Indemnity share for various types of life insurance

(*Data source*: Chinese Protecting and Supervising Association)

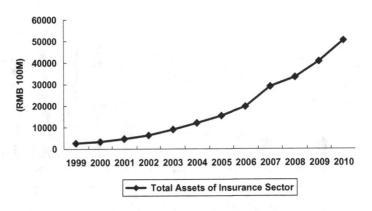

Figure 7.1.1.10   Asset growth of insurance sector

(*Data source*: Chinese Protecting and Supervising Association)

RMB 89.1 billion in 1999 to RMB 3.2136 trillion in 2010, with an annual compound growth rate up to 38.5%. Its growth rate was far higher than that of total assets. The investment/asset ratio rose from 34.2% in 1999 to 63.7% in 2010. On the contrary, though deposits also increased from RMB 92.6 billion in 1999 to RMB 1.3909 trillion in 2010, the annual compound growth rate was 27.9%, lower than asset growth rate. In addition, the deposit/asset ratio also gradually decreased from 35.6% in 1999 to 27.6% in 2010.

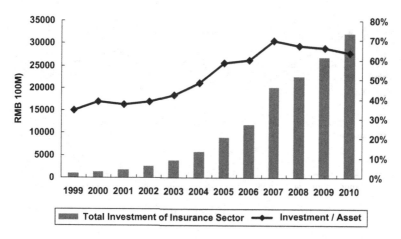

Figure 7.1.1.11 Significant investment growth of insurance sector

(*Data source*: Chinese Protecting and Supervising Association)

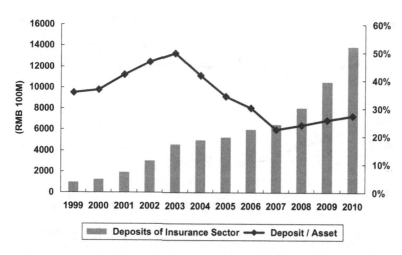

Figure 7.1.1.12 Decrease in deposits of insurance sector

(*Data source*: Chinese Protecting and Supervising Association)

7.1.2 *Overall profitability of insurance sector*

From the perspective of the overall insurance sector, the important indicator of the influence over profitability of the insurance sector is indemnity (accounting for a significant part in insurance business expenses). Moreover, the operating expense also influences the profits of insurance companies to some extent.

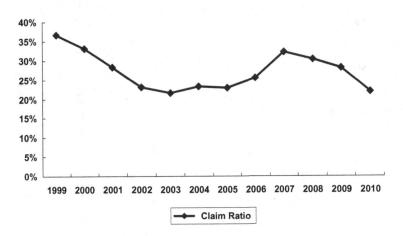

Figure 7.1.2.1   Indemnity/premium income ratio for insurance sector
(*Data source*: Chinese Protecting and Supervising Association)

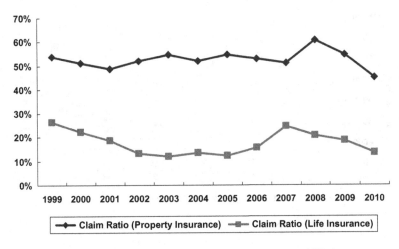

Figure 7.1.2.2   Claim ratio for property insurance and life insurance
(*Data source*: Chinese Protecting and Supervising Association)

During the 11 years from 1999 to 2010, the overall claim ratio (indemnity/premium income ratio) for the insurance sector remained within the 20%–35% interval, with an average of 27.7%. Within this period, there was a downtrend during 1999 and 2003 but an uptrend from 2003 to 2007; then after 2007 there appeared a downtrend again with a ratio of 22% in 2010.

In terms of different insurance types, indemnity/premium income ratio for property insurance was significantly higher than that for life insurance: from 1999 to 1010, this ratio for property insurance basically remained

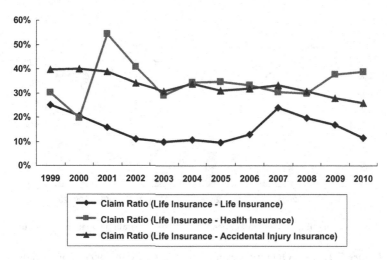

Figure 7.1.2.3　Claim ratio for various types of life insurance

(*Data source*: Chinese Protecting and Supervising Association)

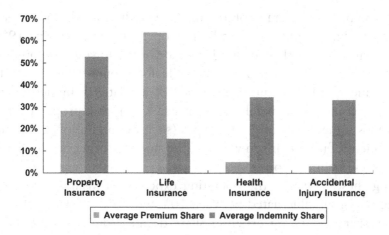

Figure 7.1.2.4　Premium share/indemnity share ratio for various types of life insurance

(*Data source*: Chinese Protecting and Supervising Association)

around 50% (the average was 52.6%); while for life insurance this ratio fluctuated between 10% and 25% (the average was 17.7%).

Among the three types of life insurance, indemnity share for life insurance is relatively lower: during the 11 years, basically fluctuating between 10% and 25%, with an average of 15.6%; by contrast, indemnity share for health insurance was relatively higher, normally above 30%, up to 40%–50% in certain years, with an average of 34.4%. Similar to the case of health insurance, for accidental injury insurance the average indemnity share was 33.1%, remaining between 30% and 40% during most of the years.

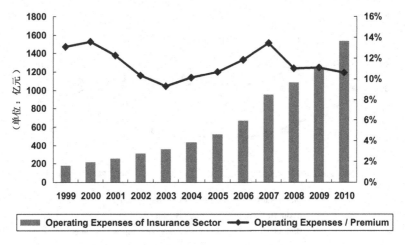

Figure 7.1.2.5 Operating expenses of insurance sector/premium ratio

(*Data source*: Chinese Protecting and Supervising Association)

If we compare the average premium share (indicating the business scale) with its average indemnity share (indicating operating costs) during 1999 and 2010, we will find out that for life insurance of the lowest indemnity share, its premium share ranks the highest; while for property insurance, health insurance and accidental injury insurance of a relatively higher indemnity share, their business scale is relatively smaller. Given that property insurance also includes some policy insurance types (such as compulsory insurance for traffic accident of motor-driven vehicle), the share for other non-policy insurance types will be much lower.

During these 11 years, the operating expenses of insurance sector/premium ratio basically fluctuated between 10% and 14%. Similar to the case of indemnity share, operating expenses share declined during 1999 and 2003 but recovered during 2003 and 2007, then after 2007 it began to decline once again with a share of 10.6% in 2010. The average share during 1999 and 2010 was 11.4%.

7.1.3 *Market prospect of China's insurance sector*

"Insurance penetration" and "insurance density" are usually adopted to measure the development degree of insurance sector in a country or region. This indicator reflects, to some extent, the development potential of the insurance sector in the country or region. "Insurance penetration" refers to the share of premium in GDP, namely premium/GDP ratio, a indicator in reflecting the importance of the insurance sector in a country's national

economy; "insurance density" refers to the per capita premium income calculated on the basis of the total population of a country, indicating the
popularization degree of insurance and development level of insurance sector
in a country.

Since 2000 the insurance penetration and insurance density of the insurance sector in China have been enjoying a rise: average insurance penetration
for all provinces in the mainland increased from 1.62% in 2000 to 2.96%
in 2009, with an annual compound growth rate of 7% (median rose from
1.53% in 2000 to 2.92% in 2009, with an annual compound growth rate
of 7.4%); average insurance density for all provinces in the mainland rose
from RMB 158.7 in 2000 to RMB 918.3 in 2009, with an annual compound
growth rate of 21.5% (median rose from RMB 89.7 in 2000 to RMB 707.3
in 2009, with an annual compound growth rate of 25.8%). Holistically speaking, the growth of insurance penetration and insurance density is reflective of
the following two characteristics:

Firstly, both insurance penetration and insurance density are below the
world level. For example, in 2003 the world average insurance penetration
was up to 8.05%, and average insurance density up to USD 469.6; by the end
of 2009, the average insurance penetration and insurance density for all
provinces in the mainland were only 2.96% and RMB 918.3 (about USD
139), with the median level much lower. Secondly, the growth of insurance
density is much faster than that of insurance penetration: during 2003 and

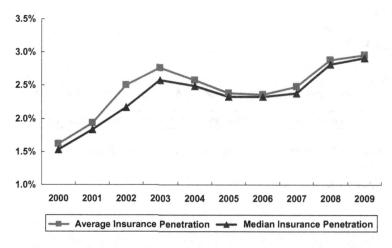

Figure 7.1.3.1   Overall situation of insurance penetration for all provinces in the Chinese
mainland

(*Data source*: People's Bank of China)

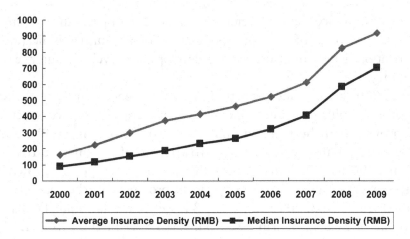

Figure 7.1.3.2 Overall situation of insurance density for all provinces in the Chinese mainland

(*Data source*: People's Bank of China)

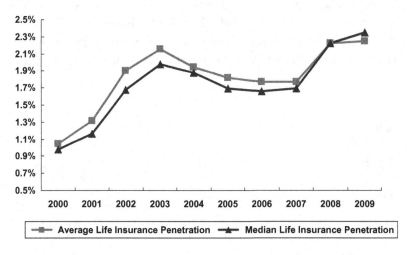

Figure 7.1.3.3 Overall penetration of life insurance for all provinces in the Chinese mainland

(*Data source*: People's Bank of China)

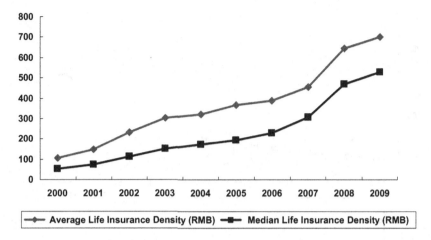

Figure 7.1.3.4 Overal density of life insurance for all provinces in the Chinese mainland
(*Data source*: People's Bank of China)

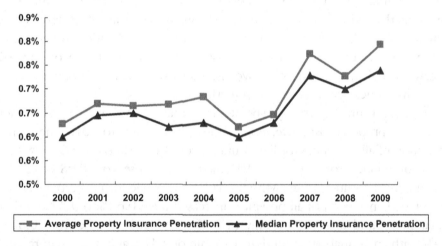

Figure 7.1.3.5 Overall penetration of property insurance for all provinces in the Chinese mainland

(*Data source*: People's Bank of China)

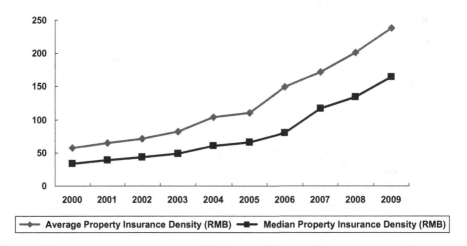

Figure 7.1.3.6 Overall density of property insurance for all provinces in the Chinese mainland

(*Data source*: People's Bank of China)

2007 insurance penetration was always fluctuating between 2.4% and 2.7%, indicating that with the overall economic growth the absolute level of per capita insurance also witnessed an uptrend, yet compared with rapid economic growth, the relatively low place of insurance sector in the economy still underwent a slow rise. In other words, there still exists a broad room for China's insurance sector to develop further.

Analyzing insurance type by type, it shows that life insurance develops more rapidly than property insurance. For example, from 2009 to 2010, the average penetration of all provinces for life insurance rose from 1.04% to 2.25%, with an annual compound growth rate of 8.9% (median level rose from 0.98% to 2.35%, with an annual compound growth rate of 10.2%); while for property insurance, the average penetration of all provinces increased from 0.63% to 0.79%, with an annual compound growth rate only of 2.7% (median level rose from 0.6% to 0.74%, with an annual compound growth rate of 2.4%), and its growth rate and penetration were both significantly lower than that for life insurance. Insurance density also witnessed a similar tendency: from 2000 to 2009, the average density of life insurance for all provinces rose from RMB 105.5 to RMB 702, with an annual compound growth rate of 23.4% (median increased from RMB 53.3 to RMB 527.4, with an annual compound growth rate of 29%); for property insurance, the average density rose from RMB 56.9 to RMB 238.3 with an annual growth rate of 17.2% (median increased from RMB 34 to RMB 164.6 with an annual compound growth rate of 19.2%); moreover, for property insurance, the growth of insurance density was significantly lower than that for life insurance.

Table 7.1.3.1 Insurance penetration in all provinces (municipalities and autonomous regions)

	2005 (%)	2006 (%)	2007 (%)	2008 (%)	2009 (%)
Anhui	2.48	2.68	2.75	3.34	3.55
Beijing	7.29	5.32	5.49	5.60	5.88
Chongqing	2.36	2.67	3.03	3.93	3.75
Fujian	2.27	2.30	2.35	2.63	2.63
Gansu	2.48	2.50	2.63	3.07	3.38
Guangdong	1.80	2.32	2.61	3.17	3.11
Guangxi	1.80	1.68	1.70	1.86	1.93
Guizhou	2.10	2.17	2.18	2.40	2.45
Hainan	1.66	1.68	1.84	2.06	2.01
Hebei	2.15	2.18	2.41	2.97	3.53
Heilongjiang	2.53	2.53	2.16	2.92	3.36
Henna	2.01	2.02	2.15	2.82	2.92
Hubei	2.08	2.13	2.28	2.82	2.90
Hunan	1.97	1.98	2.20	2.80	2.69
Inner Mongolia	1.59	1.50	1.62	1.82	1.76
Jiangsu	2.37	2.33	2.26	2.56	2.67
Jiangxi	2.21	2.13	2.08	2.64	2.47
Jilin	2.10	2.12	2.23	2.47	2.57
Liaoning	2.53	2.43	2.41	2.81	3.24
Ningxia	2.62	2.72	2.87	2.89	2.94
Qinghai	1.45	1.36	1.35	1.46	1.68
Shanghai	3.65	3.96	3.78	4.41	4.46
Shanxi	2.95	2.97	3.22	3.76	3.93
Shaanxi	2.66	2.65	2.58	3.13	3.17
Shandong	1.84	1.81	1.92	2.14	2.34
Sichuan	2.56	2.74	3.19	3.95	4.09
Tianjin	2.47	2.42	3.01	2.76	2.02
Tibet	0.60	0.40	0.78	0.82	0.91
Xinjiang	2.78	2.85	3.03	3.63	3.67
Yunnan	2.33	2.37	2.38	2.90	2.92
Zhejiang	2.40	2.38	2.43	2.80	2.89

(*Note*: Description based on map of China)
(*Data source*: People's Bank of China)

Table 7.1.3.2　Insurance density in all provinces (municipalities and autonomous regions)

(RMB/person)	2005	2006	2007	2008	2009
Anhui	204.52	249.73	302.74	483.36	582.63
Beijing	3230.90	2597.58	3027.97	3466.74	3974.90
Chongqing	233.00	294.00	442.77	706.42	855.91
Fujian	355.80	440.85	542.53	726.71	806.69
Gansu	184.60	218.20	268.84	370.80	434.10
Guangdong	468.00	556.48	724.66	1020.72	1097.06
Guangxi	149.39	163.01	199.57	277.26	306.05
Guizhou	103.56	124.41	148.45	210.70	250.73
Hainan	180.85	211.83	267.96	351.98	382.75
Hebei	317.20	368.58	480.00	689.91	854.54
Heilongjiang	365.56	411.00	406.70	655.75	727.59
Henna	218.00	268.70	328.28	550.23	595.96
Hubei	223.39	268.89	363.88	559.89	651.09
Hunan	189.02	218.76	295.78	456.08	543.94
Inner Mongolia	255.10	300.75	406.43	585.59	707.31
Jiangsu	579.78	666.68	759.25	1010.21	1175.06
Jiangxi	208.27	226.30	261.08	389.35	422.24
Jilin	283.72	336.82	433.22	586.29	674.70
Liaoning	461.66	521.53	620.62	875.23	933.26
Ningxia	263.99	320.07	392.91	514.69	628.44
Qinghai	144.66	161.32	186.22	254.50	326.90
Shanghai	2458.27	2983.10	3286.41	4405.79	4821.16
Shanxi	362.92	417.80	534.00	764.92	844.03
Shaanxi	261.82	311.06	372.04	569.57	688.22
Shandong	368.51	425.64	497.30	659.98	778.19
Sichuan	216.40	275.39	412.78	606.90	707.43
Tianjin	869.06	978.46	1353.45	1493.38	1231.82
Tibet	56.67	573.68	94.25	113.75	138.42
Xinjiang	360.72	417.00	505.56	717.01	725.77
Yunnan	181.89	211.66	248.91	363.36	393.97
Zhejiang	617.83	710.49	851.79	1113.93	1206.22

(*Note*: Description based on map of China)

(*Data source*: People's Bank of China)

Table 7.1.3.3 Insurance penetration of life insurance in all provinces (municipalities and autonomous regions)

	2005 (%)	2006 (%)	2007 (%)	2008 (%)	2009 (%)
Anhui	1.89	2.03	2.05	2.62	2.68
Beijing	6.31	4.24	4.30	4.32	4.49
Chongqing	1.69	1.98	2.16	3.12	3.03
Fujian	1.45	1.64	1.64	2.00	2.41
Gansu	1.78	1.80	1.90	2.36	2.58
Guangdong	1.26	1.59	1.80	2.42	2.33
Guangxi	1.24	1.13	1.11	1.30	1.28
Guizhou	1.36	1.41	1.33	1.54	1.52
Hainan	1.06	1.05	1.07	1.34	1.29
Hebei	1.62	1.64	1.80	2.33	2.77
Heilongjiang	2.14	2.07	1.67	2.37	2.67
Henna	1.67	1.63	1.71	2.38	2.41
Hubei	1.52	1.55	1.72	2.31	2.36
Hunan	1.51	1.53	1.68	2.21	2.11
Inner Mongolia	1.14	1.05	1.00	1.13	1.07
Jiangsu	1.86	1.77	1.65	1.96	1.99
Jiangxi	1.76	1.33	1.54	2.10	1.88
Jilin	1.69	1.68	1.63	1.97	2.00
Liaoning	1.93	1.82	0.76	2.24	2.43
Ningxia	1.86	1.92	1.96	2.03	2.06
Qinghai	0.80	0.73	0.66	0.81	0.95
Shanghai	2.68	2.97	2.80	3.42	3.44
Shanxi	2.19	2.17	2.35	2.86	3.02
Shaanxi	2.01	1.97	1.82	2.43	2.43
Shandong	1.37	1.63	1.37	1.63	1.74
Sichuan	1.90	2.02	2.30	3.07	3.04
Tianjin	1.86	1.79	2.30	2.10	1.41
Tibet	N.A.	N.A.	N.A.	N.A.	N.A.
Xinjiang	1.98	1.97	2.04	2.58	2.45
Yunnan	1.49	1.49	1.35	1.94	1.81
Zhejiang	1.59	1.53	1.50	1.86	1.84

(*Note*: Description based on map of China)
(*Data source*: People's Bank of China)

Table 7.1.3.4 Insurance density of life insurance in all provinces (municipalities and autonomous regions)

(RMB/person)	2005	2006	2007	2008	2009
Anhui	155.89	189.45	225.27	388.49	439.77
Beijing	2795.52	2071.89	2354.18	2674.24	3038.04
Chongqing	166.36	217.79	315.42	561.17	691.31
Fujian	267.03	320.70	384.28	542.91	591.37
Gansu	132.51	157.10	193.91	284.75	331.42
Guangdong	326.78	382.35	499.81	780.33	823.70
Guangxi	103.13	110.19	130.09	194.10	203.69
Guizhou	67.18	80.96	90.48	135.34	155.81
Hainan	115.30	132.01	156.21	229.14	245.56
Hebei	238.91	276.73	355.08	541.85	671.61
Heilongjiang	309.20	336.00	314.40	530.58	579.33
Henna	180.48	216.18	260.45	464.69	492.94
Hubei	163.09	195.71	274.39	458.07	530.51
Hunan	144.90	168.88	225.34	360.33	426.91
Inner Mongolia	182.25	209.48	251.01	363.55	429.27
Jiangsu	454.67	505.81	553.54	774.53	879.41
Jiangxi	166.12	174.61	193.13	309.45	322.67
Jilin	229.11	267.19	316.29	467.41	527.04
Liaoning	352.85	389.56	455.09	697.23	699.69
Ningxia	187.11	226.35	267.87	361.17	438.98
Qinghai	79.24	81.72	90.67	141.25	183.95
Shanghai	1804.95	2234.20	2436.85	3417.24	3720.62
Shanxi	268.81	305.71	381.47	582.17	648.16
Shaanxi	197.54	230.99	262.03	442.56	527.75
Shandong	273.35	311.55	354.58	502.95	578.73
Sichuan	160.53	203.17	297.78	472.47	525.73
Tianjin	654.54	723.12	1035.76	1137.77	858.94
Tibet	N.A.	N.A.	N.A.	N.A.	N.A.
Xinjiang	256.57	305.99	340.07	509.23	485.73
Yunnan	116.54	132.83	141.33	243.26	244.84
Zhejiang	408.95	456.97	526.89	742.77	766.10

(*Note*: Description based on map of China)
(*Data source*: People's Bank of China)

Table 7.1.3.5 Insurance penetration of property insurance in all provinces (municipalities and autonomous regions)

	2005 (%)	2006 (%)	2007 (%)	2008 (%)	2009 (%)
Anhui	0.59	0.65	0.70	0.72	0.87
Beijing	0.98	1.08	1.19	1.28	1.39
Chongqing	0.67	0.69	0.87	0.81	0.72
Fujian	0.57	0.63	0.69	0.67	0.70
Gansu	0.70	0.70	0.73	0.71	0.80
Guangdong	0.54	0.73	0.81	0.75	0.77
Guangxi	0.56	0.54	0.59	0.56	0.65
Guizhou	0.74	0.76	0.85	0.86	0.93
Hainan	0.60	0.63	0.77	0.72	0.72
Hebei	0.53	0.54	0.61	0.64	0.76
Heilongjiang	0.39	0.46	0.49	0.56	0.68
Henna	0.35	0.40	0.44	0.44	0.50
Hubei	0.56	0.58	0.56	0.51	0.54
Hunan	0.46	0.45	0.52	0.59	0.58
Inner Mongolia	0.45	0.46	0.62	0.69	0.69
Jiangsu	0.51	0.56	0.61	0.60	0.67
Jiangxi	0.45	0.49	0.54	0.54	0.58
Jilin	0.40	0.44	0.60	0.50	0.56
Liaoning	0.60	0.62	1.76	0.57	0.81
Ningxia	0.76	0.80	0.91	0.86	0.89
Qinghai	0.65	0.63	0.69	0.65	0.74
Shanghai	0.97	0.99	0.98	0.99	1.02
Shanxi	0.77	0.80	0.87	0.90	0.91
Shaanxi	0.65	0.68	0.76	0.70	0.74
Shandong	0.47	0.48	0.55	0.51	0.60
Sichuan	0.66	0.72	0.89	0.87	1.05
Tianjin	0.61	0.63	0.71	0.66	0.61
Tibet	0.60	0.40	0.73	0.74	0.78
Xinjiang	0.80	0.78	0.99	1.05	1.21
Yunnan	0.84	0.88	1.03	0.96	1.11
Zhejiang	0.81	0.85	0.93	0.93	1.05

(*Note*: Description based on map of China)
(*Data source*: People's Bank of China)

Table 7.1.3.6   Insurance density of property insurance in all provinces (municipalities and autonomous regions)

(RMB/person)	2005	2006	2007	2008	2009
Anhui	48.64	60.28	77.47	94.87	142.86
Beijing	435.38	525.69	673.79	792.50	936.86
Chongqing	66.64	76.21	127.35	145.25	164.60
Fujian	88.77	120.15	158.26	183.79	215.32
Gansu	52.08	61.00	74.89	86.05	102.67
Guangdong	141.22	174.12	224.85	240.39	273.36
Guangxi	46.26	52.83	69.48	83.16	102.36
Guizhou	36.68	43.45	57.98	75.36	94.93
Hainan	65.55	79.82	111.75	122.84	137.19
Hebei	78.29	91.85	120.52	148.07	182.93
Heilongjiang	56.36	75.00	92.30	125.17	148.25
Henna	37.51	52.53	67.83	85.54	103.02
Hubei	60.29	73.17	89.49	101.82	120.58
Hunan	44.12	49.88	70.44	95.75	117.03
Inner Mongolia	72.85	91.27	155.33	222.04	278.04
Jiangsu	125.11	160.87	205.71	235.68	295.65
Jiangxi	42.15	51.69	67.95	79.90	99.57
Jilin	54.61	69.63	116.93	118.89	147.66
Liaoning	108.82	131.97	165.53	177.99	233.57
Ningxia	76.88	93.72	125.03	153.51	189.46
Qinghai	65.42	79.60	95.55	113.22	142.95
Shanghai	650.32	748.90	849.56	988.55	1100.54
Shanxi	94.11	112.09	152.53	182.75	195.87
Shaanxi	64.28	80.07	110.01	127.01	160.47
Shandong	95.16	114.09	142.72	157.03	199.46
Sichuan	55.87	72.23	115.01	134.43	181.70
Tianjin	209.20	255.34	317.69	355.61	372.88
Tibet	56.67	573.68	88.11	103.11	118.10
Xinjiang	104.15	121.68	165.49	207.78	240.04
Yunnan	65.35	78.83	107.58	120.20	149.13
Zhejiang	208.88	253.52	324.90	371.16	440.12

(*Note*: Description based on map of China)

(*Data source*: People's Bank of China)

7.1.4 *Channel structure of insurance sector*

The marketing channels of the insurance sector mainly include concurrent-business insurance agencies, agency recruitments, insurance agencies, and insurance broker companies, etc. The concurrent-business insurance agencies include bank, post office, railway company, airline company, auto dealer, etc. By the end of 2009, concurrent-business insurance agency became one of the main marketing channel of the insurance sector, accounting for 40% of the total premium income; 57.1% of total premium was acquired through the channel of bank, that is to say, in 2009, the premium through bank accounted for about 23%.

Among the various concurrent-business insurance agencies, bank dominates either in quantity, premium or commission. According to statistics in 2009, bank accounted for 57% of the total number of concurrent-business insurance agencies, 68% of total premium and 51% of total commission. The case in 2010 was basically the same with that in 2009: according to the cumulative statistics by the third quarter of 2010, bank accounted for 56% of the total number of concurrent-business insurance agencies, 67% of total premium and 53% of total commission. Immediately following are auto dealer (mainly sales of automobile insurance) and post office, and railway company and airline company have a relatively lower share.

Another important marketing channel for the insurance sector is agency recruitment. In recent years, the number of agency recruitments is continuously

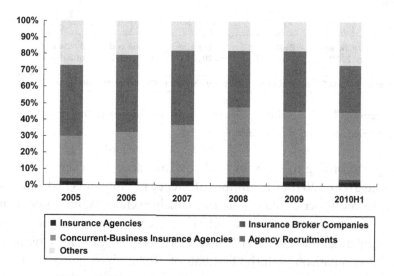

Figure 7.1.4.1 Channel structure of insurance sector

(*Data source*: Insurance Association of China)

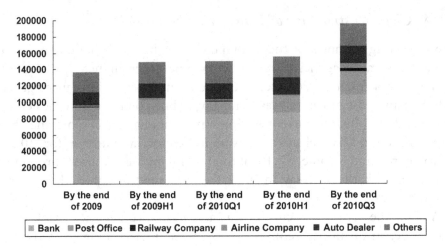

Figure 7.1.4.2   Number of concurrent-business insurance agencies

(*Data source*: Insurance Association of China)

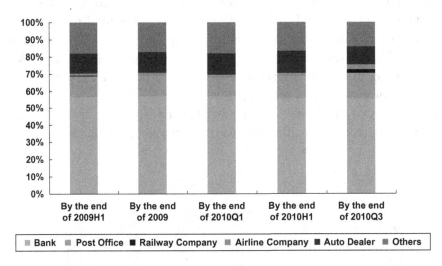

Figure 7.1.4.3   Number share of concurrent-business insurance agencies

(*Data source*: Insurance Association of China)

increasing. According to statistics made by Insurance Association of China, by the third quarter of 2010, the number of agency recruitments had surpassed 3.1 million. However, per capita premium (namely average premium generated by every person) did not witness a significant increase. Seen from the perspective of semi-annual data, for the first half of 2010, the per capita premium slightly dropped in comparison with the first half of 2009, which means that the marginal benefit generated merely by the increase in the number of salesmen is gradually declining.

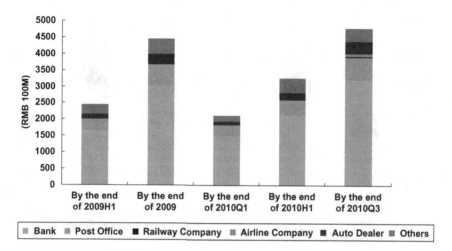

Figure 7.1.4.4   Premium of concurrent-business insurance agencies

(*Data source*: Insurance Association of China)

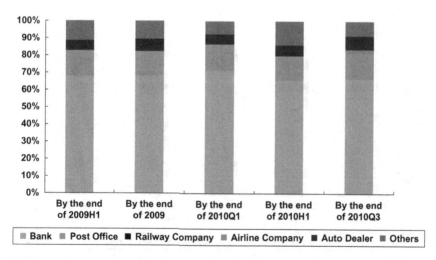

Figure 7.1.4.5   Premium share of concurrent-business insurance agencies

(*Data source*: Insurance Association of China)

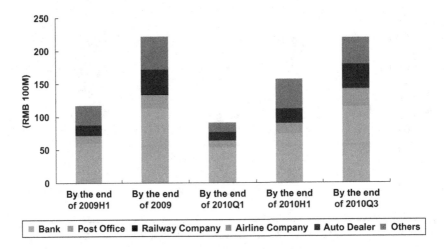

Figure 7.1.4.6   Commission of concurrent-business insurance agencies

(*Data source*: Insurance Association of China)

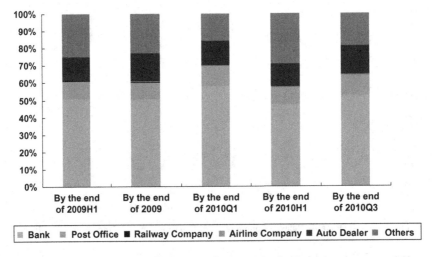

Figure 7.1.4.7   Commission share of concurrent-business insurance agencies

(*Data source*: Insurance Association of China)

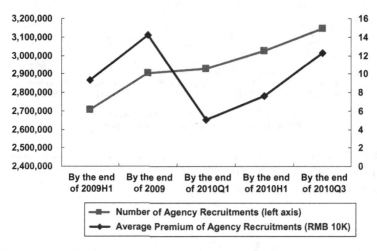

Figure 7.1.4.8 Number of agency recruitments and per capita premium

(*Data source*: Insurance Association of China)

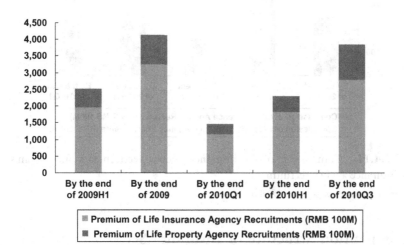

Figure 7.1.4.9 Premium of life insurance agency recruitments and premium of property insurance agency recruitments

(*Data source*: Insurance Association of China)

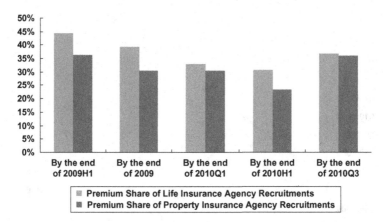

Figure 7.1.4.10   Premium share of life insurance agency recruitments and premium share of property insurance agency recruitments

(*Data source*: Insurance Association of China)

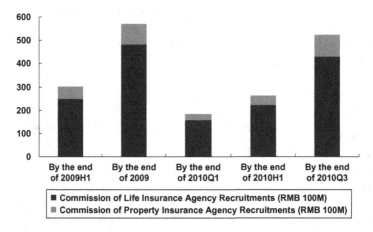

Figure 7.1.4.11   Commission of life insurance agency recruitments and commission of property insurance agency recruitments

(*Data source*: Insurance Association of China)

7.2 Competition Structure of Insurance Sector

7.2.1 *Competition structure of life insurance*

According to statistics made by the Insurance Association of China, by December of 2010, top five Chinese life insurance companies in terms of premium are China Life Insurance Company, Ping An Insurance, New China Life Insurance, China Pacific Insurance Company and Taikang Life Insurance: their premium in all accounts for 77.2% of the total premium of

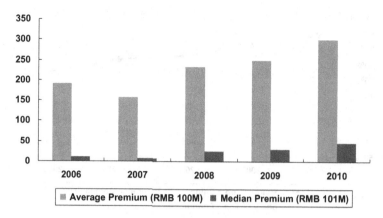

Figure 7.2.1.1 Average premium and median premium of Chinese life insurance companies (*Data source*: Chinese Protecting and Supervising Association)

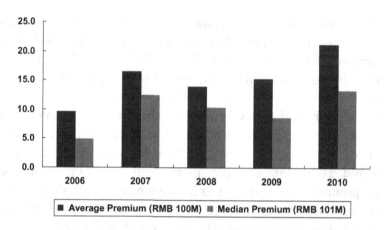

Figure 7.2.1.2 Average premium and median premium of foreign life insurance companies (*Data source*: Chinese Protecting and Supervising Association)

all Chinese life insurance companies. The top five foreign life insurance companies in terms of premium are American International Assurance (AIA), Generali Life Insurance, Huatai Life Insurance, Citic-Prudential Life Insurance and Sun Life Everbright: their premium in all accounts for 52.8% of the total premium of all foreign life insurance companies. According to historical data, from 2006 to 2010, the average premium of Chinese Life Insurance Company increased from RMB 19.1 billion to RMB 30 billion, and its median rose from RMB 1.02 billion to RMB 4.52 billion. The factor causing the relatively wide gap between average and median is that the premium mainly concentrates on the companies in the front rank.

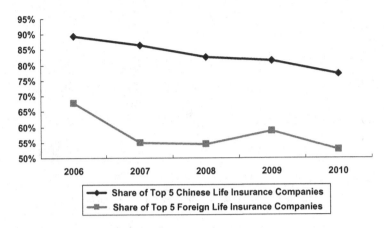

Figure 7.2.1.3   Share of top 5 Chinese and foreign life insurance companies respectively
(*Data source*: Chinese Protecting and Supervising Association)

For foreign life insurance companies, during 2006 and 2010, their average premium rose from RMB 960 million to RMB 2.11 billion, and its median increased from RMB 500 million to RMB 1.33 billion. Compared with Chinese life insurance companies, the top five foreign life insurance companies have a relatively lower premium share.

Actually, seen from the perspective of premium share of top 5 insurance companies, no matter top 5 of Chinese life insurance companies or of foreign life insurance companies, industry concentration witnessed a reduction during 2006 and 2010. For example, in the case of Chinese life insurance companies, premium share of the top 5 companies was 89.4% in 2006 up to 77.2% in December 2010. That is to say, their premium share had a drop of more than 10% during this period. The concentration of foreign life insurance companies is lower than that of Chinese life insurance companies, but the premium of its top 5 companies reduced from 67.7% in 2006 to 52.8% in 2010, with a drop of more than 10% in their premium share.

7.2.2 *Competition structure of property insurance*

According to statistics made by the Insurance Association of China, by December of 2010, the top 5 Chinese property insurance companies in terms of premium are PICC Property and Casualty, Ping An Insurance, CPIC Property Insurance, China United Property Insurance and China Continent Property & Casualty Insurance: their premium in all accounts for 75.5% of the total premium of all Chinese life insurance companies. The top 5 foreign property insurance companies are AIU, Tokyo Marine Insurance, Mitsui

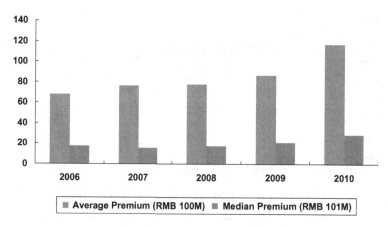

Figure 7.2.2.1 Average premium and median premium of Chinese property insurance companies

(*Data source*: Chinese Protecting and Supervising Association)

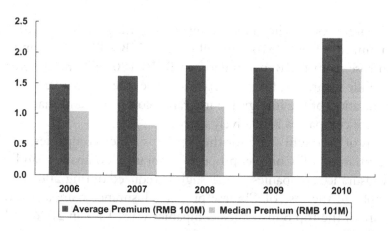

Figure 7.2.2.2 Average premium and median premium of foreign property insurance companies

(*Data source*: Chinese Protecting and Supervising Association)

Sumitomo Insurance, Liberty Mutual Insurance and Samsung Insurance: their premium in all accounts for 60.3% of the total premium of all foreign life insurance companies.

According to the historical data, during 2006 and 2010, the average premium of all Chinese property insurance companies rose from RMB 6.8 billion to RMB 11.7 billion, and median premium increased from RMB 1.75 billion to RMB 2.87 billion. The factor causing the relatively wide gap between average and median is that the premium mainly concentrates on the companies in the front rank.

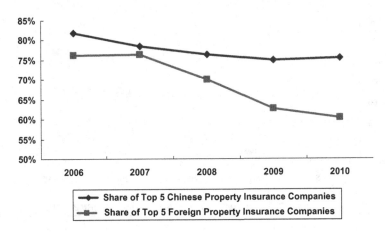

Figure 7.2.2.3   Average premium and median premium of foreign property insurance companies

(*Data source*: Chinese Protecting and Supervising Association)

For foreign property insurance companies, during 2006 and 2010, average premium rose from RMB 150 million to RMB 230 million, and median premium rose from RMB 100 million to RMB 180 million. Different from the case of life insurance, for property insurance, the gap between the industry concentration of the foreign life insurance companies and that of Chinese life insurance companies is relatively narrow.

In terms of premium share for the top 5 insurance companies, the industry concentration of Chinese property insurance companies and foreign property insurance companies as well slightly reduced during 2006 and 2010. For example, in the case of Chinese property insurance companies, the premium share of the top 5 insurance companies was 81.8% in 2006 and 75.5% in 2010. The industry concentration of foreign property insurance companies is slightly lower than that of Chinese property insurance companies, and the premium share of their top 5 reduced from 76.3% in 2006 to 60.3% in 2010.

7.2.3 *Competition structure of pension insurance*

By December of 2010, the main insurance companies in the pension insurance sector are Taiping Pension, Ping An Pension, China Life Pension, Changjiang Pension and Taikang Pension.

From 2007 to 2010, the enterprises annuity of the pension insurance companies increased from RMB 8.55 billion to RMB 35.74 billion, among which China Life Pension and Ping An Pension had a relatively higher share, 48.6% and 28.6% respectively in 2010.

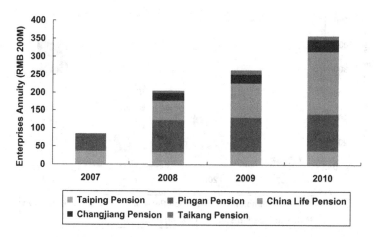

Figure 7.2.3.1 Enterprises annuity of pension insurance companies

(*Data source*: Chinese Protecting and Supervising Association)

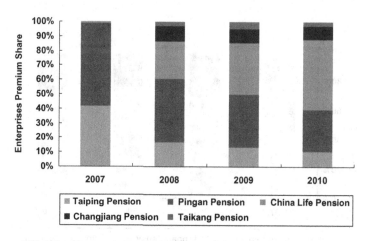

Figure 7.2.3.2 Enterprises annuity share of the pension insurance companies

(*Data source*: Chinese Protecting and Supervising Association)

During 2007 and 2010, the trustee assets of the pension insurance companies witnessed a rise from RMB 8.4 billion to RMB 103.9 billion, among which, the total share of China Life Pension and Ping An Pension approximated to over 60%, that is, 30.7% and 28.7% respectively of the total trustee assets in 2010.

During 2007 and 2010, the investment assets of the pension insurance companies rose from RMB7.97 billion to RMB 70.9 billion, among which Ping An Pension accounted for more than 50% of the total, with a share up to 54.2% in 2010.

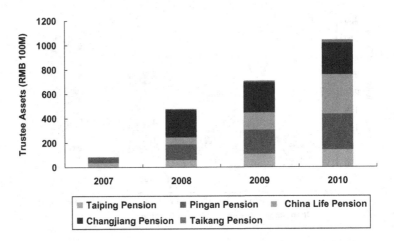

Figure 7.2.3.3   Trustee assets of the pension insurance companies
(*Data source*: Chinese Protecting and Supervising Association)

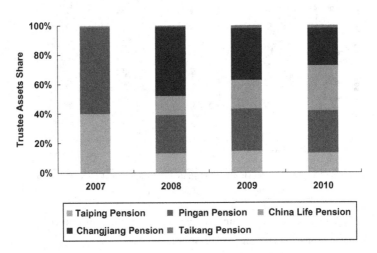

Figure 7.2.3.4   Trustee assets share of the pension insurance companies
(*Data source*: Chinese Protecting and Supervising Association)

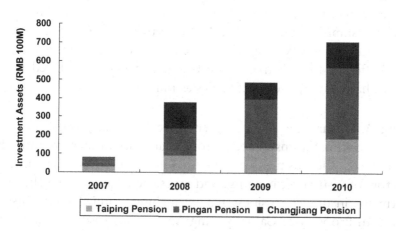

Figure 7.2.3.5 Investment assets of the pension insurance companies

(*Data source*: Chinese Protecting and Supervising Association)

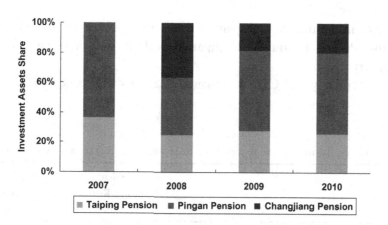

Figure 7.2.3.6 Investment assets share of the pension insurance companies

(*Data source*: Chinese Protecting and Supervising Association)

7.3 Comparison of Listed Insurance Companies

7.3.1 *Overview*

Among the insurance companies located in the Chinese mainland, there are in all 4 companies listed in Hong Kong market, including Ping An Insurance, China Life Insurance Company, China Pacific Insurance Company and PICC Property and Casualty. Among which, the first three are also listed in A-share market. Different from banking, the business structure of listed insurance companies has its unique characteristics as follows:

(1) Ping An Insurance: as a comprehensive financial group (though it is classified into the insurance sector because its primary revenue lies in insurance), the business of Ping An Insurance covers the three broad sectors of insurance, banking, and investment, among which, the platform for insurance business mainly includes Ping An Life Insurance, Ping An Property & Casualty, Ping An Pension Insurance and Ping An Health Insurance; the platform for banking is Ping An Bank; and the platform for investment includes Ping An Trust, Ping An Securities, Ping An Asset Management and Ping An Asset Management (Hong Kong), etc.;

(2) China Life Insurance Company: mainly dealing with life insurance;

(3) China Pacific Insurance Company: dealing with life insurance and property insurance;

(4) PICC Property and Casualty: mainly dealing with property insurance.

Table 7.3.1.1　　Insurance companies listed in Hong Kong market and A-share market

Name	Code listed in Hong Kong market	Code listed in A-share market
Ping An Insurance (Group) Co., Ltd. (Ping An Insurance)	02318	601318
China PICC Property and Casualty Co., Ltd. (PICC Property and Casualty)	02328	
China Pacific Insurance (Group) Co., Ltd. (China Pacific Insurance Company)	02601	601601
China Life Insurance Co., Ltd. (China Life Insurance Company)	02628	601628

7.3.2 *Comparison of major financial indicators for listed insurance companies*

As the business structures of different listed insurance companies are distinct from each other, certain financial indicators are difficult to be directly compared. However, through the comparison of some core financial indicators it is still possible to get an overall understanding of the financial status of the listed insurance companies.

In terms of return on equity (ROE), among the above 4 listed insurance companies, China Life Insurance Company has a relatively stable ROE: except for the year 2008 when it was relatively severely impacted by the global financial crisis, its ROE reduced to 11%, in recent years its ROE has remained above 14%. By contrast, China Pacific Insurance Company and PICC Property and Casualty have a significantly lower ROE: before 2008 China Pacific Insurance Company had a ROE similar to that of China Life Insurance Company, but during 2008 and 2009 (and the first half of 2010 as well) its ROE significantly fell behind that of the latter. For PICC Property and Casualty, its ROE in recent years is always lower than that for China Life Insurance Company. Ping An Insurance's ROE is comparatively higher, but was under negative influence of the global financial crisis in 2008.

In terms of return on assets (ROA), China Life Insurance Company is significantly higher than the rest of the three listed insurance companies. It is immediately followed by China Pacific Insurance Company; Ping An Insurance and PICC Property and Casualty have a relatively lower ROA.

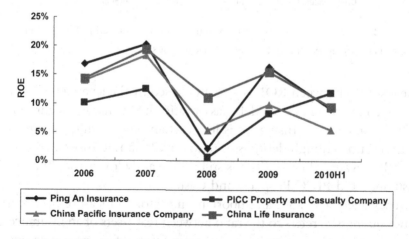

Figure 7.3.2.1 ROE of insurance companies listed in Hong Kong market

(*Data source*: Financial reports of each listed insurance companies)

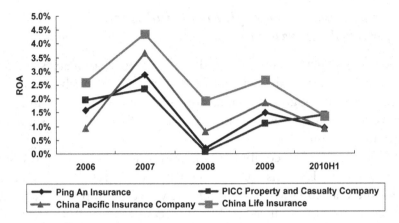

Figure 7.3.2.2   ROA of listed insurance companies listed in Hong Kong market

(*Data source*: Financial reports of each listed insurance companies)

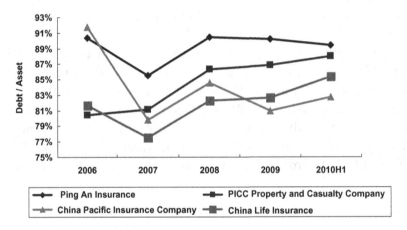

Figure 7.3.2.3   Debt/asset ratio of the insurance companies listed in Hong Kong market

(*Data source*: Financial reports of each listed insurance companies)

The disparity between ROE is actually caused by the leverage of each company. The comparison of each debt/asset ratio shows that in recent years, the high ROE for Ping An Insurance is in a certain sense resulted from its high debt/asset ratio. Though debt/asset ratio for China Life Insurance Company has slightly elevated after 2008, it is still significantly lower than that for Ping An Insurance and PICC Property and Casualty.

Solvency adequacy ratio, an important indicator to measure the security of insurance businesses, refers to the ratio between real assets of an insurance company and its minimum assets (the minimum assets of an insurance company refers to the necessary amount of assets required of the insurance company

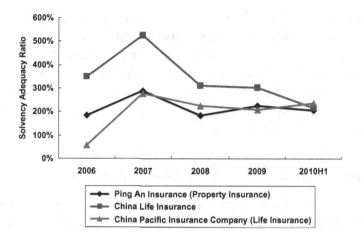

Figure 7.3.2.4 Solvency adequacy ratio of life insurance of the insurance companies listed in Hong Kong market

(*Data source*: Financial reports of each listed insurance companies)

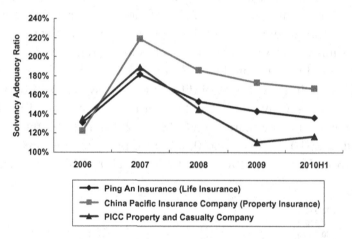

Figure 7.3.2.5 Solvency adequacy ratio for property insurance of the insurance companies listed in Hong Kong market

(*Data source*: Financial reports of each listed insurance companies)

to offset the influence on profitability by risks such as asset risk and underwriting risk, etc.; real asset of an insurance company refers to the balance between admitted assets and admitted debts). Solvency is the ability of insurance companies to repay the debts. An insurance company should possess the amount of assets corresponding to its risk and business scale so as to ensure a solvency adequacy ratio not below 100%. Historically speaking, the solvency adequacy ratio of China Life Insurance Company is higher than that for the life insurance of Ping An Insurance and China Pacific Insurance Company, but since 2009 the life insurance of the above three insurance companies have a similar solvency adequacy ratio, all basically remaining between 200% and 240%.

In respect of property insurance business, China Pacific Insurance Company has a slightly higher solvency adequacy ratio than Ping An Insurance and PICC Property and Casualty. According to data during 2009 and the first half of 2010, PICC Property and Casualty has the lowest solvency adequacy ratio, only slightly higher than 100%.

7.3.3 *Business structure of major insurance companies*

As a comprehensive financial growth company with insurance business as its basis, Ping An Insurance divides its businesses into 3 general categories and 5 sub-categories: insurance (including life insurance and property insurance), banking, and investment (including security business and trust business). From 2006 to 2009, in terms of annual compound growth rate of revenue for each category, banking income boasts the highest growth rate (its annual compound growth rate amounted to 212.7%), followed by trust income (with an annual compound growth rate of 53.1%); the growth rate for property insurance, life insurance and securities insurance remains relatively low (with their annual compound growth rate being 31.6%, 25.3% and 24.7% respectively).

The difference in growth rate of different business is also embodied in the income share of respective business. The net interest income of banking witnessed a rise in its income share from 0.38% in 2006 up to 0.66% in 2009 (for the first half of 2010 the share was 0.55%); for property business, the income share rose from 19.51% in 2006 to 21.50% in 2009 (this share was 23.53%

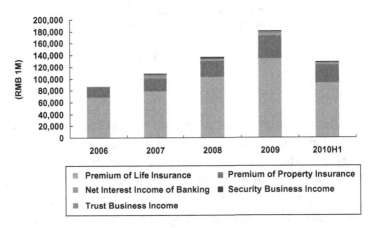

Figure 7.3.3.1   Income variation of each business of Ping An Insurance

(*Data source*: Financial reports of Ping An Insurance)

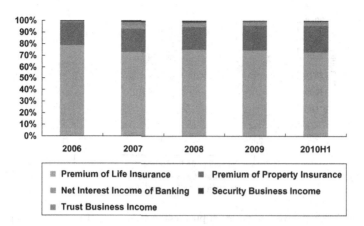

Figure 7.3.3.2 Income share for each business of Ping An Insurance

(*Data source*: Financial reports of Ping An Insurance)

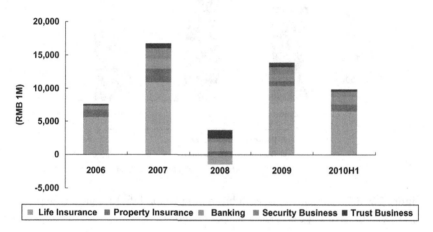

Figure 7.3.3.3 Net profits variation for each business of Ping An Insurance

(*Data source*: Financial reports of Ping An Insurance)

for the first half of 2010). By comparison, the income share for life insurance and security business slightly decreased (respectively from 78.52% and 1.47% in 2006 down to 74.57% and 1.37% in 2009).

In terms of net profits, banking boasts the highest growth rate: during the 3 years from 2006 to 2009, its annual compound growth rate amounted to 147.77%; trust business still ranked the second in this respect with an annual compound growth rate of 46.18%. For both life insurance and security business, the annual compound growth rate during the 3 years remained between 21% and 22%. The net profits from property business witnessed a drop during this period with an annual compound reduction rate of 13.64%.

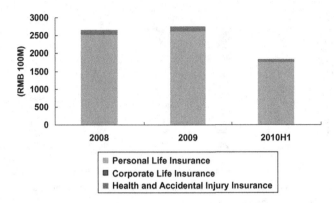

Figure 7.3.3.4   Income of each business in China Life Insurance Company
(*Data source*: Financial reports of China Life Insurance Company)

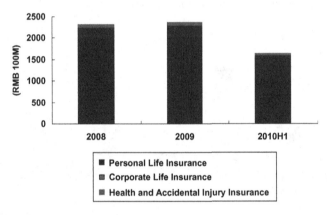

Figure 7.3.3.5   Indemnity of each business in China Life Insurance Company
(*Data source*: Financial reports of China Life Insurance Company)

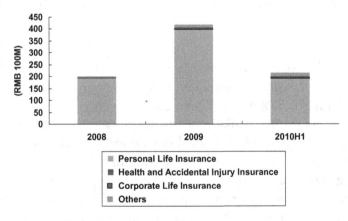

Figure 7.3.3.6   Pretax profits of each business in China Life Insurance Company
(*Data source*: Financial reports of China Life Insurance Company)

According to data by the end of 2009, life insurance is still the primary business of Ping An Insurance, with a profit share of 75.14%; banking and security business rank second and third, with a share of 7.82% and 7.76% respectively; the net profit share for property insurance and trust business stays at the bottom, 4.89% and 4.39% respectively.

As a company dealing with life insurance, China Life Insurance Company focuses its main business on personal life insurance. From 2008 to the first half of 2010, the income share of personal life insurance is always above 95%, accounting for over 96.5% of its indemnity. The second largest businesses are accidental injury insurance and health insurance, with an income share less than 5%, about 3% of their indemnity; for corporate life insurance, the income share remains between 0.1% and 0.2%.

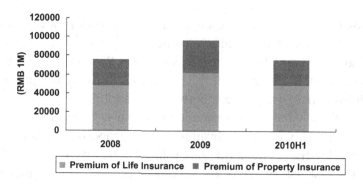

Figure 7.3.3.7   Revenue of life insurance and property insurance in China Pacific Insurance Company

(*Data source*: Financial reports of China Pacific Insurance Company)

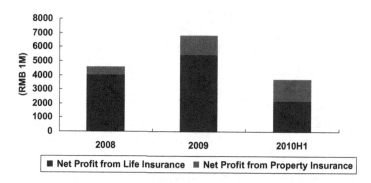

Figure 7.3.3.8   Net profits of life insurance and property insurance (attributed to parent company) in China Pacific Insurance Company

(*Data source*: Financial reports of China Pacific Insurance Company)

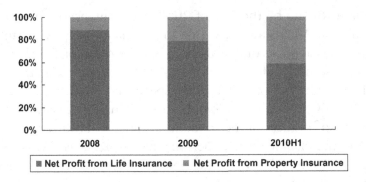

Figure 7.3.3.9   Net profit share for property insurance in China Pacific Insurance Company enjoys a gradual increase

(*Data source*: Financial reports of China Pacific Insurance Company)

In terms of contribution of each business to pretax profits, personal life insurance still enjoys an absolute advantage over income share: for 2008 and 2009, the average annual pretax profit share was 95% with a slight drop for the first half of 2010, down to 89%. The next are accidental injury insurance and health insurance, with a share between 2% and 3%.

Different from China Life Insurance Company, China Pacific Insurance Company deals with both life insurance and property insurance, and the income share for these two kinds of business is relatively balanced. During 2008 and the first half of 2010, the income share for life insurance in China Pacific Insurance Company basically remained between 63% and 64%. However, seen from the perspective of net profits, though in 2008 the net profit share for property insurance was only 11.8%, it rose to 20.8% in 2009 and further up to 41.2% for the first half of 2010.

Chapter 8

SECURITY, FUND AND TRUST

8.1 Development of Security Sector

8.1.1 *Expansion of security sector*

With the continuous development of China's security market, the development of security firms — the main agent of security market also witnesses a rapid advance. According to statistics about security firms that published their financial reports during 2005 and 2009, the total assets of security firms increased from RMB 298.6 billion in 2005 to RMB 2.2538 trillion in 2009, the latter being more than 5 times of the former, and the annual compound growth rate amounted to 65.7%. Moreover, along with the increase in assets size was the gradual rise in the total assets of the security firms: during the same period the equity of security firms rose from RMB 56.6 billion to RMB 501.9 billion, with an annual compound growth rate of 72.6%, higher than total assets growth rate.

In respect of business scale, the total revenue of security firms increased from RMB 12.3 billion in 2005 to RMB 234.7 billion in 2009 with an annual compound growth rate of 109%. The business profits and net profits reverse the tide of loss in 2005, amounting to RMB 131.6 billion and RMB 99.1 billion respectively in 2009.

However, from the perspective of data about revenue, operating profit and net profit for the security sector, profitability of this sector badly relies on the trend of stock market. For instance, during the downturn of A-share in 2005, the security sector as a whole witnessed a loss; while with the arrival of bull market in 2007, the revenue and profits of the security sector came to a peak during the recent years; but in 2008 when the market fell due to the impact of the global financial crisis, the revenue and profitability of the security sector underwent a large-scale decline once again.

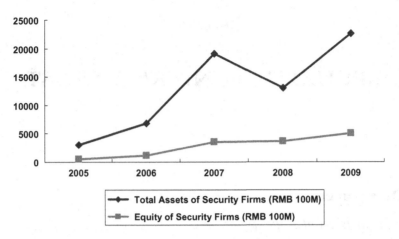

Figure 8.1.1.1   Increase in total assets of security firms
(*Data source*: Securities Association of China)

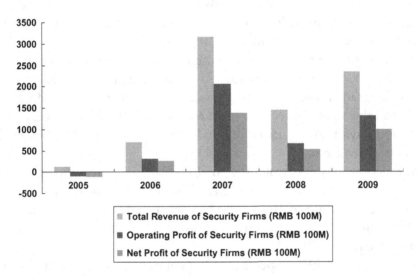

Figure 8.1.1.2   Increase in total business scale of security firms
(*Data source*: Securities Association of China)

In terms of assets size and the distribution of revenue and net profit, in 2009 nearly half (48%) of all security firms found that their total assets were lower than RMB 10 billion and only 5 security firms had total assets of more than RMB 100 billion (one of them had a total asset of above RMB 200 billion). Similarly, nearly half (47%) of security firms found that their revenue was below RMB 1 billion, with a share of less than 3%. On the aspect of net profit,

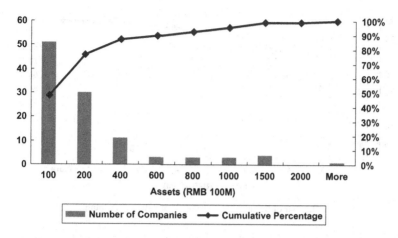

Figure 8.1.1.3   Asset distribution of the security firms in 2009

(*Data source*: Securities Association of China)

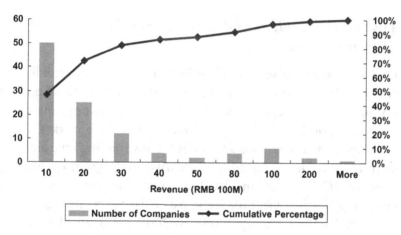

Figure 8.1.1.4   Revenue distribution of the security firms in 2009

(*Data source*: Securities Association of China)

in 2009, 18% of security firms saw their net profit going below RMB 100 million, and about half (51%) of security firms found their net profit diving below RMB 500 million, and only less than 10% of security firms had a net profit over RMB 3 billion, with only 2 security firms' net profit surpassed RMB 5 billion and a share of less than 2%.

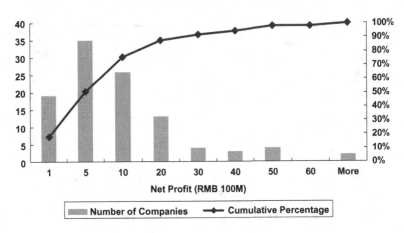

Figure 8.1.1.5   Net profit distribution of the security firms in 2009

(*Data source*: Securities Association of China)

8.1.2 *Overall profitability and anti-risk capability of security firms*

Since the main business of security firms in China's mainland still lies in brokerage business, during 2005 and the first half of 2010 the overall profitability of security firms largely depends on the trend of the security market. Since 2005 to the year 2007, with the gradual rising of A-share market, ROA and ROE of security firms also witness an uptrend. However, with the arrival of the bear market in 2008, the profitability of security firms rapidly declines.

In terms of ROE median and ROA median (since certain security firms have a rather high or low yield for some particular years, average can hardly reflect the overall status), during 2005 and 2009 the ROE of security firms remained around 16% and 17%, and their ROA between 2% and 3%.

In terms of anti-risk capability, according to *Regulations on Risk Control Indicator Management of Security Firms* issued by China Securities Regulatory Commission (CSRC) on 5th July, 2006 (amended on 4th March, 2008), one important indicator of measuring the overall risks of security firms is "net capital". Net capital refers to one's comprehensive risk control indicator that has undergone risk adjustment about certain projects and businesses relevant to debt on the basis of equity and with reference to the business scope of security firms and liquidity of the company's debt. The basic formula for calculating net capital goes as follows:

Net capital = equity-risk adjustment about financial assets-risk adjustment about other financial assets − risk adjustment about debt (if any) −/+ other

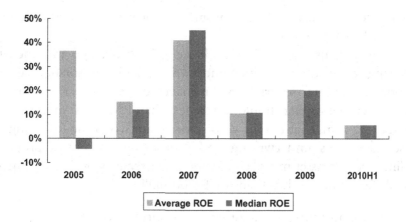

Figure 8.1.2.1 Overall ROE of security firms

(*Data source*: Securities Association of China)

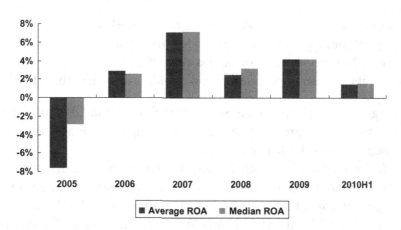

Figure 8.1.2.2 Overall ROA of security firms

(*Data source*: Securities Association of China)

adjustments identified or approved by China Securities Regulatory Commission.

China Securities Regulatory Commission specifies net capital standards for security firms that operate different categories of business:

- For security firms that operate securities brokerage, their net capital should not be less than RMB 20 million.
- For security firms that operate one of the following businesses: securities underwriting and sponsorship, securities proprietary trading, security asset

management and other security businesses, their net capital should not be less than RMB 50 million.

- For security firms that operate both securities brokerage and one of the following businesses: securities underwriting and sponsorship, securities proprietary trading, security asset management and other security businesses, their net capital should not be less than RMB 100 million.
- For security firms that cover two or more than two of the following businesses: securities underwriting and sponsorship, securities proprietary trading, security asset management and other security businesses, their net capital should not be less than RMB 200 million.

Meanwhile, security firms shall constantly confirm to the following (overall) risk control indicator standards:

- Net capital/total of various risk reserves ratio should not be less than 100%;
- Net capital/equity ratio should not be less than 40%;
- Net capital/debt ratio should not be less than 8%;
- Equity/debt ratio should not be less than 20%;
- Current assets/current liabilities ratio should not be less than 100%.

Among the above-mentioned 5 risk control indicators, 3 involve net capital, indicating the significant place of net capital management in risk management for security firms.

For the convenience of comparison, we analyze 68 security firms whose net capitals for 2009 and the first half of 2010 have been published. In 2009, the average net capital of these 68 security firms was RMB 5.03 billion (median is RMB 2.57 billion), the highest net capital being RMB 34.9 billion and the lowest being RMB 550 million. In 2010, the average net capital of the 68 firms was RMB 4.97 billion, slightly lower than that for 2009 but its median rose to RMB 2.66 billion. Comparing the situations in 2009 and the first half of 2010, net capital distribution was basically stable, among which, the number of security firms whose net capital is between RMB 5 billion and 10 billion enjoyed a slight increase.

In terms of the net capital/equity ratio, in 2009, among these 68 security firms, the lowest ratio was 45%, and the highest was 111.8%, with an average net capital/equity ratio of 78.2% (median was 80.1%); in 2010, this average ratio basically kept stable — 79.9% (median was 78.8%, the highest being 177.2% and the lowest being 50.5%). Seen from ratio distribution, for the majority of security firms, their net capital/equity was within the interval between 70% and 90%.

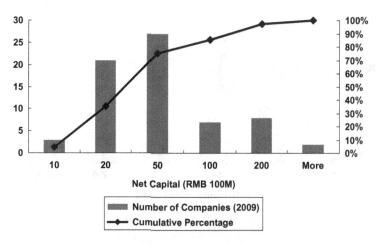

Figure 8.1.2.3   Net capital distribution of the 68 security firms in 2009

(*Data source*: Securities Association of China)

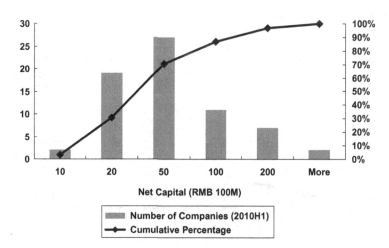

Figure 8.1.2.4   Net capital distribution of the 68 security firms during the first half of 2010

(*Data source*: Securities Association of China)

Comparing 2009 and the first half of 2010, it is found that for the first half of 2010, net capital/equity ratio of the above-mentioned 68 security firms amounted to more than 50%, and the number of firms whose ratio was between 70% and 80% increased, while the number of firms whose ratio was between 80% and 90% decreased.

Among the 68 security firms, in 2009 one was not up to the standard specified by China Securities Regulatory Commission — "net capital/debt ratio shall be more than 8%", its ratio being 7.4%. Besides, for the 68 firms, the highest net capital/debt was 90% with an average ratio of 25.7% (median was 21%);

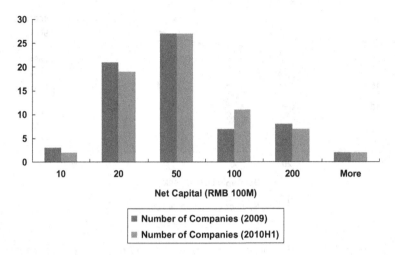

Figure 8.1.2.5 Comparison of net capital distribution of the 68 security firms between 2009 and the first half of 2010

(*Data source*: Securities Association of China)

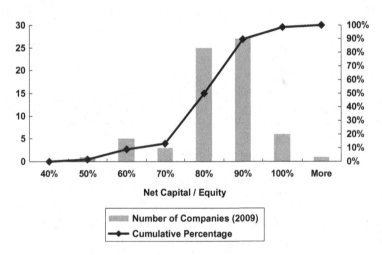

Figure 8.1.2.6 Net capital/equity ratio distribution of the 68 security firms in 2009

(*Data source*: Securities Association of China)

by the first half of 2010, the 68 firms have been all up to this standard, the lowest ratio being 13.3% and the highest being 101.5%, with an average of 32.4% and a median of 24.8%, which saw a significant rise in comparison with 2009. Seen from the comparison, for the first half of 2010, the number of firms whose equity/debt ratio was less than 20% significantly declined, while the number of firms whose ratio was above 30% significantly increased.

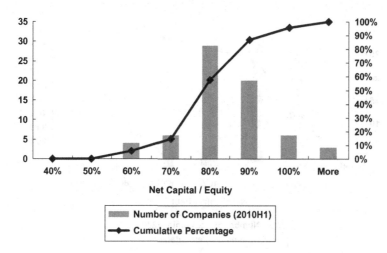

Figure 8.1.2.7 Net capital/equity ratio distribution of the 68 security firms for the first half of 2010

(*Data source*: Securities Association of China)

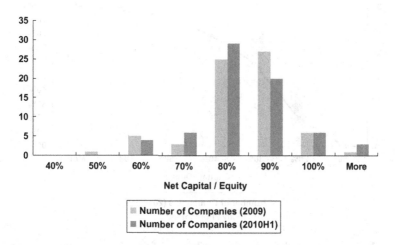

Figure 8.1.2.8 Comparison of net capital/equity ratio distribution of the 68 security firms between 2009 and the first half of 2010

(*Data source*: Securities Association of China)

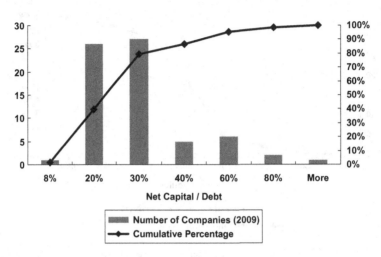

Figure 8.1.2.9   Net capital/debt ratio distribution of the 68 security firms in 2009

(*Data source*: Securities Association of China)

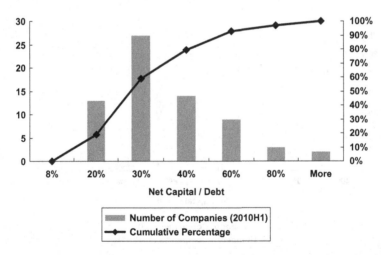

Figure 8.1.2.10   Net capital/debt ratio distribution of the 68 security firms for the first half of 2010

(*Data source*: Securities Association of China)

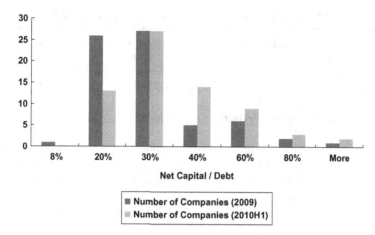

Figure 8.1.2.11   Comparison of net capital/debt ratio distribution of the 68 security firms between 2009 and the first half of 2010

(*Data source*: Securities Association of China)

8.1.3 *Listed security firms*

In 2005 there were in total 8 listed security firms. In recent years the number of listed security firms significantly increased. By far, there are 15 security firms listed in A-share market directly or indirectly (given the need of using data for 2009, the following comparison does not include Guangfa Securities listed in 2010 by means of backdoor listing through Yan Bian Road Construction Co., Ltd).

In 2009, the average assets of the 14 listed security firms was RMB 54.97 billion, the first three security firms in total assets being CITIC Securities, Haitong Securities, and Huatai Securities. For the first half of 2010, the average assets of the above 14 firms dropped to RMB 50.39 billion, with the above-mentioned three firms still ranking the top three in terms of total assets.

In 2009, the average net capital of the 14 listed security firms was RMB 11.01 billion, the first three being CITIC Securities, Haitong Securities and Everbright Securities. For the first half of 2010, this average net capital declined to RMB 10.51 billion, the first three being Haitong Securities, CITIC Securities and Everbright Securities.

In terms of profitability, by the end of 2009, the average ROE of the listed security firms was 18.4%, the first three being Northeast Securities, Huatai Securities and CITIC Securities; by the end of the first half of 2010, this average ROE was 5.5%, the first three being Hongyuan Securities, Guojin Securities and Shanxi Securities.

Table 8.1.3.1   Listed security firms and their stock code

A-share market stock code	security firms	A-share stock code	security firms
601788	Everbright Securities Co., Ltd.	600030	CITIC Securities Co., Ltd.
000562	Hongyuan Securities Co., Ltd.	000783	Changjiang Securities Co., Ltd.
601688	Huatai Securities Co., Ltd.	000686	Northeast Securities Co., Ltd.
002500	Shanxi Securities Co., Ltd.	600109	Guojin Securities Co., Ltd.
601099	Pacific Securities Co., Ltd.	000728	Guoyan Securities Co., Ltd.
601377	Industrial Securities Co., Ltd.	600837	Haitong Securities Co., Ltd.
600999	Merchants Securities Co., Ltd.	600369	Southwest Securities Co., Ltd.
000776	Guangfa Securities Co., Ltd.		

(*Data source*: Xinhua Finance)

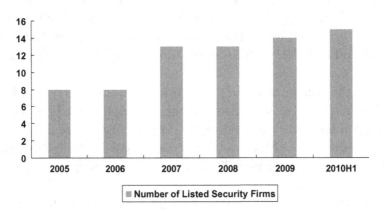

Figure 8.1.3.1   Number of listed security firms

(*Data source*: Xinhua Finance)

By the end of 2009, the average ROA of the above 14 security firms was 4.5%, the first three being Pacific Securities, Southwest Securities and Northeast Securities; by the end of the first half of 2010, this average ROA was 1.6%, the first three being Hongyuan Securities, Guojin Securities and Shanxi Securities.

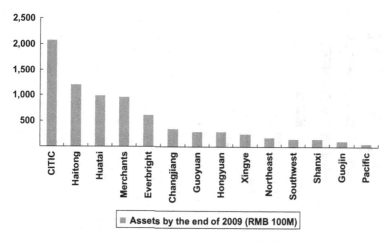

Figure 8.1.3.2   Total assets of listed security firms by the end of 2009
(*Data source*: Financial reports of various listed security firms)

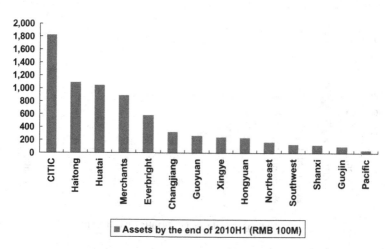

Figure 8.1.3.3   Total assets of the listed security firms by the end of the first half of 2010
(*Data source*: Financial reports of various listed security firms)

In respect of anti-risk capability, by the end of 2009 the average net capital/equity ratio of the listed security firms was 74.1%, among which, firms of the highest ratio included Guojin Securities, Pacific Securities and Guoyuan Securities; by the first half of 2010, this average ratio dropped to 67.4%, the first three still being Guojin Securities, Pacific Securities and Guoyuan Securities.

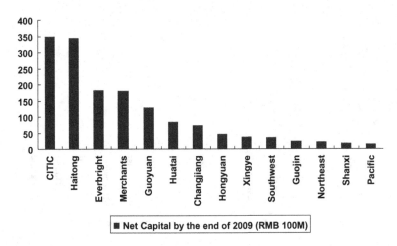

Figure 8.1.3.4   Net capital of the listed security firms by the end of 2009

(*Data source*: Financial reports of various listed security firms)

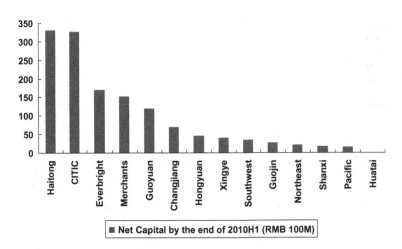

Figure 8.1.3.5   Net capital of the listed security firms by the end of the first half of 2010

(*Data source*: Financial reports of various listed security firms)

By the end of 2009, the average net capital/debt ratio of the listed security firms was 31.2%, among which Guoyuan Securities enjoyed the highest ratio, immediately followed by Everbright Securities and Haitong Securities successively; by the first half of 2010, the above average was 35.1%, with Guoyuan Securities, Pacific Securities and Haitong Securities ranking the top three.

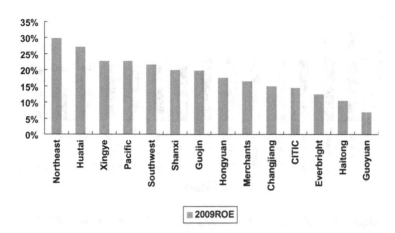

Figure 8.1.3.6   ROE of the listed security firms by the end of 2009

(*Data source*: Financial reports of various listed security firms)

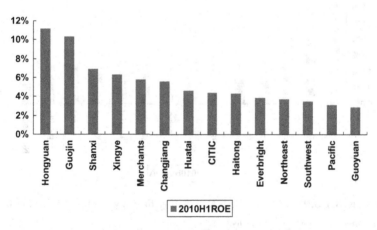

Figure 8.1.3.7   ROE of the listed security firms by the first half of 2010

(*Data source*: Financial reports of various listed security Firms)

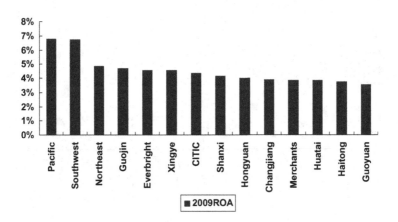

Figure 8.1.3.8   ROA of the listed security firms by the end of 2009

(*Data source*: Financial reports of various listed security firms)

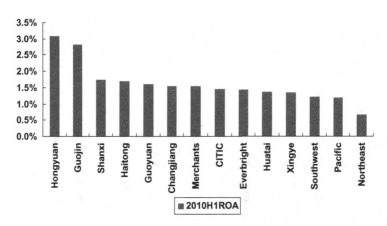

Figure 8.1.3.9   ROA of the listed security firms by the first half of 2010

(*Data source*: Financial reports of various listed security firms)

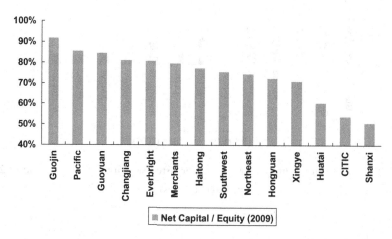

Figure 8.1.3.10 Net capital/equity ratio of the listed security firms by the end of 2009

(*Data source*: Financial reports of various listed security firms)

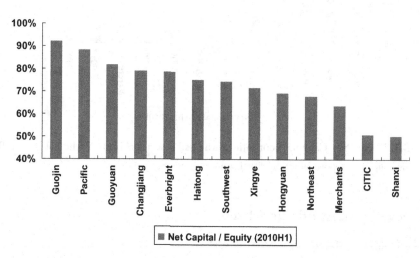

Figure 8.1.3.11 Net capital/equity ratio of the listed security firms by the first half of 2010

(*Data source*: Financial reports of various listed security firms)

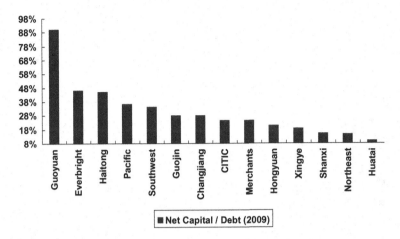

Figure 8.1.3.12   Net capital/debt ratio of the listed security firms by the end of 2009
(*Data source*: Financial reports of various listed security firms)

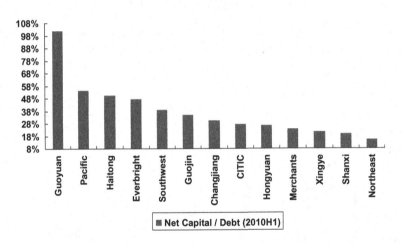

Figure 8.1.3.13   Net Capital/ debt ratio of the listed security firms by the half of 2010
(*Data source*: Financial reports of various listed security firms)

8.2   Development of Fund Sector

8.2.1   *Overall status of fund sector*

By the end of the fourth quarter of 2010, the 61 fund management companies covered in our statistics have cumulatively managed 816 funds, among which there are 775 open-ended funds and 41 close-ended funds. Each fund management company manages 13 funds on average (median is 12) and each fund company on average manages 13 open-ended funds (median is 11).

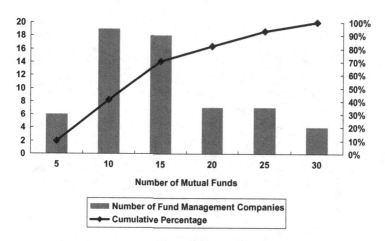

Figure 8.2.1.1   Number of funds by the end of the fourth quarter of 2010

(*Data source*: Securities Association of China)

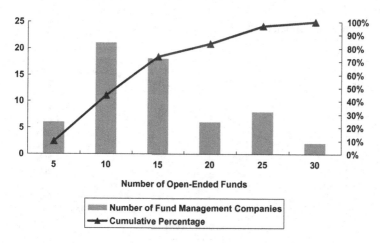

Figure 8.2.1.2   Number of open-ended funds by the end of the fourth quarter of 2010

(*Data source*: Securities Association of China)

Seen from company number distribution, about 40% of fund management companies manage fewer than 10 funds, and about 40% of fund management companies manage 10–20 funds. Among the fund management companies that manage more than 20 funds, 4 companies manage more than 25 funds. By the end of the fourth quarter of 2010, about 45% of fund management companies manage no more than 10 open-ended funds, and 10 fund management companies manage more than 20 open-ended funds.

By the end of the fourth quarter of 2010, for the top ten fund management companies in terms of fund number, there are in total 254 funds

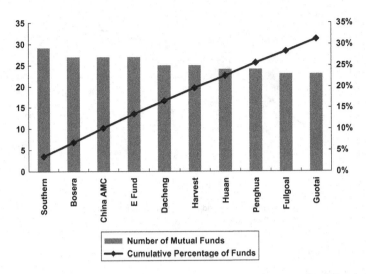

Figure 8.2.1.3   Fund management companies that manage the most funds by the end of the fourth quarter of 2010

(*Data source*: Securities Association of China)

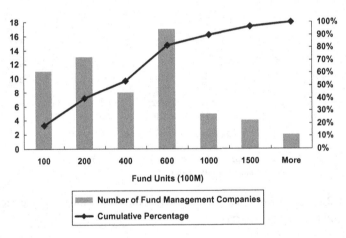

Figure 8.2.1.4   Fund units distribution among the fund management companies by the end of the fourth quarter of 2010

(*Data source*: Securities Association of China)

(among which 233 are open-ended funds), accounting for 31% of total fund number. In terms of fund number, the top 4 companies are Southern Fund Management Company, Bosera Fund Management Company, China AMC Fund Management Company and E Fund Management Company, all of which manage more than 25 funds. Among the top ten fund management companies, they manage 23 funds at least and 29 at most.

By the end of the fourth quarter of 2010, the 60 fund management companies covered in our statistics have 2.5 trillion fund units, with each company managing 42.4 billion funds on average (the median is 31.7 billion). In terms of distribution, nearly 20% of fund management companies have fund units less than 10 billion, and about 40% of fund management companies manage funds less than 20 billion. There are in total 6 fund management companies whose fund units are over 100 million (accounting for 10% of the total within our statistic range), among which 2 companies manage over 150 million funds.

Among the above 60 fund management companies, the total fund units of the top ten companies in terms of total fund units are 1.18 trillion, accounting for 46.5% of the total of each fund management companies. In terms of the share of fund units for the top ten companies, their fund unit concentration is larger than the concentration of fund number. Among these 10 companies, the fund units of China AMC Fund Management Company and Harvest Management Company surpass 150 billion; the lowest fund units are 67.1 billion and the largest are 188.6 billion.

By the end of the fourth quarter of 2010, net asset value (NAV) of the above 60 fund management companies amounted to RMB 2.4 trillion, with each company's equity being RMB 40.3 billion on average (the median was RMB 27.5 billion). Among them, about 10% of companies had a NAV less than RMB 5 billion, about half of the companies had a NAV below RMB 25 billion, and 6 companies had a NAV above RMB 100 billion.

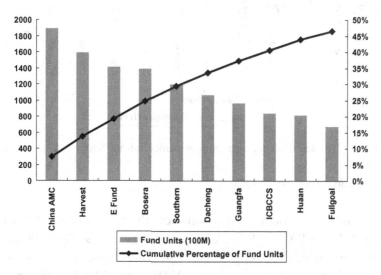

Figure 8.2.1.5   Top ten fund management companies in fund units by the end of the fourth quarter of 2010

(*Data source*: Securities Association of China)

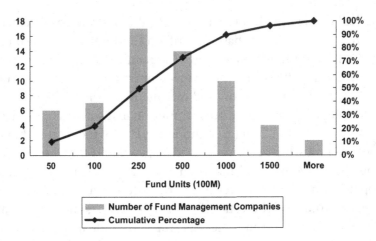

Figure 8.2.1.6   NAV distribution of the fund management companies by the end of the fourth quarter of 2010

(*Data source*: Securities Association of China)

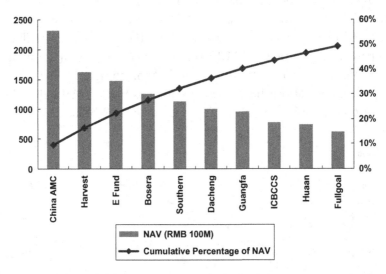

Figure 8.2.1.7   Top ten fund management companies in total NAV by the end of the fourth quarter of 2010

(*Data source*: Securities Association of China)

Among the above-mentioned companies, the top ten companies in NAV have a total NAV of RMB 1.19 trillion, accounting for 49.2% of the total NAV of the 60 companies. Among these 60 companies, China AMC Fund Management Company boasts the largest NAV, over RMB 200 billion, followed by E Fund Management Company and Harvest Management Company in order. Among the top ten companies here, the lowest NAV is RMB 61.5 billion.

8.2.2 *Qualified foreign institutional investors (QFII) and Qualified domestic institutional investors (QDII)*

Given the market regulation of China's capital market, QFII mechanism and QDII mechanism are still the major channels for foreign investors to invest in A-share market and investors in Chinese mainland to invest in foreign markets. By the end of the third quarter of 2010, the cumulative approved QFII quota and approved QDII quota are USD 18.97 billion and USD 66.904 billion.

The comparison of historical data shows that during the 3 years from 2004 to the third quarter of 2010, approved QFII quota tends to remain stable: in 2007 approved QFII quota was relatively low, only amounting to USD 0.95 billion, while for 2006, 2008 and 2009 the approved QFII quota was relatively higher, amounting to USD 3.4 billion, USD 3.398 billion and USD 3.227 billion respectively. Contrary to QFII, in 2007 QDII quota ranked the highest, amounting to USD 30.445 billion, while in 2008 approved QDII quota remained at the lowest (not including the year 2005 that did not approve QDII quota), only USD 3.255 billion and lower than QFII quota approved in 2008. The comparison between approved QFII quota and approved QDII quota together with the consideration of A-share market trend manifests that when A-share market is in bull market (e.g. in 2007), constraints on the approval of QDII quota tend to be less; by contrast, when A-share market witnesses a bear market (e.g. in 2008), the approval of QDII quota tend to be tight while the constraints on the approval of QFII quota will be less. The characteristic of "reverse-market-trend operation" by the regulators in quota approval is pretty significant.

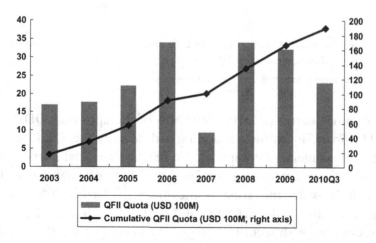

Figure 8.2.2.1   Approved QFII quota by the end of the third quarter of 2010

(*Data source*: State Administration of Exchange Control)

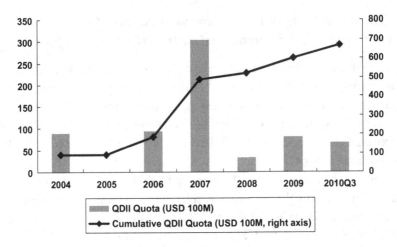

Figure 8.2.2.2   Approved QDII quota by the end of the end of 2010

(*Data source*: State Administration of Exchange Control)

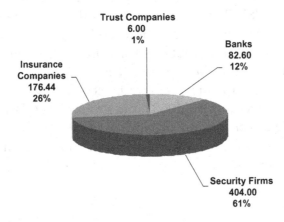

Figure 8.2.2.3   Financial institution share of each category in terms of cumulative approved QDII quota by the third quarter of 2010

(*Data source*: State Administration of Exchange Control)

By the third quarter of 2010, over 60% of the approved QDII quota is possessed by financial institutions dealing with security (i.e. QDII fund issued by each fund management company); the next are financial institutions dealing with insurance, accounting for 26%; the share of financial institutions dealing with banking and trust is the lowest, 12% and 6% respectively. However, after 2007 the majority of QDII quota is issued to financial institutions dealing with security.

Table 8.2.2.1 Summary of QDII quota approval for each category of financial institution between 2004 and the third quarter of 2010

(USD 100M)	Banks	Security	Insurance	Trust	Total QDII Quota
2004			88.90		88.90
2005					0.00
2006	71.80	5.00	17.38		94.18
2007	7.50	230.00	66.95		304.45
2008	0.30	32.00	0.25		32.55
2009	0	74.00	0.79	6.00	80.79
2010Q3	3.00	63.00	2.17		68.17
Cumulative QDII Quota for the Financial Institution	82.60	404.00	176.44	6.00	669.04

(*Data source*: State Administration of Exchange Control)

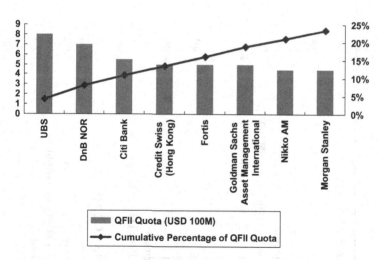

Figure 8.2.2.4 Top 8 financial institutions in cumulative approved QFII quota by the third quarter of 2010

(*Data source*: State Administration of Exchange Control)

Table 8.2.2.2 Summary of GFII quota approval (By the end of the third quarter of 2010)

QFII name	Cumulative approved QFII quota	QFII name	Cumulative approved QFII quota
United Bank of Switzerland	8.00	HSBC Global Investment Management (Hong Kong) Co., Ltd.	3.50
Nomura Securities	3.50	Sumitomo Mitsui Asset Management Company, Limited	3.50
Citigroup Global Markets	5.50	Den Norske Bank	7.00
Morgan Stanley & International Limited	4.00	Pictet Asset Management Limited	1.00
Goldman-Sachs Assets Mangement International	3.00	Columbia University	1.00
Hongkong and Shanghai Banking Corporation Limited (HSBC)	4.00	PRUDENTIAL ASSET MANAGEMENT CO., LTD	0.75
Deutsche Bank AG	4.00	Robeco Institutional Asset management B.V	1.50
ING	4.00	KBC Asset Management N. V.	1.50
JP Morgan Chase Bank	1.50	Future Asset Management	2.50
Credit Suisse (HK) Limited	5.00	Platinum Investment Company Limited	1.50
Nikko Asset Management	4.50	State Street Global Advisors Asia Ltd.	0.50
Standard Chartered Bank (Hong Kong) Ltd.	0.75	Quebec Savings Investment Group	2.00
Hang Seng Bank Limited	1.00	SAMSUNG Investment Trust company	3.00
DAIWA SECURITIES CO.LTD.	0.50	Oversea-Chinese Banking Corporation	1.50
Merrill Lynch International	3.00	Alliance Bernstein Limited	1.50
Lehman Brothers International (Europe)	2.00	Anda International Holdings Ltd.	1.50
Bill and Melinda Gates Trust Foundation	3.00	Harvard University	2.00
Algemene Bank Nederland	1.75	Prosynx International	1.10
Societe Generale	0.50	Daiwa Securities, Investment Trust company	1.00
Barclays Bank	4.00	ABU Dhabi Investment Authority	2.00
Banque Paribas	2.00	Allianz Global Investors	1.00
Dresdner Bank AG	0.75	Mitsubishi UFJ Securities Co., Ltd.	1.00
Fortis Bank	5.00	Capital International	1.00

(*Continued*)

Table 8.2.2.2 *(Continued)*

QFII name	Cumulative approved QFII quota	QFII name	Cumulative approved QFII quota
Power Corporation of Canada	0.50	Credit Suisse	2.00
Banque de l'indochine	0.75	Emerging Markets Management, L.L.C.	0.50
Invesco Asset Management	2.50	First State Investment Management (UK) Limited	1.20
Government of Singapore Investment Corporation	3.00	Han Hwa Investment &Trust Management Co., Ltd.	0.70
Goldman Sachs Asset Management International	5.00	UOB AM	0.50
Martin Currie Investment Management Limited	1.20	Bank Negara Malaysia	2.00
Temasek Fullerton Alpha Investments Pte Ltd	3.00	DWS Investment Management Limited	2.00
AIG Global Investment Corp.	0.50	Lloyd George Investment Management (Hong Kong) Limited	0.50
Dai-ichi Mutual Life Insurance Company	2.00	Korea Development Bank	1.00
DBS Bank Limited	1.00	Templeton Investment Consulting	2.00
JF ASSET MANAGEMENT	2.75	Shell Asset Management	1.00
KBC Financial Products UK Ltd.	1.00	East-Asia Luen Fung Investment Management Co., Ltd.	1.00
Bank of Nova Scotia	1.50	Woori Bank	0.50
La Compagnie Financiere Edmond de Rothschild Banque	1.00	Korea Investment & Trust Co., Ltd.	1.00
Yale University	1.50	Sumitomo Trust and Banking	0.50
AMP CAPITAL INVESTORS LIMITED	3.00	Baring Asset Management Limited	2.00
Morgan Stanley Investment Management Inc.	4.50	Anshi Investment Management Co., Ltd.	2.00
Prudential Asset Management Limited	3.00	Nomura Asset Management Co., Ltd.	2.00
Stanford University	1.00	Manulife Asset Management (HK) Co., Ltd.	2.00
UOB Bank	0.50	ToYo Investment & Trust	1.00
Schroder Investment Management Limited	2.00	Royal Bank of Canada	1.00
GE Asset Management Incorporated	3.50	Ivy Asset Management	1.00
UBS Global Asset Management (Singapore) Ltd.	2.00	Dayi'an Asset Management	1.00
Shinko Securities Co., Ltd.	0.50		

(*Data source*: State Administration of Exchange Control)

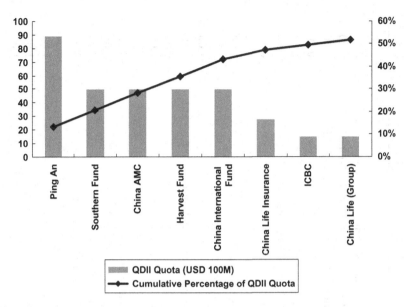

Figure 8.2.2.5   Top 8 institutions in cumulative approved QDII quota by the end of the third quarter of 2010

(*Data source*: State Administration of Exchange Control)

By the third quarter of 2010, the top 8 financial institutions in cumulative approved QFII quota has a total QFII quota of USD 4.45 billion with a share of 23.5%. The first 3 of these 8 institutions — United Bank of Switzerland (UBS), Den Norske Bank (DnB NOR) and Citigroup Global Markets (Citi Bank) all acquire a QFII quota of more than USD 500 million. Among these 8 institutions, the lowest quota is USD 450 million and the highest is 800 million.

By the end of the third quarter of 2010, the top 8 institutions in acquiring QDII quota have a total of USD 34.64 billion, with a share of 53.8%, among which Ping An Group boasts the highest QDII quota amounting to USD 8.89 billion, and Southern Fund, China AMC, Harvest Fund and China International Fund each have a QDII quota of USD 5 billion.

Table 8.2.2.3a Summary of QDII quota approval for banks (by the third quarter of 2010)

Institution name	Time of approving investment quota	Approved quota
Bank of China Limited	2006.07.10	10.00
Industrial and Commercial Bank of China Limited	2006.07.11	15.00
Bank of East Asia (China) Limited	2006.07.20	1.00
Bank of Communications Limited	2006.07.27	5.00
China Construction Bank Limited	2006.07.27	7.00
HSBC Bank (China) Company Limited	2006.08.07	7.00
China Merchants Bank Limited	2006.09.05	5.00
China CITIC Bank	2006.09.18	2.00
Hang Seng Bank (China) Limited	2006.09.27	0.30
Citi Bank (China) Limited	2006.09.27	5.00
Industrial Bank	2006.10.18	5.00
Standard Chartered Bank (China) Limited	2006.10.24	7.00
China Minsheng Bank	2006.11.08	1.00
China Everbright Bank	2006.11.23	1.00
Bank of Beijing	2006.12.11	0.50
Bank of China (Hong Kong) Limited, Mainland Branch	2007.01.11	0.30
Credit Suisse (Shanghai)	2007.01.30	0.30
Agricultural Bank of China	2007.02.09	6.00
NCB (China) Limited	2007.04.29	0.30
Deutsche Bank AG (China) Co., Ltd.	2007.08.17	0.30
Shanghai Pudong Development Bank	2007.08.31	0.30
Bank of Shanghai	2008.01.24	0.30
DBS Bank (China) Limited	2010.07.28	1.00
Banque Paribas (China) Limited	2010.07.28	1.00
Societe Generale (China) Limited	2010.09.01	1.00

(*Data source*: State Administration of Exchange Control)

Table 8.2.2.3b   Summary of QDII quota approval for financial institutions dealing with security (fund) (by the end of the third quarter of 2010)

Institution name	Time of approving investment quota	Approved quota
Hua An Fund Management Co.	2006.09.05	5.00
Southern Fund Management Company	2007.09.04	50.00
China AMC Fund Management Company	2007.09.10	50.00
Harvest Management Company	2007.09.26	50.00
China International Fund Management	2007.10.12	50.00
ICBC Fund Management	2007.12.05	10.00
Fortune Sgam Fund Management	2007.12.28	10.00
China International Capital Corporation Limited	2007.11.16	10.00
Fortis Haitong Investment Management	2008.03.11	10.00
Yinhua Investment Management	2008.04.03	10.00
Merchants Securities Co., Ltd.	2008.05.04	2.00
Bank of Communications Schroder Fund Management Co., Ltd.	2008.05.22	10.00
E Fund Management Corporation Limited	2009.10.19	10.00
China Merchants Fund Management Co., Ltd.	2009.10.19	5.00
Boshi Fund Management Co., Ltd.	2009.11.06	10.00
China Universal Asset Management Co., Ltd.	2009.11.09	10.00
GF Fund Management Co., Ltd.	2009.12.08	10.00
Penghua Fund Management Co., Ltd.	2009.12.08	8.00
Changsheng Fund Management Co., Ltd.	2009.12.11	7.00
Guotai Fund Management Co., Ltd.	2009.12.30	7.00
Ubs Sdic Fund Management Co., Ltd.	2009.12.30	7.00
Jianxin Fund Management Co., Ltd.	2010.03.12	7.00
CITIC-Prudential Fund Management Company Ltd.	2010.03.12	5.00
Lion Fund Management Co., Ltd.	2010.03.12	5.00
Everbright Pramerica Fund Management Company	2010.03.12	5.00
Fuligoal Fund Management Co., Ltd.	2010.03.12	8.00
Da Cheng Fund Management Co., Ltd.	2010.03.12	5.00
BOC Investment Managers	2010.03.12	7.00
Taida-Manulife Funf Mangement	2010.04.20	5.00
Huatai Securities Co., Ltd.	2010.04.14	2.00
Guotai Junan Securities	2010.05.31	2.00
Chang Xin Asset Mangement	2010.07.23	5.00
Huatai-PineBridge Fund Management	2010.07.28	5.00
Everbright Securities Co., Ltd.	2010.07.28	2.00

(*Data source*: State Administration of Exchange Control)

Table 8.2.2.3c Summary of QDII quota approval for financial institutions dealing with insurance (by the end of the third quarter of 2010)

Institution name	Time of approving investment quota	Approved quota
Ping An Insurance (Group) Company of China, Ltd.	2004.12.14	88.90
China Life Insurance Company Co., Ltd.	2006.12.14	15.00
China PICC Property and Casualty	2006.12.14	2.38
China Life Insurance Company Co., Ltd.	2007.04.10	27.50
Taikang Life Insurance Company Co., Ltd.	2007.06.22	13.85
Generali China Life Insurance Co., Ltd.	2007.06.22	0.15
The People's Insurance Company (Group) of China	2007.08.13	0.15
ING Capital Life Insurance Company Ltd.	2007.08.16	0.09
China Reinsurance (Group) Company	2007.10.18	3.50
China Pacific Insurance (Group) Company	2007.09.17	5.37
China Pacific Property Insurance Co., Ltd.	2007.09.17	4.00
PICC Health Insurance Company Ltd.	2007.09.24	0.15
The People's Life Insurance Company (Group) of China	2007.09.26	0.14
An Bang Insurance Company Limited	2007.10.10	1.60
Taiping Life Insurance Co., Ltd.	2007.10.31	5.70
Hua An Insurance Company Limited	2007.11.15	1.20
Huatai Insurance Company Limited	2007.11.15	1.30
Huatai Asset Mangement Limited	2007.04.23	1.30
AIA International Assurance, Mainland Branch	2007.12.24	0.82
Bohai Property Insurance Co., Ltd.	2007.12.18	0.05
AXA-Minmetals Assurance Company Limited	2007.12.28	0.08
Du Bang Insurance Company Limited	2008.01.23	0.25
Pacific Property Insurance Company Limited	2009.12.30	0.79
Ming An Insurance Company (China) Limited	2010.04.14	0.25
China Property Reinsurance Company Limited	2010.05.31	1.92

(*Data source*: State Administration of Exchange Control)

Table 8.2.2.3d Summary of QDII quota approval for financial institutions dealing with trust (by the end of the third quarter of 2010)

Institution name	Time of approving investment quota	Approved quota
China Credit Trust Co., Ltd.	2009.12.08	2.00
Shanghai International Investment and Trust Company	2009.12.08	2.00
Zhonghai Trust Co., Ltd.	2009.12.30	2.00

(*Data source*: State Administration of Exchange Control)

8.2.3 *Classified statistics of major fund categories*

Currently funds issued in A-share market and bond market in China's mainland cover various categories. These funds can be classified into "open-ended" and "close-ended" by their means of redemption. In addition, finds can also be classified, according to the major investment objectives of the fund, into equity fund, bond fund, money market fund and mixed fund.

(1) According to whether or not to track index (investment objective), equity fund can be categorized into index fund and common equity fund:

- Index fund can be further categorized, in terms of its relation with objective index, into exchange traded fund (ETF), general-index replicated fund and index enhanced fund;
- Common equity fund can be further categorized, in terms of investing style, into value fund and growth fund, etc.

(2) According to whether the fund is only invested in bond, can be invested in subscription of new stock, or in secondary stock market, bond fund can be categorized into absolute bond fund, level I bond fund and level II bond fund:

- Absolute bond fund: it does not participate in stock investment, only in fixed-income financial instruments, thus is at a relatively low risk level;
- Level I bond fund: except for fixed-income financial instruments, it also participates in new-stock investment in primary market, thus is at a medium and low risk level;
- Level II bond fund: except for fixed-income financial instruments, it befittingly participates in stock trading in secondary market, but also in new stock investment in primary market, thus is at a medium and low risk level;

(3) Mixed fund can be categorized, according to the different shares of equity asset and bond asset in portfolio, into equity mixed fund, bond mixed fund and balanced mixed fund.

Presently there are in total 15 ETFs issued and traded in A-share market. By the fourth quarter of 2010, the total is RMB 67.68 billion. Among these 15 ETFs, 11 ETFs' objective is Shanghai SE Index Series (such as Shanghai SE Index Series, 50 and Shanghai SE Index Series, 180, etc.), with a total NAV of RMB 40.26 billion and a share of 59.5%; only 3 ETFs takes Shenzhen SE Index Series as their objective (such as Shenzhen Component SE Index and Shenzhen SE MSE Index), with a total NAV of RMB 26.86 billion and

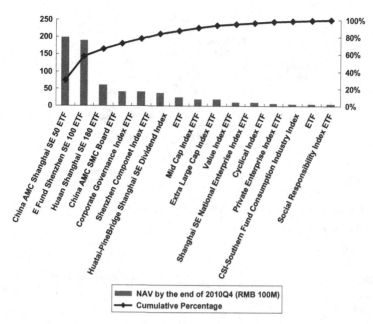

Figure 8.2.3.1 NAV of ETFs by the end of the fourth quarter of 2010

(*Data source*: Xinhua Finance)

a share of 39.7%; and for ETFs whose objective is CS Index Series, their total NAV is RMB 560 million, with a share of 0.8%.

Among the above ETF, the largest AV size is that of "China AMC, Shanghai SE Index Series, 50 ETF": by the end of the fourth quarter of 2010, its NAV approximates to RMB 20 billion, with a share of 29.5%. The average size of the above 15 ETFs is RMB 4.51 billion (median is RMB 2.01 billion).

By the end of the fourth quarter of 2010, the 61 general-index replicated funds included in our statistics (including ETF jointing fund) gained a total NAV of RMB 221.76 billion, the average size being RMB 3.64 billion (median is RMB 1.81 billion). Among these 61 funds, 40 of them take CS Index Series as their objective (including Shanghai-Shenzhen 300 Index and CS Index Series exclusive CSI300); 19 funds track take exchange tracking index as their objective (including Shenzhen Stock Exchange and Shanghai Stock Exchange); and the rest 2 funds track other indexes (e.g. FTSE Index Series and CNInfo Index Series, etc.).

If the calculation is based on NAV of the fund, then among the above 61 funds, funds tracking Shanghai-Shenzhen 300 Index within CS Index Series have a total NAV up to RMB 119.94 billion, with a share of 54.1%; immediately following are the funds tracking Shenzhen SE Index Series and CS Index Series exclusive CSI300, whose total NAV amounts to RMB 40.4 billion, each

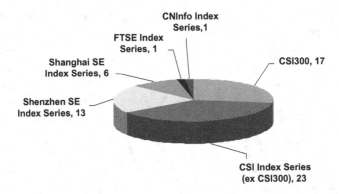

Figure 8.2.3.2   Index distribution of general-index replicated funds

(*Data source*: Xinhua Finance)

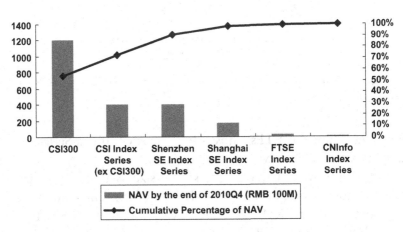

Figure 8.2.3.3   NAV distribution of general-index replicated funds

(*Data source*: Xinhua Finance)

with a share of 18.2%. For funds tracking CS Index Series including Shanghai-Shenzhen 300 Index, their total NAV is RMB 160.34 billion with a share of 72.3%.

By the end of the fourth quarter of 2010, the top 7 general-index replicated funds all have a NAV over RMB 8 billion, with a NAV share of more than 50%. Among these 6 funds, 5 funds have a NAV above RMB 10 billion, with a cumulative NAV share of 43.2%. The first two — Harvest CSI300 Index fund and China AMC CSI300s have a NAV over RMB 30 billion and RMB 20 billion respectively and both take SCI300 as their tracking objective.

By the end of the fourth quarter of 2010, the total NAV of the 277 common equity funds included in our statistics is RMB 1.08 trillion, with an average

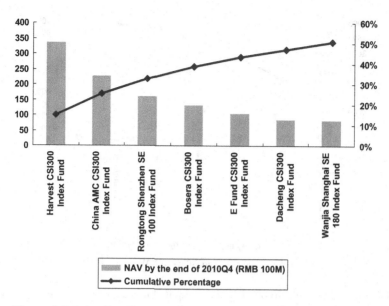

Figure 8.2.3.4 Top 7 general-index replicated funds in terms of NAV
(*Data source*: Xinhua Finance)

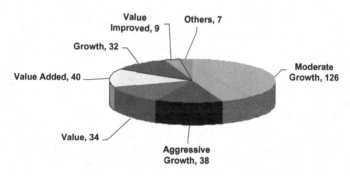

Figure 8.2.3.5 Number of common equity funds of different investing styles
(*Data source*: Xinhua Finance)

size of RMB 3.91 billion (median is RMB 2.42 billion). In terms of different investing styles, moderate growth funds boast largest number, followed successively by value added funds and aggressive growth funds, 40 and 38 respectively.

In terms of NAV share, moderate growth funds ranks the first, with a share of 34%,; the second and third are aggressive growth funds and value funds, with a share of 18.3% and 17.4% respectively. The above three types of funds in total has a NAV share of around 70% among the common equity funds.

Seen from the overall NAV distribution, among the common equity funds, funds with a size less than RMB 500 million accounts for about 20%;

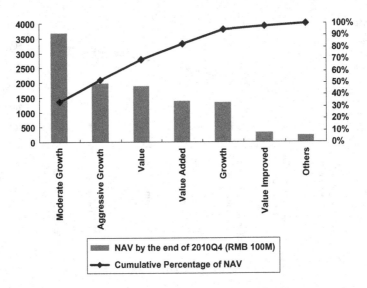

Figure 8.2.3.6   NAV distribution of common equity funds of different investing styles by the end of the fourth quarter of 2010

(*Data source*: Xinhua Finance)

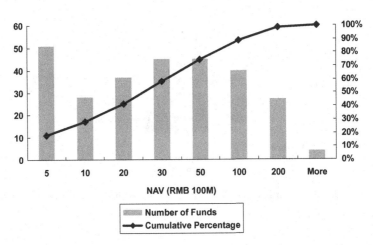

Figure 8.2.3.7   NAV distribution of common equity funds by the end of the fourth quarter of 2010

(*Data source*: Xinhua Finance)

nearly 60% of funds have a size below RMB 3 billion; funds with a size over RMB 10 billion has a share of less than 10%, with the largest size being RMB 26.2 billion, and the smallest size being less than RMB 100 million.

By the end of the fourth quarter of 2010, the 171 bond funds covered in our statistics have an average size of RMB 1.32 billion (median is RMB 850

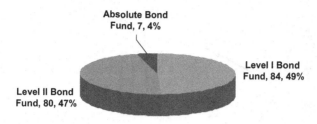

Figure 8.2.3.8 Number of bond funds of different investing styles

(*Data source*: Xinhua Finance)

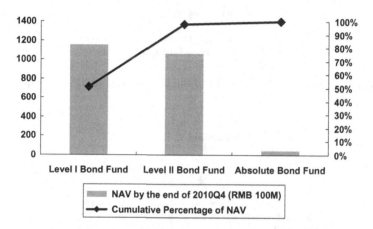

Figure 8.2.3.9 NAV distribution of bond funds of different investing styles by the end of the fourth quarter of 2010

(*Data source*: Xinhua Finance)

million). Among them level I bond fund possesses the largest number, 84 in all; next is level II bond fund, with a total of 80; absolute bond has the lowest number of only 7.

In terms of NAV share, the total NAV of level I bond fund was 115.2 billion, with a share above 50%; while the total asset size for absolute bond fund is RMB 4.74 billion, with a share of 2.1% only.

In terms of NAV distribution, funds with a size less than RMB 500 million accounts for over 35%; around 75% of funds have a size below RMB 2 billion; the share for funds of a size below RMB 4 billion is about 5%. Among these bond funds, the largest size is RMB 6.08 billion, and 7 funds have a size less than RMB 100 million.

By the end of the fourth quarter of 2010, the total NAV of the 162 mixed funds included in our statistics amounts to RMB 693.9 billion, with an average size of RMB 4.28 billion (median is RMB 3.09 billion). Among these

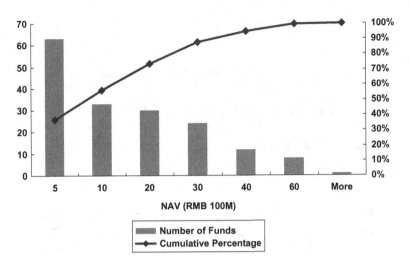

Figure 8.2.3.10 NAV distribution of bond funds by the end of the fourth quarter of 2010

(*Data source*: Xinhua Finance)

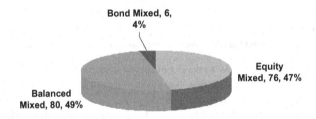

Figure 8.2.3.11 Number of balanced funds of different investing styles

(*Data source*: Xinhua Finance)

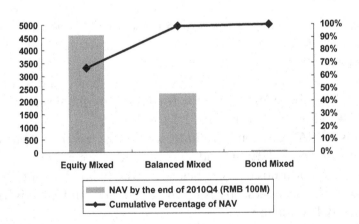

Figure 8.2.3.12 NAV distribution of balanced funds by the end of the fourth quarter of 2010

(*Data source*: Xinhua Finance)

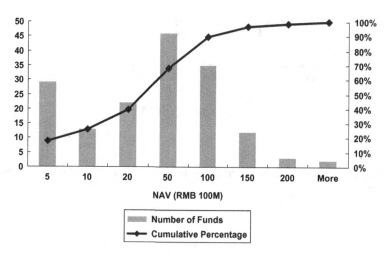

Figure 8.2.3.13 NAV distribution of balanced funds by the end of the fourth quarter of 2010

(*Data source*: Xinhua Finance)

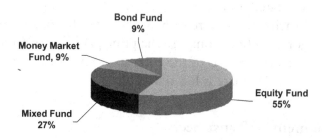

Figure 8.2.3.14 NAV distribution of funds of each category

(*Data source*: Xinhua Finance)

mixed funds, the number of balanced mixed fund is the largest, 80 in total; next is that of equity mixed fund, 76 in all; bond mixed funds have the lowest number, only 6.

In terms of NAV share, the total NAV of equity mixed fund is RMB 458.76 billion, with a share close to 2/3, while the total NAV of bond mixed fund is RMB 5.95 billion with a share less than 1%.

In terms of overall NAV distribution, among mixed funds, the funds with a size less than RMB 500 million accounts for 20%, and approximately 40% of funds have a size below RMB 2 billion; funds with a size over RMB 10 billion accounts for about 10%. The largest fund size is RMB 26.15 billion and 5 of them have a size less than RMB 100 million.

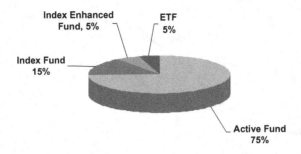

Figure 8.2.3.15 NAV distribution of funds of each category by the end of the fourth quarter of 2010

(*Data source*: Xinhua Finance)

In summary, by the end of the fourth quarter of 2010, the NAV share of funds of each category in China's market is as follows: the share for equity funds is 55% (among equity funds, common equity funds have a share of 75%, general-index replicated funds have a share of 15%, and ETF and index enhanced funds each have a share of 5%); the share for mixed funds is 27%. These two categories of fund comprise the principal funds in China's market, accounting for 80% and above of the total size. For bond fund and money market fund, their NAV share is less than 10%.

8.3 Development of Trust Sector

8.3.1 *Business development and expansion of trust sector*

The business development of the trust sector is always in a status of "developing along with regulation". Before 1999, the trust sector was at the exploratory stage, symbolized by the founding of China International Trust and Investment Corporation (CITIC) in October 1979. At this stage, a large number of trust companies were established in many regions, but since the relevant policies, regulations and regulatory means failed to keep up, basically these trust companies did not operate trust businesses in the real sense.

During 1999 and 2002, a series of laws such as *Trust Law of People's Republic of China, Administrative Measures for Trust and Investment Companies,* and *Provisional Measures for the Management of Investment and Trust of Trust* and *Investment Companies* were successively issued, and every trust company was required to re-register. After re-registration the number of trust companies was 59 in total. Then during 2002 and 2007, *Provisional Measures for the Management of Investment and Trust of Trust and*

Investment Companies was officially issued and implemented, which together with *Trust Law* and *Administrative Measures for Trust and Investment Companies* laid the cornerstone of laws for China's trust sector. Besides, the regulatory authority also successively issued some auxiliary documents such as *Provisional Measures for the Management of Entrusted Foreign Financing*. For trust companies, business at this stage was mainly about self-employment, and entrusted financing of a real sense was not substantially launched.

After 2007, with the issuance of *Administrative Measures for Trust and Investment Companies* and *Administrative Measures for Assembled Funds Trust Scheme*, the trust sector is required to make entrusted financing as the major business and from then on the trust sector witnessed a rapid development. As the *Administrative Measures for Net Capital of Trust companies* issued by China Banking Regulatory Commission in 2010 will lead the trust sector to develop active-management trust business, the business quality of trust companies will be further improved.

According to statistics about trust companies who published financial reports during 2005 and 2009, the total assets of the aforesaid trust companies rose from RMB 85.6 billion in 2005 to RMB 167.4 billion in 2009, increasing by about twice within these 4 years, with an annual compound growth rate of 18.3%. Meanwhile, with the rise in asset size, the total assets of trust companies also witnessed an increase: during the 4 years, the total equity of trust companies (attributed to parent companies) rose from RMB

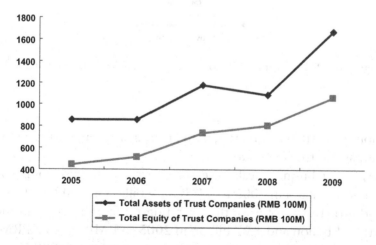

Figure 8.3.1.1   Asset size growth of trust companies

(*Data source*: China Trustee Association)

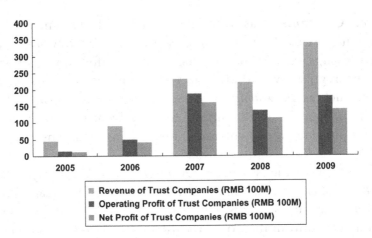

Figure 8.3.1.2 Total business scale growth of trust companies

(*Data source*: China Trustee Association)

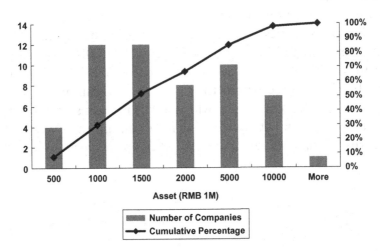

Figure 8.3.1.3 Asset distribution of trust companies by the end of 2009

(*Data source*: China Trustee Association)

44.2 billion to RMB 106.3 billion, with an annual compound growth rate of 24.5%, surpassing that of the total assets.

In respect of business scale, the total revenue of trust companies rose from RMB 4.57 billion in 2005 to RMB 33.9 billion in 2009, with an annual compound growth rate of 65%; the operating profit and net profit increased from RMB 1.4 billion and 1.27 billion in 2005 to RMB 17.9 and RMB 13.9 billion respectively, with an annual compound growth rate of 88.5% and 82% respectively.

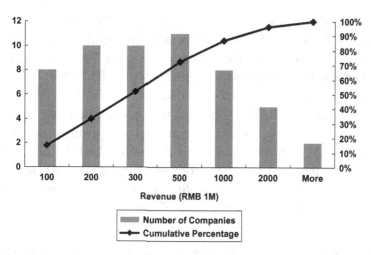

Figure 8.3.1.4   Revenue distribution of trust companies by the end of 2009

(*Data source*: China Trustee Association)

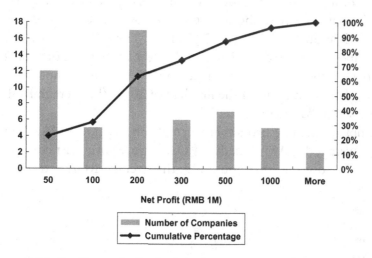

Figure 8.3.1.5   Net profit distribution of trust companies by the end of 2009

(*Data source*: China Trustee Association)

Seen from the perspective of distribution of asset size, revenue and net profit, in 2009 among the 54 trust companies covered in our statistics, the average asset size is RMB 3.1 billion, with a median of RMB 1.47 billion, about 30% of which have a total asset below RMB 1 billion, and about half of which have a total asset less than RMB 1.5 billion. There are in all 8 trust companies with an asset size of RMB 5 billion (one of them has an asset size over RMB 10 billion), with a share of about 15%.

For the above-mentioned trust companies, in 2009 the average revenue was RMB 62.8 billion, and the median was RMB 25.06 billion, among which 1/3 of the trust companies had revenue less than RMB 200 million, and about half of which (51.85%) had revenue less than RMB 300 million. There were in total 7 trust companies with revenue over RMB 1 billion (one of them had revenue over RMB 10 billion) with a share of 13%.

In terms of net profit, in 2009 the average net profit of the above trust companies was RMB 25.8 bullion with a median of RMB 14.6 billion. About 30% of trust companies had a net profit less than RMB 300 million; about 13% of trust companies had a net profit over RMB 500 million, and 2 trust companies had a net profit over RMB 1 billion.

8.3.2 *Profitability and anti-risk capability of trust companies*

Since 2007 the profitability of trust companies has been witnessing a significant rise. During 2005 and 2006 for the trust and investment companies included in our statistics, the average ROE and median ROE were both below 6%; while during 2007 and 2009 the average ROE and ROE median were both above 10%. Even in 2008 — the year when the global financial crisis exerted a significant impact, the median ROE of trust companies remained at the level of 11%, and during the first half of 2010, the average ROE of trust companies was 6.3% (median was 5.9%).

The improvement of profitability can also be seen in ROA: during 2005 and 2006, average ROA and median ROA of the above trust companies were both below 5%; during 2007 and 2009, this average ROA and median ROA

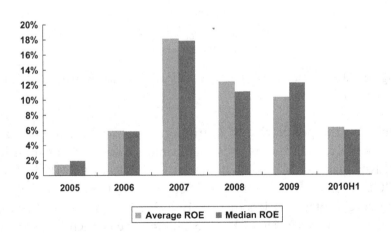

Figure 8.3.2.1   ROE of trust companies

(*Data source*: China Trustee Association)

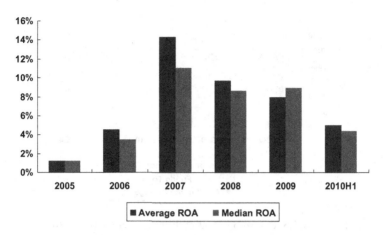

Figure 8.3.2.2   ROA of trust companies

(*Data source*: China Trustee Association)

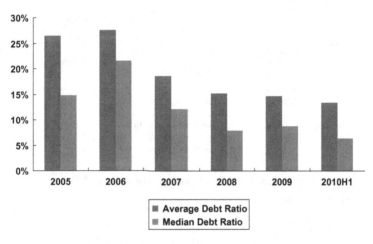

Figure 8.3.2.3   Debt ratio (debt/asset) of trust companies

(*Data source*: China Trustee Association)

were both above 8%; for the first half of 2010, the average ROA of trust companies was 5% (median was 4.4%).

On the other side, after 2007 the debt ratio (=debt/asset) has significantly declined. During 2005 and 2006, the average debt ratio of trust companies remained above 25%, and the median of debt ratio was above 14%; while after 2007 this average debt ratio kept below 20% and decreased year by year, with the median level remaining below 10%, which indicates a rise in anti-risk capability of the trust companies.

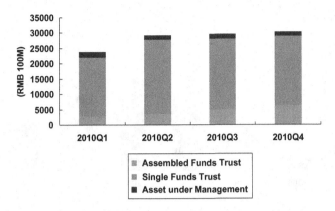

Figure 8.3.3.1   Amounts of each trust asset source in 2010

(*Data source*: China Trustee Association)

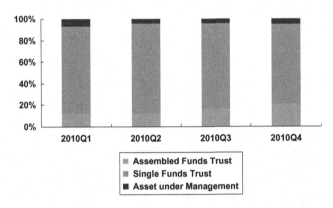

Figure 8.3.3.2   Trust asset source share in 2010

(*Data source*: China Trustee Association)

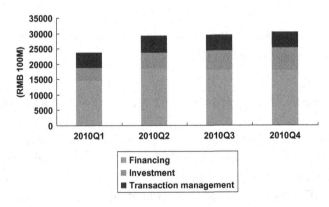

Figure 8.3.3.3   Amounts of each trust asset function in 2010

(*Data source*: China Trustee Association)

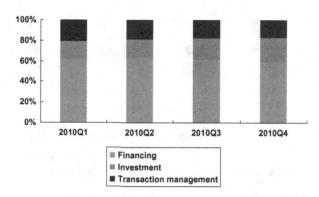

Figure 8.3.3.4 Trust asset function share in 2010

(*Data source*: China Trustee Association)

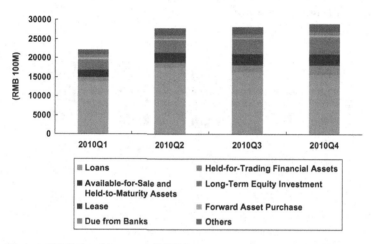

Figure 8.3.3.5 Amounts of different ways to use trust assets in 2010

(*Data source*: China Trustee Association)

8.3.3 *Classified statistics of trust business*

The Trust sector abounds with asset sources: by the end of the fourth quarter of 2010, the asset source balance of trust companies is RMB 3.04 trillion, among which the share for single funds trust ranks the highest, between 75% and 80%; next is assembled funds trust, around 10% and 20%; and assets under management was below 10%. The distribution of asset sources for trust companies in terms of their functions will show that the share for financing is around 60%, and that for investment and transaction management each was about 20%.

Among various ways to use trust assets, loans boasts the primary share, about 60%; followed by long-term equity investment and by available-for-sale and held-to-maturity assets, about 15% and 10% respectively; the share for

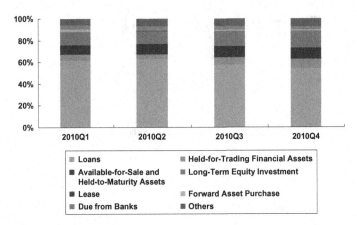

Figure 8.3.3.6   Share of different ways to use trust assets in 2010
(*Data source*: China Trustee Association)

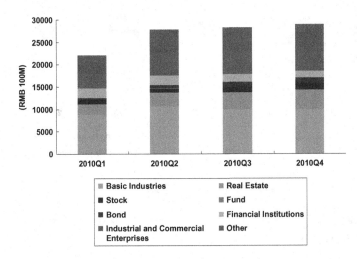

Figure 8.3.3.7   Amounts of different investment orientations of trust assets in 2010
(*Data source*: China Trustee Association)

held-for-trading financial assets is about 6%; the other ways to use the rest of the 10% assets include due from banks, forward asset purchase, loans, etc.

In terms of the investment orientation of trust assets, investment in basic industries accounts for around 35% and 40%, real estate accounts for around 10% and 15%, and financial institutions and industrial and commercial enterprises for about 7% and 18% respectively.

Among security investment trust, the major part is portfolio, with a share around 55%; the next main part is secondary market investment, with a share around 40% and 50%; for primary market investment and fund investment, their share is relatively low, with a total share about 5%.

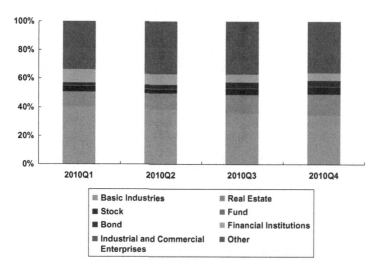

Figure 8.3.3.8   Share of different investment orientations of trust assets in 2010

(*Data source*: China Trustee Association)

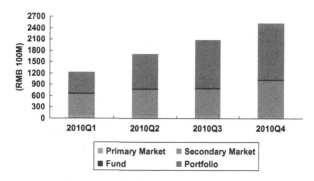

Figure 8.3.3.9   Amounts of different security investment trusts in 2010

(*Data source*: China Trustee Association)

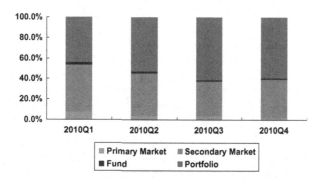

Figure 8.3.3.10   Share of different security investment trusts in 2010

(*Data source*: China Trustee Association)

Chapter 9

CONCLUSION

The day when the Chinese version of the present book was completed coincided with the convening of the fourth meeting of the 11th National People's Congress in Beijing. One of the important agendas of this meeting was to inspect and approve "the 12th five-year plan of national economic and social development" (abbreviated as "National 12th Five-Year Plan"). From the published suggestions for the "National 12th Five-Year Plan," we have delightedly observed that many significant measures relevant to the financial sector have been listed in the plan, such as elevating residents' property income, compelling the reform for the marketization of interest rates and RMB exchange rates, establishing a sound and systematic defensive and early warning system for financial risks and disposal mechanism, improving the mechanism of state-owned financial assets management, etc.

The development history of the global economy shows that, if a country wants to become a developed economy, its financial sector must be at a significantly high level of development; also, the development of the financial sector can add impetus to the development of a country, and improve its development speed and quality. Just as what we have observed, the development of China's finance during these recent years has equipped it with scale and strength to a certain degree. Nevertheless, non-balance in the real economy is reflected, to a large extent, in China's financial sector: one big impediment in the developing course of China's financial sector lies in scarcity of financial product variety and simplification of financial businesses, which is in bad need of being overcome properly.

With the growth of China's economy and the increasingly close attention to people's well-being, there is good reason to expect that in the near future, the affluence level of Chinese residents will enjoy a significant elevation, and when national wealth reaches a certain level, there will be a substantial leap in the demand for financial services. This leap not only signifies (even not mainly means) that we are in need of a market and banks of larger scales, but also means that we need more bountiful financial products to meet the demands of investors at different wealth levels and with different risk preferences.

The continuous rise of China's economy in the global economy also signifies the stronger interrelation between China's economy and the global economy. It is reasonable to expect that the interrelation between China's financial sector and the global financial sector will correspondingly become stronger. In a more complex and more dynamic global environment, ensuring the stability of the financial sector not only entails strict risk monitoring, but also risk diversification through multi-layer and multifarious financial intermediaries.

The year 2011 is the first year of China's "National 12th Five-Year Plan". For China's economy, the 12th five-year period is not just simply a development stage of another 5 years. In a sense, the forthcoming 5 years is highly likely to determine the basic orientation and basic model of China's economic growth and social development in the decades to come. We are expecting to see that within this new 5-year period, China's financial sector will witness a development towards the objective of being more marketized in mechanism, more modernized in business, and more pluralized in products.